PRAISE FOR

BARE KNUCKLE

"Stayton Bonner's BARE KNUCKLE is a remarkable debut.
It's ROCKY, only with an outlaw street fighter and mobsters—
and, even better, it's all true."

—DON WINSLOW

BARE
KNUCKLE

BARE KNUCKLE

BOBBY GUNN, 73–0 UNDEFEATED.
A DAD. A DREAM. A FIGHT LIKE YOU'VE NEVER SEEN.

STAYTON BONNER

BLACK
STONE
PUBLISHING

Copyright © 2021 by Stayton Bonner
Published in 2023 by Blackstone Publishing
Cover design by Sean M. Thomas
Book design by Kathryn Galloway English

Some names and identifying details have been changed
to protect the privacy of individuals.

Printed in the United States of America

First edition: 2023
ISBN 978-1-9826-5071-1
Sports & Recreation / Boxing

Version 1

CIP data for this book is available
from the Library of Congress

Blackstone Publishing
31 Mistletoe Rd.
Ashland, OR 97520

www.BlackstonePublishing.com

For Catherine, for everything

CONTENTS

PART I
FIRST BLOOD

CHAPTER 1
WELCOME TO THE UNDERGROUND

Bobby Gunn is pacing the concrete floor of an auto-body shop somewhere in the industrial badlands of a large northeastern city. "I'm worried," he says, wringing his mallet-size hands. "I've heard this guy today is a head-butter."

More pacing, more hand-wringing, as Gunn sinks deeper into a momentary funk amid the garage's taxidermy heads and faded American flags. Today's opponent, a former marine, has a reputation for dropping his head during matches—an old trick among gloveless fighters who can easily fracture a hand by striking the skull. Gunn has pulled the maneuver himself many times. He's broken his right hand just as often. Another fracture could end his career.

"Everybody wants to take me down, brother, and make a name for himself," he says, punching a wall of rubber tires. "I've gotta watch my back."

Whap, whap, whap.

Gunn pounds the tread, keeping his hands slightly open until just before impact, loosening up the knuckles. He has black hair, blue eyes, and 235 pounds of muscle, his 5-foot-11 frame supported by the bowlegged gait of a cowboy. Every morning, he wakes up at six, shaves with a straight razor and rubbing alcohol, puts on his standard uniform—denim jacket, jeans, gray Henley, black Pumas, cell-phone holster—and bangs out two hundred push-ups. He has no tattoos and does not drink. His favorite book is the Bible. "I'm a hugger," he'll say, nearly crushing your torso in a full embrace.

Gunn used to step into matches without so much as cracking a knuckle, but now he needs a warm-up. An extensive one. He is forty-two, an age when most fighters have long since retired. He has broken his right hand six times and dislocated his fingers so often, he now resets them with his teeth during matches. He has no cartilage left at all in his nose and can press it flat against his face like a rubber prosthetic. He's also broken two bones in his back, fractured his elbow, and severely broken his right foot after falling from a two-story roof on a construction site in 2000. After that last accident, one that left eighteen screws and bolts in his foot permanently, doctors told him he would never walk again. Within a year, he was back in the ring, fighting with a new stance.

Gunn usually knows what to expect from an opponent in the underground, but soldiers are wild cards. With pro boxers and MMA fighters, he can anticipate a real fight. With neighborhood toughs like bouncers and bodyguards—usually washed-up linebackers adept at tossing frat boys to the curb—he can finish it quickly. But military guys are different. They have formal training in hand-to-hand combat, but not the years inside a ring to temper it. Soldiers are unpredictable, and that makes them dangerous. "Anytime you get a marine or army guy, they're usually a stupid ass," Gunn says. "They make mistakes. They think with their heart more than their head."

Whap, whap, whap.

Gunn is fighting in a midday match in October 2015, in a run-down neighborhood clinging like lint to the interstate. The auto-body shop is a long way from Caesar's Palace. It is a cavern-ous space with twenty-foot ceilings, oil-stained floors, and tool chests lining the walls. A baby-blue vintage Mustang sits atop a hydraulic lift. A wild-eyed bear's head hangs on the wall. In the corner, an industrial fan blows grease-soaked air. The shop's double-bay rolling door is closed, so the only entrance is through the cluttered front office, where the owner admits the last of the stragglers, hangs the "Closed" sign, and locks the door.

[Figure 1.1] An auto-body shop at an undisclosed location (Photo by author)

In the center of the garage, about thirty men and one woman stand in a loose circle. As with most bare-knuckle fights, the crowd is blue-collar: old men with faded tattoos and beer guts, a construction foreman in a polo, a pair of roofing contractors on lunch break. The lone woman wears a black tank top and cut-off shorts. "This is exciting because it's illegal," a man says.

For this match, the promoter sent a single email to a small group of regular fight goers. The crowd is not paying a cover charge, but they are gambling. Gunn and his opponent will be paid upward of $5,000 apiece.* This is less money than Gunn usually makes for a fight, but it's not about the purse. As champion of the underground bare-knuckle circuit, Gunn has an undefeated 71-0 record, a legendary status earned in blood from channel docks to highway overpasses, to mobster McMansion dens. He has his name at stake. "I'm going to pick my shots and take him out fast," he says, breathing steadily. "My record is everything."

Whap, whap, whap.

Gunn grunts, increasing his tempo. Punching the tires takes him back to his childhood, back to the Shamrock Boxing Club in Niagara Falls, Ontario, the town his people, the Irish Travelers, would always circle back to come fall. Back then his father would wrap tire tread around a punching bag and make Gunn alternate between hitting the rubber and leather, working the bag until his knuckles bled, until they hardened.

In Niagara Falls, Robert Williamson Gunn—descended from a long line of nomadic brawlers—trained his only son to uphold the family legacy. He taught him to rub a leather belt over his eyebrows to toughen them up, and to pour kerosene on his cuts to heal them more quickly. He taught him how to take pain, wrapping a baseball bat with foam and duct tape and hitting his son repeatedly in the midsection to harden his abs. Most importantly, Gunn's father taught him always to be ready for battle. Grinning, eyes like glass, a Marlboro Red dangling from his mouth, Robert would rouse him in the middle of the

---

* Gunn and other fighters are often cagey about the exact amounts of their purses in underground fights. In this book, I give a precise amount when verified. Otherwise, I give an approximation, when told to me, or no number at all. "They don't want attention from the IRS," says an underground fight promoter. "Bobby will tell you he's only made enough off bare knuckle to buy a Subway sandwich. It's more like he's made enough to buy a Subway sandwich franchise."

night from their motel rooms and trailer parks to fight grown men he had brought home from the bar. He gambled up to $1,000 on the child brawler he had molded since birth. "He would say, 'Can you beat that boy right there?'" Gunn recalls. "'How much do you want to bet?'"

Whap, whap, whap.

Gunn gives a clipped yell and steps back. He stretches his tree-stump neck from side to side. He opens and closes his mouth, dancing back and forth on the balls of his feet. "I'm nervous," he says. "I don't know what he's going to do."

At Gunn's side are his trainer, Dominick Scibetta, and his nineteen-year-old son, Bobby Jr. Bobby Jr. has attended all his father's fights, from the pro boxing bouts in 20,000-seat stadiums to the darkened battles in abandoned warehouses, and worries about how much longer his old man can last. "I feel nervous," he says, arms crossed, chewing gum, staring straight ahead. "It hurts my chest."

Dom, an aging boxer from Boston with sleepy eyes and a growing paunch, has other concerns. He has been with Gunn through dozens of underground fights, seen scores more over the decades, and knows what it takes to win. More importantly, he knows how little it takes to lose. Once a promising pro boxer, Dom folded when he made it to Madison Square Garden in 1988, so nervous he could barely walk through the crowds after leaving the locker room. His career lasted only another year after that. He knows that Gunn shouldn't be worried about today's opponent, a relative nobody. But he also knows that in the fight game, anything can happen—especially if you let in doubt. "Anxiety can break you down," he says. "But Bobby has dealt with it over the years and can wash it out. He's an old-school tough guy."

Dom leans in, putting his mouth right in Gunn's ear. "*He's* the one who's pacing back and forth," Dom says, pointing past the crowd, to the front office of the body shop. "*He's* the one who's worried."

Gunn shakes his head. "I don't know."

"Trust me."

Gunn looks toward the door.

He turns back to the tires.

Whap, whap, whap.

* * * * *

Wooooosssaaaaaaa.

Outside the auto-body shop, Gunn's opponent, Jim McClendon, sits in his car and meditates. "Before fights, some guys pray and some guys do breathing exercises, what I call the 'woo-sa.'" He breathes in, holds it, exhales. *Wooooosssaaaaaaa.*

"You got to get mentally focused," he says. "Or you'll get knocked the fuck out."

McClendon, twenty-eight, is the last guy you'd expect to find in a bare-knuckle fight. He is an accountant, a marine, and a devoted father to his eleven-year-old daughter. His favorite magazine is *The CPA Journal.* "I help small businesses who can't afford a private accountant," he says. "Have you ever tried to hire one? Those guys are expensive."

McClendon is 6'3" and 200 pounds, a ropy, muscled natural athlete with a handsome smile and easygoing attitude. He wears a white T-shirt, acid-wash jeans, and black sneakers. He is the only Black man at the fight today. "Not a lot of Black dudes do this," he says, shrugging.

After graduating from high school in Philly, McClendon played semipro basketball for a year in Japan. When the NBA neglected to call, he joined the marines, completing two campaigns as a corporal with the First Light Armored Reconnaissance Battalion in southern

Iraq in 2008–2009.[1] There, he learned two skills: accounting and fighting. "It's not like the army, where you do just one job," he says. "If you're a marine, then you're an accountant and a killer, too."

After the war, McClendon returned to Philly, got a CPA job, bought a car and a house, and began helping to care for his eight-year-old daughter, the one he'd had back in high school, back before he was ready to be a father. Everything seemed to be on track. But McClendon was tortured. "I have PTSD pretty bad," he says. "It was some shit in Iraq."

When his best friend from his platoon committed suicide, McClendon suffered a nervous breakdown. He lost his job, his house, his car. He fell just about as far as a man can go, homeless and living on the streets for years, arranging to meet his daughter in public parks. "My PTSD went untreated, you know, because, as marines, we're tough, we don't want to go to the hospital, that's being a pussy, blah blah blah," he says. "But then, when my best friend killed himself, I was like, 'Maybe I should get some help.'" After a two-year wait, McClendon got into a VA hospital, began treatment, and secured a loan to rent an apartment. He parked cars to pay the bills and eventually started his own business, keeping the books for small and midsize companies. On Instagram, he recently posted a photo of himself with his now-teenage daughter, both of them smiling as they go over tax forms in his apartment. "Tons of transactions to do, and guess who is helping me?" the caption said.

So after enduring such hell, after finally coming out on top, why on earth is McClendon fighting in a seedy underground bare-knuckle match, risking jail and serious injury? The answer is complicated. Yes, the PTSD he battles stems from the carnage he witnessed overseas. But it's also born of the anxiety and depression he feels since returning to an antiseptic world of Costcos and swipe-right binge dating where everyone texts but nobody talks. A world where total strangers thank him for his service but no one knows the difference between Sunnis and Shiites. McClendon knows that it sounds strange, but he misses war. He misses the bonds he forged in battle, where decisions truly mattered, where he and his platoon members lived and died for each other. He misses that cocktail of adrenaline and purpose, that primal satisfaction he can now find only in bare knuckle. "It's weird, but I love to fight," he says. "I'm not a marine anymore, so bare-knuckle boxing gets the 'I just want to fuck somebody up' out of me. And it's in the name of brother-hood. People think bare-knuckle boxing is barbaric, but dudes shake hands afterwards."

McClendon saw his first underground fight as a marine stationed at Camp Pendleton in California—a roped-off match in a nightclub basement. He was mesmerized. Now he's working on making his own name in the sport. So when the promoter reached out about today's bout—a last-minute call-up, as often happens in the circuit—he knew that it was a rare opportunity. If he beats Gunn—a man thirty-five pounds heavier, fourteen years more experienced, and with sixty-five more underground victories—he will make money and achieve instant fame. He will take the title.

Wooooosssaaaaaaa.

McClendon stops meditating, steps out of the sedan, and enters the body shop's front office. Standing amid the metal file cabinets and out-of-date calendars, he looks through the shop's grimy interior window, his eyes moving to a hulking man in the corner. Gunn.

"It was the first time I'd seen him in my life," McClendon later says. "He's built like a wall. He took his jacket off, and I was like, 'Oh, my God.'"

* * * * *

[Figure I.2] The crowd gathers (Photo by author)

"I'm the boss, I'm the boss, I'm the boss, I'm the boss."

Gunn mutters his mantra over and over and over and over. It's the closing lines from Martin Scorsese's 1980 film *Raging Bull,* the ultimate boxing movie, starring Robert De Niro as middleweight champion Jake LaMotta. At this point in the movie, LaMotta is an overweight has-been still hungry for the limelight, quoting lines from Marlon Brando's "I could have been a contender" dialogue from *On the Waterfront* while shadowboxing in front of a mirror, unable to accept the ravages of time.

But Gunn sees the scene differently. Growing up, he watched the film constantly on a VHS tape in whatever run-down motel room or trailer his family was living in, drawing inspiration from LaMotta's defiance, his refusal to give an inch to a world that told him he was a failure. Now before every fight, Gunn repeats the line to himself like a prayer, dancing back and forth on the balls of his feet while punching the air, jacking up his adrenaline. "I always say that because I *am* the fucking boss," Gunn says. "Nobody else."

Even in middle age, Gunn is a spark plug of muscle and pent-up energy, a bullet with a flattop shaved head. Wearing a black tank, jeans, and sneakers, he looks straight ahead as Dom gets right in his face, whispering instructions. Typically a laconic lug, Dom looks as if he is about to have a seizure. "Hands high, hands high," he says. "Chin down."

Gunn nods, shifts his feet, moves his mouth. Dom fakes a punch to the gut and then spreads his arms like an ump calling a runner safe. Gunn nods. That's it, the killing shot.

Gunn is fearless in the legal boxing ring, where he won twenty-two pro bouts, including the 2006 International Boxing Association world cruiserweight belt, and took on world champions like Tomasz Adamek. But it is his reputation in the underground that has made him famous. Over the years, he has fought for cash in every underground venue imaginable, from midtown Manhattan bars to desert outposts to a Boston mobster den with a caged lion in the corner. He has been carjacked by the Latin Kings, had guns pointed at his forehead by the Russian and Albanian mobs, and been robbed at gunpoint by Irish gangsters. Even when bouts have become "rough-and-tumble"—that is, all rules are thrown out and anything goes—he has never backed down. "I've seen it all," he says. "Scary things. Men trying to kill me. Unfortunately, this is the world we live in."

Gunn claims not to be bothered by all this. "It's nothing to me, pal," he will say, shrugging his massive shoulders. But, of course, that isn't true. All fighters get scared. The key distinction is that Gunn doesn't worry about a battle until right before it begins. And it is then, in those moments when the world goes still and he looks at his opponent, the man threatening to take everything away from him in a fight that can always turn lethal, that Gunn allows himself to embrace the one fear he harbors deep within his battle-scarred body—that he will somehow fail his family. He thinks about the simple terror he endures each morning as he walks his seven-year-old daughter, Charlene, into the private school he pays for with his bare-knuckle winnings. He prays the other suburban parents don't discover his side hustle, prays the world never shuns his little girl for his own sins. "The other parents have no idea who I am," he says, "and I don't want them to." Gunn pauses. "The last thing my little girl told me this morning was, 'Please, Daddy, don't come home with a black eye.'"

Gunn shakes his head and walks into the center of the garage. The chatter dies down. The crowd's circle tightens. The only noise is the whir from an industrial fan. The referee, Danny Provenzano, an ex-con who served five years in a state prison and who also happens to be the grand-nephew of Anthony Provenzano, a key figure in the disappearance of Jimmy Hoffa, looks at the aging fighter.[2]

"You ready?"

Gunn nods.

* * * * *

[Figure I.3] **Fighting Jim McClendon** (Photo by Barcroft Media/Getty)

The two men circle. McClendon seems jittery. He feints and jabs while dancing on his toes, exhaling loudly with each punch. A few land, but most miss. By contrast, Gunn has undergone a stark transformation. He is calm, relaxed, his feet planted squarely on the concrete, keeping time with his opponent, dodging and weaving with his upper body. He throws fewer punches—sharp jabs, mostly to the body—but lands all of them. "*Oof,*" McClendon says, shaking his head after a shot to the chin.

"Bring it to the body," Dom calls.

About a minute into the fight, the men clench in a sweaty embrace, catching their breath, slowing their racing hearts, diagnosing each other's exhaustion. Then Gunn pushes McClendon away.

The end is sudden. Gunn shoots a left hook to the stomach, a right hook to the kidney, and a devastating deep left hook straight to the heart. As his opponent doubles over, Gunn delivers a final jab to the chin. McClendon goes down. "Get him up! Get him up!" Gunn yells, jacked up, marching back and forth.

On the ground, McClendon shakes his head.

"That's it, that's it," the ref says. "No fight."

Gunn helps his opponent up. "Good punch, dog," McClendon says. Gunn holds him by the shoulders, staring at him fully as if for the first time. They smile and embrace. The fight is over.

"I don't know if you ever took a sledgehammer to the face," McClendon later says. "But it was pretty equivalent to that. I'm actually surprised that my mouth is still moving."

The crowd cheers. Gunn is some $5,000 richer, but he looks like a guy who just missed his train.

"I'm tired of fighting in the shadows like this," he says, rubbing his knuckles while a mechanic slides the garage doors open and sunlight fills the room.

"I want to make this sport legal."

CHAPTER 2
THE BLOOD'S RED AND THE MONEY'S GREEN

Bobby Gunn parks his truck in a "No Parking: Loading Zone" space and hangs a fake police badge from the rearview mirror. He walks through a chain-link gate, down a narrow alleyway, past two snarling pit bulls, through a metal door, and into Ike and Randy's Boxing Gym in Paterson, New Jersey. On a Saturday morning in May, eight months after his victory over Jim McClendon, Gunn begins working a heavy bag, sweat flying off his massive shoulders. "I'm banging really hard right now," he says. "I believe God is saving the best for last."

Ike's is a cramped, low-slung, windowless space with brick walls the color of smoker's teeth. It has a full-size boxing ring and a rack of sledgehammers for swinging at a six-foot tire. A former auto-body shop, Ike's is sandwiched between a bar and a Baptist church in the Fifth Ward, the most crime-ridden neighborhood of Paterson, recently ranked as one of the most dangerous cities in the United States.[1]

"There are gangs on the corner, guys with AK-47s and AR-15s," says Richard Pierson, a former area drug dealer who now trains at Ike's. "You have to get past your fear of dying just to get here." Around the corner is Eastside High School, whose onetime baseball bat–wielding principal Joe Clark was immortalized in the 1989 Morgan Freeman film *Lean On Me*. Like Clark, Gunn also carries a wooden bat, which he keeps wedged between the bench seat and rear window of his truck. He once used it to beat a man attempting to carjack him outside the gym. Another time, while training, he heard gunshots, finished his workout, and emerged to find police cars and the chalk outline of a body on the street.

These days, Gunn has his own version of a security system: the fake police badge. "If you want to fight monsters," he says, "you got to train with them."

Gunn loves it here, pounding the duct-taped bags, sparring the local talent, keeping himself always ready for the underground. In preparation for his big-money bare-knuckle matches, he pits himself against the fiercest sparring partners he can find, local heavyweights who troll gyms looking to pick fights, men willing to go ten rounds for $50. "I don't even know their last names," Gunn says. "They're like pool sharks. These are professional gym bums who will fight me in the morning and then move to another gym in the afternoon, looking to make a few bucks as sparring partners. And some are killers—it's a hairline difference between them and a world heavyweight." Gunn has a standing offer of $100 to anyone who can knock him down. So far, he hasn't had to pay up. "If you want to look good and put on your headphones and lift some weights, then go to Bally," he says. "If you want to prepare for the belly of the beast, then go fight the young lions who look at you like a piece of steak."

For Gunn, Ike's is more than just a gym—it's also his main connection to the underground. Bare-knuckle boxers tend to come up in places like these, impoverished training grounds bridging the fight world and the criminal underbelly. In these shadow economies, journeyman fighters share information on quick-cash bouts, promoters look for prospects, and trainers and gym managers act as conduits for everyone, cherry-picking the top talent for underground gloved boxing and MMA matches, known as "smokers," as well as bare-knuckle bouts in which participants can risk their lives for up to $50,000 in a brown paper sack.* "You get a reputation in the gym and then get in," says

[Figure 2.1] The entrance to Ike's (Photo by author)

Steve Pellegrino, a former bare-knuckle brawler who now trains fighters in the Signature Strength and Nutrition gym in Las Vegas. "The connected guys would get their fighters from the gyms. It's always word of mouth."

Gunn stops working the bag and points to a custard-colored landline phone the size of a toaster, sitting on a metal desk. "This is where everyone knows to reach me for a fight," he says. "I'll come here to spar and see a note taped above the phone: 'Yo, Gunn—call this number.'"

From New York to LA, to Moscow, to London, and down to the cartel lands of Mexico, bare-knuckle boxing thrives in the

---

* According to popular theory, "smoker" boxing matches get their name from World War II, when sailors would stage impromptu unsanctioned fights on the smoking decks of battleships and aircraft carriers. "We used to charge ten dollars a head for smokers in barroom clubs in the South," recalls Mike Hopper, a pro boxing trainer. "You'd have old tobacco-spitting cowboys, farmers, sheriff's deputies, and preachers with a Bible in one hand and a whiskey bottle in the other. We'd do twenty, thirty fights a night, nothing sanctioned about them. It was crazy."

underworld. Like a modern-day gladiator arena, the sport almost exclusively features men, although there are tales of women who fight in bare-knuckle bouts staged by the Italian mob on Coney Island. Essentially boxing bouts without gloves or rounds, bare-knuckle fights last until one man either drops or says he has had enough. Fighters wear street clothes rather than trunks, the better to blend in with the crowd should the cops burst in. The sport is dangerous, bloody, and illegal almost everywhere, the bouts staged by bikers and gangland dons in warehouses, parking lots, and mobster manses. "The scene is crazy," Pellegrino says. "There are stabbings and guns. Gambling and drinking. People betting on everything. I used to drink shots of Jack Daniel's before I'd go out. Down south they some-times didn't want to pay, so you'd have to assert yourself. I remember one time I knocked out some guy who was supposed to be the shit from where he came from. His guys got so angry with him for losing that they mud-stomped him to a bloody pulp and put him in the hospital. He had injuries he never recovered from."

[Figure 2.2] "Yo, Gunn—Call this number." (Photo by author)

The sport does, however, have one redeeming grace: the winner takes all. As Joey Eye, a Philadelphia cut man and former under-ground promoter, says, "The blood's red and the money's green."

The circuit is not an organized association. There is no website. You cannot call a spokesperson to gain access. Instead, it is run by a loose confederation of regional promoters who keep tabs on prospects, arranging fights and bringing in talent from across the country. For years, Gunn worked with a man named Johnny Varelli (now deceased), a matchmaker based in New York and Chicago. Gunn was first given Varelli's number by a gym manager in Pittsburgh after winning his first major underground match—a biker bout—at age nineteen. He never once met Varelli in person. "You'd call Johnny, tell him you want to fight, and he'd call back a week later with all the details," Gunn says. "If you're anybody, they'll know your name."

Sometimes, bare-knuckle matches are put on by organized crime, much like the underground gambling circuits for dog- and cockfighting. (In the Southwest, cartel-funded events often include all three types of bouts.) Sometimes, they are staged by small-time promoters and may include gloved boxing. Sometimes, they're spur-of-the-moment challenges for cash, the brawlers' reputations then spreading across the country. "It exists everywhere," says Larry Willis, a former bare-knuckle fighter in Houston. "You go to certain places and it's more prevalent—Vegas, Florida, Philly, New York—but it's also in Colorado, Wyoming, and Indian reservations. There used to be a ton of activity around here, but, hell, maybe I'm older."

For its sheer number of bouts, its deep boxing culture, and its concentrated mix of organized crime and hard-luck contenders, New York has long been the heart of bare-knuckle boxing, and its feeder system is entrenched. Like the bouts themselves, Ike's and other hard-bitten Northeast boxing meccas—Champs in Philly, Morris Park Boxing and el Maestro in the Bronx—are almost impossible to find. They don't advertise. They don't really have signs. They're typically in the middle of residential neighborhoods, nondescript row houses that also function as the owners' homes. Yet everyone who keeps tabs on the local fight world knows where to find them. In 2008, Brandon Jacobs, then a star running back for the New York Giants, who had just won the Super Bowl, parked his sports car outside Ike's, stationed a bodyguard by it, and walked through the metal door, donning sparring gloves. A former amateur heavyweight from Napoleonville, Louisiana, Jacobs wanted to test his stuff. But after a couple of sessions with local boxers, the 6'4", 265-pound behemoth got dropped to one knee by Gunn's left jab to the body and hasn't been seen since. Even an NFL star accustomed to bone-crushing tackles from 330-pound linemen couldn't survive Ike's. (While this story was confirmed by other fighters at Ike's, Jacobs did not respond to repeated requests for interviews.) "Guys don't know Bobby's a pro," trainer Ray Henderson says with a gold-toothed grin. "But he's a force to be reckoned with."

At some underground fights, over a hundred spectators will pay up to $100 a head to gamble on multiple matches, security patting down entrants while beer and liquor are served at makeshift bars. At others, a small cluster of fans will meet at the last minute. No matter the venue or the prize money, chances are, at least one person there will know of Gunn, the first recognized bare-knuckle boxing champion in the United States in over 120 years—a legendary brawler who has fought his way through the underground for decades. "There's only one champion of bare-knuckle boxing," world heavyweight boxing champ Tyson Fury said on a Twitter video in 2016, "and that's Bobby Gunn."

* * * * *

At Ike's, Gunn circles the hundred-pound bag, pushing it, teasing it, and then, suddenly, demolishing it with torrents of punches, crying out with each shot. "Bop-bop-bop-bop-bop!"

"Ay, ay, ay, ay, ay!" A few feet away, Gunn's French bulldog, Max, sits on his haunches, chewing a sock. In the corner, Bobby Jr. works a speed bag, keeping time with the Kendrick Lamar blasting on Ike's boom box, the gym a swirl of pulsing bass, swinging sledgehammers, and gloved jabs. "You smell that?" asks Ossie Duran, the dreadlocked Ghanaian

[Figure 2.3] Working the hundred-pound bag (Photo by author)

immigrant and middleweight fighter who manages Ike's. "That smells like sweat. It smells like *war.*"

Gunn is massive, muscular, the biggest he's ever been, and says he is at the top of his game. But recently, there have been rumblings in the underground that he is aging out, that the circuit's top fighter is finished, that his era is over. "I would never say this to Bobby, but I can tell he's slowing down," an underground promoter says. "He's changed the way he fights. He can still hit like a horse, pull off these incredible side shots that nobody sees coming, but he's not the same. He's slower."

To this, Gunn has a response. "Nobody's beating me, pal," he says, grabbing the swinging bag. "I'm doing a young man's game but take care of myself—God is good to me."

Raised on the icy shores of Niagara Falls by Irish Travelers—a nomadic tribe of people who shun the outside world, speak their own language, and devote themselves almost entirely to family, religion, and fighting—Gunn has made his way with his two fists since leaving school after the second grade. When his pro boxing career fizzled, he began earning his keep by laying asphalt and fighting bare-knuckle bouts in the quick-cash underworld, getting in daily gym sessions while raising a family. Now, from the phone at Ike's, he books bouts from LA to Texas, to Florida, as well as countless matches in his own backyard. He once met two Russian mobsters from Brooklyn at a nearby Starbucks. "They said, 'We pay you very financial good,'" Gunn recalls. "Lovely gentlemen."

In the underground, Gunn is a fabled figure, a ghost, a man famed for his undefeated bare-knuckle record and 40,000 Twitter followers but, until recently, rarely seen except on a handful of blurry YouTube videos.* "He becomes almost mythical," says Steve Janoski, a newspaper reporter in New Jersey who watched Gunn fight in a warehouse match in 2011—a bout that has since been viewed online over 1.2 million times.[2] "It carries more weight because you don't know exactly what happened at most of these fights. You just know the bare bones. Even down to the name, he was born to do this—you can't become an accountant with a name like Bobby Gunn."

Gunn floors opponents with his precise punches, bare-knuckled strikes that penetrate deeper than gloved hits, going straight to the internal organs. Unlike gloved boxers, who

---

* So how can we confirm Gunn's complete 72-0 record? We cannot. But no one has ever disproved it or publicly claimed to have beaten him, either. "If someone beat me, trust me, you would know about it," Gunn says. "It would be all over Facebook and Twitter." Gunn says he has kept a personal tally of each fight, and makes claims to dozens more street bouts that were not for money and hence not included in this figure, but doesn't want to reveal the whole list, for fear of possible prosecution in some cases. (In this book, almost every specific fight I recount has been corroborated by at least one eyewitness.) When asked for his take, fight reporter Janoski offers this: "I don't doubt Bobby with his number, because he has no reason to inflate himself, and fighters are incredibly accurate with the day and how they fought and who they fought. It's always amazed me." This has been my experience as well. Gunn has often corrected stories told to me by others about his exploits, even when the truth is less compelling.

wear thick sixteen-ounce gloves and can therefore punch as often and as hard as they want, Gunn and other bare-knuckle fighters must punch with less force to keep from breaking their hands, targeting only certain areas of the body to avoid hitting hard bone. As a result, Gunn's bare-knuckle fights are not classic wars of attrition—the endless back and forth of boxing matches—but more like duels, each man waiting for the perfect opportunity to strike. "Bobby Gunn is a very skillful guy in bare-knuckle boxing," says Joe Rogan, a commentator for the Ultimate Fighting Championship (UFC). "I like watching him fight. He doesn't throw full-power punches, because he'd break his hand. So he chips away at guys and breaks them down. When you see him fight, you can tell he's been doing it for a long time. What Bobby Gunn is doing—that's real boxing."

Gunn, able to pinpoint the exact pressure points to topple an opponent, starts out by targeting the eyes, opening cuts to bloody the vision and striking behind the ears to upset equilibrium. He then moves on to his opponents' forearms, punching tendons and causing them to drop their hands. Avoiding the hard bone of the forehead, he instead aims for a three-inch-wide gap from the eyes to the upper lip, staying clear of his opponent's teeth since they can cut skin and cause infection. The chin is fair game but still relatively hard, so he aims for pressure points along its side and up to the ear, often throwing a corkscrew punch, twisting his wrist at the last moment to strike his opponent knuckle-first and better tear the skin, resulting in less trauma to his hand while still delivering a knockout blow.[*]

---

[*] The corkscrew punch—a favorite technique in bare knuckle and boxing in general—is said to have been invented in the late nineteenth century by pro boxer Charles "Kid" McCoy, who came up with the idea after watching a cat strike a ball of yarn. Created in an era when boxing gloves were thin, the punch safeguards the fighter's hand by stabilizing his wrist with its angle, the fighter turning his palm down at the last moment. It also protects his thumb by ensuring that his knuckles hit first, resulting in fewer broken bones while delivering devastating power.

Mostly, however, Gunn just works the body, pivoting to strike opponents from both the front and the back, punching deep to the kidney, liver, and heart with the precision of a sniper, unleashing terrible pain. "It's like getting hit with a ball peen hammer," Janoski says. "A liver shot feels like your ass drops out of your ass." All the while, Gunn must ensure he never actually kills an opponent—jail time always hanging over his head, the thought of his daughter, Charlene, never far from his mind. While sparring, Gunn sometimes wears fight trunks adorned with the Star of David—an acknowledgment not of the Jewish religion, but of the diminutive future king who singlehandedly brought down the giant Goliath with a single precise blow to the head. "The idea is to break a man down without breaking yourself down," Gunn says. "I'm like a surgeon."

Surprisingly, Gunn also credits bare knuckle with keeping him healthy. While the skin-on-skin contact may result in more blood and superficial wounds and look more gruesome, the overall use of less force appears to result in fewer concussions and fewer cases of chronic traumatic encephalopathy (CTE), a neurodegenerative disease common among former boxers and NFL players. In 2021, a two-year study published in the journal of the Physician and Sports Medicine found that bare-knuckle fighters suffered lacerations and hand fractures, but fewer concussions than gloved boxing. "Intuitively, it makes sense that BKF might not necessarily increase concussion risk, as the absence of hand padding may reflexively make fighters more selective about where they land their punches or lead to less force being administered with each strike," stated the study's authors.[3] Bare-knuckle fighters hit each other with less force than contestants do in either of the other two sports.[4] "Out of boxing, MMA, and bare knuckle," says Randy Gordon, a former athletic commissioner of New York, "bare knuckle is the safest." *

* Amazingly, in combat sports, relatively little research has been done on

Gunn, having fought bare knuckle for most of his life—far more often than he has boxed—says the sport has likely saved his sanity. "Believe me, at my age, I'm taking MRIs," he says, breathing hard, sizing up the swinging bag. "And don't think I'm not worried about those head scans. But I haven't had so much as a trace of a concussion. I was taught the old forgotten art, how to roll your head and shoulders with the shot. You know, people have in their minds that bare knuckle is barbaric, but it's actually safer. This isn't barroom brawls. This is a totally different art. It's what kept me in the game this long."

To his fellow fighters at Ike's, Gunn is something even more threatening than a bare-knuckle knockout artist: a nice guy. He demolishes sparring partners in the ring and then sits them down to ask if they have allowed Christ into their hearts. He is a family man who arrives every morning with Bobby Jr. and Max—a papaya-size dog that would not be out of place in a Rodeo Drive handbag—and then gives classes on how to elbow opponents while the ref isn't looking. He is a middle-aged Scotch-Irishman who goes out of his way to train brutally with fighters half his age in a predominantly Black gym in a Black neighborhood ruled by the Paterson Bloods, and then sits back with them to discuss

---

the relationship between glove weight, headgear, and concussions. Yet, numerous studies link gloved combat and CTE—fueling a growing argument for fighting without padding. The International Boxing Association, for instance, requires Olympic boxers not to wear headgear, citing internal studies showing that it results in more acute brain injuries. State athletic commissions in the United States, by contrast, have not followed suit, sometimes citing the need for more research. According to some researchers, the fight over bare knuckle and safety will become an increasing issue in combat sports—perhaps resulting in lawsuits. "When we have rules that require the use of gloves and headgear, alongside research that says it looks like it's putting us at a greater risk for brain injury, then it's not unreasonable to sue the entities involved," says Jason Thalken, a PhD scientist in computational condensed metaphysics, senior machine-learning scientist at Amazon, and author of *Fight Like a Physicist*. "The requirements of the Athletic Commissions and insurance companies are actually putting you in greater danger."

career choices or dole out family advice or talk about how he has overcome oppression as a Traveler. "Not many white guys here," says Pierson. "And Bobby is *white* white. Like, he wears stone-washed jeans."

Pierson laughs. "But he can fucking fight. I mean, inside of the ring he is brutal. He was showing me moves like how to catch a guy with an overhand right and finish it off with a little tip of your elbow. I was like, 'This is dirty.' And he said, 'No no, bro, my blood is gypsy. This is not dirty. This is fighting.' And then when he got out the ring, he was a generous teddy bear. When I went through custody shit with my four kids, he would give me a pep talk and never judge me. I listened to him speak, and it was always about peace and God, and I was like, 'There's something wrong with him.'"

Today at Ike's, Gunn is building a sweat. He lifts 120-pound barbells and jumps rope—along with more unusual bare-knuckle workouts like hoisting rope-tethered weights from his clenched teeth to strengthen his neck muscles, massaging Epsom salts and

[Figure 2.4] Preparing for war (Photo by author)

rubbing alcohol onto his brow to tighten the skin against cuts, and soaking his clenched hands in buckets of dry ice, squeezing them in the subzero temperatures to harden the muscles and tendons. Sometimes, he dons a World War I–style gas mask to simulate training at altitude, wearing it until he nearly collapses, gulping for air. He exercises the way he fights, with a Styrofoam cup of Dunkin' Donuts coffee at his side. No stretching. No water. Sometimes, he doesn't even bother to change out of his jeans. But today, he wears a black tank, black shorts, and ten-year-old black high-top boxing shoes that reach halfway up his shins. Today, he is preparing for war.

Gunn steps back from the bag, straps on his jeans, and scoops up Max, cradling the tiny dog like a football as he exits past the snarling pit bulls. No shower. No warm-down. Gunn has to move fast if he's going to make it back for his second workout later today.

In recent weeks, the phone at Ike's has finally rung.

Gunn has a new fight.

A tattooed young boxer approaches. "Whoa," he says, admiring Gunn's footwear. "Those are old-school."

Gunn smiles, sweat gleaming on his face, the pit bulls pulling at their chains.

"*I'm* old-school."

CHAPTER 3
SUBURBAN BRAWLER

Gunn is up at dawn six days a week, cruising for jobs in his truck, a black extended-cab Z71 with paving equipment in the bed, ladders strapped to the top, a chrome Jesus fish on the tailgate, and the slogan "Powerwashing Roofs and Driveways: Protective Coatings for All Surfaces" in big block letters alongside an American flag on the rear window. Max sits in his lap. Bobby Jr. sits shotgun. On the doors, yellow metal decals in the shape of New Jersey read "Serving the Tri-State Area for Over 20 Years." At night, Gunn removes them, wiping off the bug splatter and placing them inside a protective sheath.

"I'm a clean freak," he says, pulling out from Ike's, heading to the morning's job. "I wash this truck inside and out twice a week."

This is Gunn's office, the space he works from most of his day. The truck's interior includes a wallet-size photo of his family seated around a shopping-mall Santa Claus, a wooden baseball bat, a pair of championship boxing belts tucked beneath the seat, and a small bottle of Listerine from which he occasionally gargles and swallows. At stoplights, he takes out a straight razor and shaves his face in the rearview mirror—no shaving cream—afterward patting his skin

with rubbing alcohol. Aspirin bottles are everywhere, Gunn preferring pain relievers, homemade remedies of whiskey and cough
syrup (the only time he touches alcohol), and pulling his own teeth
and setting his own bones over modern medicine. "Who's going
to hire me for a job if they see a cast on my hand?" he asks. The
SiriusXM channel is permanently set to the Elvis station, Gunn
periodically joining in. *"Retuuuurn to sender! Ad-dress un-known!"*
Coffee cups and Pepsi bottles abound. Gunn never drinks water. "I
got tired of it," he says, shrugging.

[Figure 3.1] [Figure 3.2] Cruising the streets of New Jersey (Photos by author)

While driving, Gunn constantly fields calls and tweets from
fighters, promoters, lawyers, trolls, fans—whoever. At one point,
a man caller-ID'd as "Tony the Rhino" rings. "You're nothing but
a big sausage!" Gunn says, laughing, by way of greeting. A pause,
his face suddenly serious. "Was he being a cunt?" Whether it's
praise or a fight offer or a death threat, Gunn answers every call
using an earbud dangling off the left side of his face. Once a day,
he checks in with his father, Robert Williamson Gunn. "Are you
okay, old boy?" Gunn will ask.

[Figure 3.3] Family photo (Photo courtesy of Bobby Gunn)

Robert lives alone in a room at the Three Diamond Inn, an aging single-story motel in Niagara Falls, Ontario. To reach him, Gunn calls his room, lets the phone ring three times, hangs up, and then immediately calls back. Only then will Robert pick up, knowing that it's his son and not one of his local enemies. Suffice it to say, he and Gunn have a complicated relationship. For years, Robert withheld affection from his only child, brutally training him as a fighter while never giving a word of praise. Now they are locked in another kind of fight. A hardened bare-knuckle brawler, the seventy-two-year-old widower recently punched out a man thirty years his junior in a bar. Also, after falling on a construction job, he has begun to turn back to the bottle. Gunn is trying to return him to God. "When my mom died, my dad actually died," Gunn says. "He's never been the same. So I visit and give him his wee haircut, clean the bottles from his room, and say, 'Come on, you gotta pull together, old boy; I got big things cooking.'"

Today, Gunn is slated to work an asphalt-sealing job in Bayonne, New Jersey. An independent contractor, he hustles for every job he can scrounge, and is now trying to get today's client, a man who said he wanted his mother's driveway seal-coated, on the phone. "Hello, Robert Gunn here," Gunn says, leaving a message. "We can do your mom's house right now. Please call."

Gunn has been working six days a week since leaving school

after the second grade, doing everything from painting grain silos to banging nails, but his true specialty, the craft of his father and grandfather before him, is sealing asphalt. In the bed of Gunn's truck is his prized possession, a heavy-grade aluminum box the size of a dog's coffin, filled with the black tarry liquid he uses to tack-coat and weatherproof roads, driveways, parking lots, roofs, and chimney flashings. It is sticky, sweltering, backbreaking work. Gunn sprays, pours, rolls, and brushes the hot rubberized coating by hand, filling in cracks in asphalt while dodging low-hanging electrical lines and angry dogs. He rarely wears protective gloves or a dust mask. He once nearly died from falling off a roof—the same injury that forever altered his fighting style. "I landed on my left heel, bone fragment shooting out my toenail," Gunn recalls. "Blood was everywhere, squishy, so I took a bungee cord off my ladder rack, wrapped my foot, and then waited on the ambulance."

Sometimes, Gunn lands a lucrative gig that lasts for months, like when he helped repave the Bayonne industrial docks after Hurricane Sandy in 2012. Most of the time, however, he trudges the back roads of New Jersey, New York, or Connecti-cut—sometimes even traveling as far as Arizona or California for work—passing out fliers, knocking door to door, waiting on

[Figure 3.4] Gunn's French bulldog, Max (Photo by author)

referrals, making anywhere from $100 to $400 a job and occasionally getting outright stiffed or nearly killed. He even seeks work with other Travelers, the group in constant communication about good regions to find paving jobs, places where it can be easy to jump on an asphalt crew or work day labor, banding together to canvas towns and counties—often encountering danger along the way.

[Figure 3.5] Decal on the door of Gunn's truck (Photo by author)

Once, in 2016, after driving halfway across the country to work alongside Travelers based in Texas, Gunn and another Traveler he was with pulled into a ranch near Fort Worth to ask whether they wanted any paving, only to be confronted by a posse of gun-toting men. "It was a father and his bunch of young bucks trying to be wiseguys," Gunn recalls. "They thought they were going to pull the bluff on me, and I didn't take the bluff too good. I told one of them I'd break his jaw, and the Traveler boy with me got out and said, 'Do it and we'll have an OK Corral gunfight, because I'll pull my gun.' Even though he didn't have a gun." Gunn laughs. "Anyway, they put the guns down and I left the area. They don't play in Texas, baby."

For his entire run in the underground, Gunn has fought

while working construction, taking on underworld bouts during mornings, lunch breaks, nights, and even while en route to job sites with other contractors. "One time, we were on our way to paint a house in Union, New Jersey, and Bob said he had to make a pit stop," says Mike Normile, a Traveler who has known Gunn since childhood. "We pulled into a warehouse, he knocked this guy out with two punches, and then we got back in the van and went and painted the house." Normile shakes his head. "This stuff doesn't bother him—it's just part of what he does."

Today, at one point, while waiting on the client's call, Gunn stops in front of a run-down shopping center in Hackensack, New Jersey, and stares at a boarded-up store. "Eight years ago, when this was a cell-phone place, I fought a guy here at eleven thirty in the morning," he says. "Beforehand, in the parking lot, I sat right here, drinking coffee, watching my opponent pace back and forth by the shop's back door. Before fights, I get zoned in, and sometimes the look of a person can set me off. And this guy here was a cocky bastard. A kickboxer."

Gunn sips his coffee. "And that was his problem. When we went to fight, he was thinking too much with his legs. So while he was doing that, I cracked him three on the chin and knocked him out cold. Boom. Stiff. I picked his head up, told his handler to give him some water, and got my five thousand. Went outside and got another coffee and went to work."

Asphalt work and underground brawling is a brutal way to make a living—one that either crushes a man's spirit or hardens it into a bedrock of resilience. Gunn is the latter. The Visa may be maxed out and he's down to $369 in the bank account—the odd jobs and bare-knuckle fights never quite bringing in enough, especially in the wake of the recession—but he still gives a dollar tip when buying his Dunkin' Donuts regular with extra sugar at the drive-through. "It's all I can do to keep up with the cost of living," he says. "But I've had doors closed on me so many times in my life, I like giving back—I know people appreciate it."

Gunn's income all goes toward one goal: letting his family enjoy the upbringing he never had. The Gunns go everywhere together: paddle-boating with the swans in Central Park, watching Pixar movies at the mall, attending Baptist church at 7:00 a.m. on Sundays. Eschewing the caravan parks Gunn knew as a child, his family lives in a tidy apartment building nestled between a Home Depot and the New Jersey Turnpike. Gunn has been married to his wife, Rose, a blond Traveler from Florida, for twenty-two years. She has never approved of her husband's fighting, never liked seeing him hurt, which Gunn appreciates.

"It tells me how much she loves me she don't come," he says. "It keeps me grounded." Bobby Jr., a rising middleweight boxer, lives at home and works asphalt and trains with his father. "My dad is involved in every aspect of my career," he says. "He's my manager, trainer, promoter—everything." Then, finally, there is pigtailed Charlene—the one member of the family who can completely dominate her father. "I always get told, 'Daddy, you do this and do that,'" Gunn says, smiling. "God help the boy that gets her."

Every weekday morning, Gunn drives Charlene to a private Baptist school, chatting about her classes and friends. He can't really afford the school's $800 monthly tuition, but he loves watching her walk in wearing her uniform—just another normal suburban kid. Gunn can sign his name only with a simple X, and does not want the same for his two kids. "I've always dropped off my children at school because I never had that growing up," he says. "My wee girl gives me a hug at night before she goes to bed. She has a wee room with all the wee stuff she likes." He pauses. "That's what it's about. That's what I fight for."

On a recent morning, Gunn was driving Charlene to school when a surprising topic came up: bullies. Four feet tall with freckles, auburn hair, and a pink ballerina backpack, Charlene is a sweet girl who loves her friends, her guitar and keyboard piano, and her father, clutching his paw of a hand wherever they go. But like the rest of the Gunn clan, she can also be an unflinching negotiator, never giving an inch, whether it's kids on the playground or her own

[Figure 3.6] Charlene (Photo courtesy of Bobby Gunn)

gospel-spouting dad. This morning, there were many pressing issues to settle during the fifteen-minute drive: the tooth fairy, who had recently visited, Charlene's new favorite song, "God of Angel Armies," a contemporary Christian pop hit she could play on guitar, and the oft-recited Pledge of Allegiance. And then Charlene—feet dangling over the edge of Gunn's backseat, a gap in her front teeth—got to another topic, one that had been worrying her: a bully. "John is a bad kid," she said, furrowing her brow. "He never listens to the teacher." *

"She wants me to fight him," Gunn said, giving a tight smile.

Charlene said something in Cant, the secret Traveler language.

"He's a bully?" Gunn asked.

"He's a bully," Charlene said.

"Oh, don't worry about him," Gunn said. "It's best not to fight, Charlene. Always be friends."

"Okay," she said, looking out the window, the matter abruptly resolved. "God told me to stop fighting. I want to be a good kid."

"So you're not going to argue with John no more?"

* This is a pseudonym.

[Figure 3.7] Day at the park
(Photo courtesy of Bobby Gunn)

"He's not in school no more anyway," she said, shrugging.

Gunn grinned.

"Good deal."

Gunn uses his winnings to help keep his family in their nice apartment, to splurge on occasional fishing trips upstate, and, most especially, to fund Charlene's $9,600-a-year school. "Am I broke doing it?" he asks. "Yes. And it's worth it, my brother. At the end of the day, if you can't do that for your family, what does being a champion really mean?"

Being the blue-collar dad with a secret illegal night job doesn't come easy. Sometimes, on the way to school, the discussions turn to Gunn's fights. Charlene doesn't like them. "Mommy gets upset, and it makes me upset too," she says. "Sometimes he gets punched and sometimes he gets cut, but I know he'll be safe."

[Figure 3.8] Dancing
(Photo courtesy of Bobby Gunn)

Gunn, on the other hand, loves the feeling of power and rhythm that fighting conjures in an otherwise unsure world. But he doesn't savor the rage, preferring to keep that part of himself separate from his family. "I don't like the feeling," he says about unleashing the "monster" in the ring—a statement only partly true. "My grandfather always said to leave the bums at the gym. If you fight the monster long enough, you become the monster, so I separate my life—I want to quickly get back to my family afterward and pretend it never happened." More importantly, he worries his actions will somehow harm his daughter, disrupting the fairy-tale upbringing he sweats and bleeds to provide. "It's hard when I walk into the school and see the other parents," he says. "If they really knew who I was, they wouldn't look at me as a normal person—'Oh, my God, this guy is ferocious.' But it isn't the case."

[Figure 3.9] Fishing on Sunday (Photo courtesy of Bobby Gunn)

Gunn has promised his wife, Rose, that this is his last year in the ring. It is a promise he has broken repeatedly. However, at forty-three, he admits it's getting harder. "My body don't heal the same way anymore," he says. "My hands are breaking. My joints are going out. Every night, I wake up and feel like my shoulders are out of socket. I have to rotate them thirty times in the shower every morning just to get going—I can't lift my hands above my head."

Yet despite his injuries, Gunn knows he needs one last fight, a match to help set up his family for a better future, a win for enough money to maybe even build out his construction business and finally leave the underground behind for good. Now, he hopes, it has finally arrived. "For years, I beat everybody they put in front of me," he says. "Now I don't care no more—I've got one more fight and then I'm out."

In June, Gunn is slated to fight MMA journeyman and

longtime underground brawler Shannon Ritch in a $100,000 bare-knuckle bout in western Miami—a showdown that could finally yield a decent payday. Ritch, forty-five, is one of the original MMA fighters, a brawler who has been competing since the nineties, back when MMA was illegal and the fighters didn't wear gloves. He is a ripped 205 pounds, his biceps and pecs adorned with fire-breathing dragon tattoos, his Mohawk a sort of Guy Fieri number spiked and bleached and running down the back of his skull like a moussed pelt of roadkill.

The son of a cotton farmer raised on the Mexican border in Arizona, Ritch has worked as a bouncer, a Blackwater security contractor in Iraq, and, in addition to his legal MMA matches, a bare-knuckle brawler with a 25-2 record in fights from LA to Houston, to Mexico. He and Gunn once shared billing on the same underground event in the early 1990s, a two-card bare-knuckle match in a warehouse in Albuquerque. Both fighters won their

[Figure 3.10] Ritch in Iraq in 2004 (Photo courtesy of Shannon Ritch)

bouts. Now, in the twilight of his career, Ritch is training around the clock in Yuma, Arizona, with one goal in mind: to beat the ever-living hell out of Gunn. "Back in the day, everybody knew Bobby was the champ," Ritch says, taunting his opponent. "But now he looks like shit. I'm going to smash him."

Gunn has other plans.

[Figure 3.11] Shannon the Cannon (Photo courtesy of Shannon Ritch)

"A hundred thousand ain't chump change," he says, pausing at a traffic light. "He's brought out the beast—I'm the fucking bastard he's going to wish he'd never seen."

CHAPTER 4

TAKING THE KID TO MEET BIG DADDY BANG

Gunn shrugs his shoulders. "He's probably sitting in a bar somewhere and just said, 'Fuck it, I don't want to talk today.'"

Gunn and Bobby Jr. are eating lunch at the Crow's Nest,
a cavernous pub just off the Interstate in Hackensack. Gunn
has repeatedly called and texted the day's client, but, as often
happens, the man has not picked up. So Gunn decides to grab
a bite instead: a Pepsi, fried mozzarella sticks, and a French dip
sandwich for himself, a Pepsi and a plate of spaghetti Bolog-
nese for Bobby Jr. Nearby sit a table of nuns in full habit. Old
men occupy the bar. Outside, Max is curled asleep in the truck,
which has been left running with the doors locked, the air
conditioning on full blast. Gunn was counting on today's $400
job, but in the asphalt game, as in the fight game, nothing is
assured, so he shrugs and settles in for a leisurely lunch. "Thank
you, my angel," he says, winking at the tired-looking waitress
who refills his Pepsi. He then looks at his son, who sits famished
from the morning workout. "They say the leaf don't fall far from
the tree," Gunn says. "But I don't believe it. I'm hard on Bobby,
but not like my dad. I want to give my boy a better life."

Gunn is constantly scrounging, hustling, and chasing dreams, but there is one commitment he considers his greatest responsibility. He will help Bobby Jr. become a world-champion boxer. "I want to give him what I could never have," he says. "I want him to be a top-class professional boxer." There's just one condition. No bare knuckle.

"It's not my interest," Bobby Jr. says, forking a meatball. "Never done it and never will. Boxing has always been my dream."

At nineteen, Bobby Jr.'s star is rising. He's a super-middleweight talent with an 8-0 record, six of those wins coming from knockouts. "I see a lot of ability in Bobby's son," says Randy Gordon, a former New York boxing commissioner and cohost of *At the Fights* on SiriusXM radio. "If he moves correctly and learns his craft, the kid could make some noise down the road."

[Figure 4.1] Bobby Jr. (Photo by author)

A muscular 154 pounds with freckles and a pompadour, Bobby Jr. is a lot like his old man. He tweets Bible verses to his six thousand followers, is unfailingly polite—and is also capable of dropping you like a wet sack of Idaho's finest. "He looks like a wee boy," Gunn says, "but God help the poor bastard that picks a fight with him."

Bobby Jr. is also very much a teenager, constantly on his phone, meeting friends at the mall, texting with his girlfriend—but with one major difference. Whereas many kids his age are graduating from high school and entering college, Bobby Jr.

awakens every day to punch the bags at Ike's and then work the same job he's known since leaving school at age twelve after the seventh grade: laying asphalt alongside his old man.* "I go to work with my dad every day," he says. "Before I train, after I train—I do anything he wants me to do."

Every morning, Bobby Jr. takes his shotgun seat in Gunn's truck, heading out for the day's job. The duo travel everywhere together, training at Ike's, laying asphalt, attending fights in the underground. Whereas most kids might be bitter about staying at home and working for their fathers, Bobby Jr. is relentlessly upbeat, seemingly pleased to be living as a Traveler and slinging gravel with Gunn—even if it means abstaining from alcohol, tobacco, and, in accordance with Traveler custom, sex until marriage, at which point he'll finally leave the nest.

"It means a lot to me," Bobby Jr. says about his Traveler heritage. "It's our name—trying not to be a Traveler is like telling a zebra to lose his stripes." When asked about not attending college, Bobby Jr. says he has no regrets, adding that white-collar jobs are forbidden for Travelers anyway. Corporate America, like high school, is an ungodly influence. "I have to do a line of work in line with our people," he says. "I mean, I'd like to be a millionaire or movie star, but I wouldn't trade the Traveler life for nothing."

Bobby Jr. never complains about standing in Gunn's shadow. In fact, he idolizes his father, obeying his every word and often acting as counsel, a level head long accustomed to cleaning up and clarifying in his father's hulking wake. "He's a smart kid," an underground promoter tells me. "Sometimes, after Bobby gets upset about something, Bobby Jr. will take me aside and say, 'Don't worry about it, I'll talk with him.'"

Bobby Jr. can recite Gunn's wars like a litany, vividly recalling

* Bobby Jr. was then homeschooled through a religious program.

the first time he saw him bleed in a boxing ring, how it shook him. "I was nine years old when my dad fought for the world title against Shannon Landbergh," Bobby Jr. says. "He got a little nick in the first round and I started crying. I was terrified."

Gunn, for his part, dotes on his son. "Bobby is a great father," says Richard Pierson, a boxer at Ike's. "To see how Bobby Jr. looks up to him is inspiring—it makes me want to be a better father."

Yet the Gunns' relationship isn't always smooth. Bobby Jr., like any teenager, can sometimes chafe against his father. At fight conferences, he often looks bored—stone-faced, wearing aviator sunglasses, scrolling his Facebook feed. He also doesn't seem to relish constantly having to check in with Gunn whenever he goes to Disney World with his Traveler teenage friends. (During these trips, his father worries about him getting cornered into a fight, the family name being an invitation for brawling.) And Bobby Jr. certainly doesn't want to talk about his personal life, bristling at one point when asked why he and his girlfriend—a young Traveler—became briefly engaged only to see the whole thing unravel when both sets of parents had a falling-out. "I don't want to talk about it," Bobby Jr. says.

But perhaps the biggest break between Bobby Jr. and Gunn is over bare knuckle—he will never practice the sport of his father. "I respect the sport, but it just isn't my thing," he says. "I want to focus on my professional career." For Bobby Jr., being the son of Gunn—the most famous bare-knuckle fighter in the world—is already hard enough, the name bringing constant threats from both Travelers and gym rats. "I've had circumstances where it's gotten out of hand," Bobby Jr. says. "If they beat me, they beat Bobby Gunn's son. That's what they think." He doesn't want to deal with that kind of pressure in the underground as well. "It's hard," Bobby Jr. says. "I have a target on my head because my dad is Bobby Gunn. I've had to deal with it since my first fight ever."

For his part, Gunn claims he never pushed his son into

fighting. He says he is only helping guide what is already there. "It's in his breeding," Gunn says. "Our family is like a pack of pit bulls. Put my boy in a fight and he naturally goes for the throat."

Bobby Jr. will tell you the same. "This was programmed into me," he says. "From the minute I was born, I was bred to fight."

They work daily together to mold Bobby Jr. into a seasoned pro, working the bags at Ike's and then getting in roadwork on Garret Mountain, a 568-acre park in the congested heart of Passaic County, New Jersey. "I'm building my boy up the way I should have been done, giving him what I never had," Gunn says. "From my mouth to God's ears, he'll be a world middleweight champion by twenty-two."

Gunn oversees every aspect of Bobby Jr.'s career, training him, booking his pro boxing matches, driving him fourteen

[Figure 4.2] Sparring with Bobby Jr. (Photo by author)

hours straight to fights ranging from makeshift arenas in Harley Davidson dealerships in West Virginia to two-thousand-seat venues in Indianapolis. At all these fights, Gunn stands ringside, coaching his son, treating his cuts, cheering him on. Gunn is so adamant about Bobby Jr.'s career that he fired his own longtime trainer, Dominick Scibetta, after they disagreed over his son's technique. "Dom told me I couldn't train a dog to take a shit," Gunn says. "But look how my boy is doing."

So far, Bobby Jr. has a perfect winning record. In the coming months, he will even qualify to fight for the Canadian world middleweight title, a belt that could elevate his status, finally allowing him to move out from his father's shadow. "I have a lot to prove," Bobby Jr. says. "I carry a lot of weight on my shoulders. My dad should have been middleweight champion of the world when he was twenty-three, but God willing, I can be."

He pauses.

"I believe I can be the new world champion of boxing."

* * * * *

In Bobby Jr., Gunn sees the future he always wanted for himself, the respectable career of a pro boxer, and won't endanger his son's prospects by putting him in the underground. "I couldn't bear for my boy to go through the violence I went through," he says.

He has cause to worry. Bare-knuckle fights are illegal. Laws vary from state to state, but generally, if busted by police, an underground fight's venue owner, promoter, and combatants can face charges of disorderly conduct—hefty fines that, for repeat offenders, can lead to imprisonment. More damningly, a state athletic commissioner can revoke promoters' and fighters' professional licenses, destroying careers. Throw in illegal gambling and the fact that many people participating in these bouts already have

[Figure 4.3] [Figure 4.4] A family tradition (Photos courtesy of Bobby Gunn)

well-worn rap sheets, and you can see why so few fights make the Internet. Recording with phones is almost always forbidden. "It's illegal," says J. C. Wilfork, a former bare-knuckle fighter in West Palm Beach, Florida. "Nobody wants these videotaped."

For years, Gunn has been chased by authorities. In 2011, Tim Lueckenhoff, then head of the Association of Boxing Commissions, condemned bare knuckle as "abhorrent, barbaric, egregious, in contravention of a multitude of federal, state, and tribal boxing laws and regulations, and, perhaps, criminal." And most state boxing commissioners appear to agree. In particular, Greg Sirb, executive director of the Pennsylvania State Athletic Commission—the longest-serving state commissioner in the United States—has seemingly made it his personal mission to bury the sport.· A compact man with a drill sergeant's build and a perpetual frown, Sirb has repeatedly tried to stop Gunn and others from competing in underground fights—even when they fall outside his jurisdiction. "Greg Sirb is a bastard," Gunn says. "He said if you're not on the side of the law, then you're an outlaw. I've been tortured. That's why I'm so scared to say

---

* Sirb retired from the Pennsylvania State Athletic Commission in 2023.

where these fights are. And that's why I don't want my son in the circuit—his pro boxing career is too precious."

There is also something deeper at work behind Gunn's decision. By not training Bobby Jr. for the underground, he is breaking from the tradition of his forefathers, of his Traveler people. While he followed Traveler custom by pulling his son from school at age twelve so he wouldn't assimilate with other children, and has brought him into the family asphalt trade, he draws the line at bare-knuckle fighting, the sport of his people. The violence is just too much to bear. "I would never do that to my boy," he says. "I want to bring him up the right way."

Gunn and the other bare-knuckle fighters are men with customs and traditions and beliefs in many ways unrecognizable to the white-collar professionals on the coasts. For better or worse, they have older values and skills. They look to ritual, to church, and to sport for comfort and identity—for an America they can recognize. "Fighting is a poor man's sport," says Gunn's father, Robert. "A rich man goes to college, and a poor man goes to the gym."

For these men living on the marginalized edges of society, bare-knuckle boxing is a shot at redemption. It's a way to win sorely needed cash. But more than that, it is a means to prove one's worth. It is a quantifiable, ancient contest—the most ancient in human history—in which a warrior can affirm his status and rise in the ranks. It is a sport that exists outside the realm of the law, but one that has very clear rules, one that can be understood in this age of chaos, one that can bind a tribe, one in which a man can embrace his opponent afterward and feel a profound bloodied satisfaction. It is a sport in which a certain type of man can find peace.

What Gunn knows, and wants to keep from his son, is that bare-knuckle fighters live in a brutal realm, a world where respect means everything and where perceived weakness can mean one's life. R. J., one of Gunn's opponents—a professional fighter and underground bare-knuckler—has a story about a match that occurred in a maximum-security state prison along the Mexican border in the 1990s.* At the time, R. J. had finished a stint in the army, studied advertising on the GI Bill, and, unable to find an industry job, moved back to his hometown for the only available paycheck: work as a prison guard. "Every day was an adventure," he says. "There were fights on the yard; guys got shanked; fires broke out. Yeah, it was nuts." One day, for whatever reason, a twenty-year-old inmate serving two consecutive life sentences for murder began threatening R. J. in the yard and wouldn't stop. After a few months of constant confrontations, the army vet finally decided to take action by appeal-ing to the prison's top authority—Gusto Jiménez, the head of the Mexican mafia.† "People think guards run the prison," R. J. says. "But inmates run the prison. They know where you work, what you drive, what you do. So I went to Jiménez and said, 'Hey, one of your guys is jumping in my face all the time. I want to fight him straight up.' And he said, 'Don't worry about it, R. J. We'll handle it.'"

Soon, R. J. was handed a "kite," a prison note, stating that Torres, his tormentor, would have mop duty in the commissary the following night.‡ R. J. ensured that the space was empty save for himself, Torres, two members of the Aryan Brotherhood—"be-cause I'm white"—and two members of the Mexican mafia. "Now, this is crazy, but I take off my shirt, my handcuffs, and my radio," R. J. says, "and I bring him into the vegetable room." Nestled deep in the kitchen, the vegetable room was essentially a concrete-floored windowless cage lined with crates of produce—tomatoes, cucum-bers, onions—with only one door in and out. As their secondaries stood vigil, the prison guard and his prisoner stripped to their pants, walked into the cage, and clanged the door shut behind

* At his request, I have used a pseudonym.
† This is also a pseudonym.
‡ "Torres" is also a pseudonym.

them. "I wanted to fight him straight up," R. J. recalls. "I'm just that type of guy. It was time to finish it, man-to-man."

From the beginning, R. J. was in control, drawing on his military background to land devastating body shots, Torres bleeding all over the surrounding crates, the air tomb-like and cold. Sensing that the fight was over, R. J. began to turn his back—and Torres pulled a shank, stabbing the stunned prison guard in the leg. Crumpling to the floor, R. J. looked up to see Torres standing over him as the other members of the Mexican mob filed into the room behind him. "The other guys run in and I think, 'Well, I'm dead,'" R. J. says. "They're going to kill me." In a final desperate move, R. J. tackled Torres and threw him to the ground, trying to grab the knife, when suddenly he was lifted off his opponent, the large prisoners then tossing him aside to do the last thing he had ever expected: pouncing on their own gang member, Torres, beating him so badly he was sent to the infirmary.

By pulling a weapon in what was supposed to be a fair underground fight, the young prisoner had violated the terms of the match—and disrespected the head of the Mexican mafia in the process. Soon, there was a contract out on Torres's life, and he sought protective custody, getting transferred to another unit. Even among thieves, murderers, and gangbangers, the honor code of bare-knuckle fighting was sacrosanct. "He more or less just disappeared off the yard," R. J. says. "And after that, I didn't really have any problems. They knew I was a stand-up guy."

When asked about R. J., about the mentality needed to confront the worst depths of the underground, Gunn just smiles. "Rough-and-tumble, baseball bats, chains—you got to steel your mind to survive," he says. "But my boy will have nothing to do with that world."

* * * * *

After lunch, Gunn drives to one last stop: a Polish neighborhood in a town whose name he doesn't want to disclose, a block of seemingly ordinary brick townhouses secretly run by organized crime. "This whole neighborhood is owned by the Polish mob," he says, gesturing at the midday bustle. "Everything. That auto-body garage is actually a chop shop."

We pass a bald man standing on a street corner—a mob soldier Gunn recognizes—drive down a dead-end street, and turn left onto a narrow dirt alleyway shaded by an Interstate overpass. To our right is a small gravel construction site surrounded by a

[Figure 4.5] Walking the streets of Hackensack (Photo by author)

chain-link fence. From the neighborhood streets, it is completely invisible. "The Poles love me," Gunn says, stepping outside to piss. "I've fought here eight times and seen at least twenty other bare-knuckle fights over the years. They happen very, very quickly, and then everyone disappears."

Gunn may not allow Bobby Jr. to fight in the underground, but that doesn't mean he won't take him along as backup. On the face of it, this logic can seem strange, but Gunn simply shrugs. "He goes everywhere with me."

Accompanying his father to bare-knuckle fights, Bobby Jr. has had guns pulled on him, survived a carjacking, and even occasionally gotten a piece of the action. In one bare-knuckle bout that occurred on this patch of gravel in 2007, Gunn fought a man called Big Daddy Bang, a 240-pound boxer hailing from the Bloods street gang in South Jamaica, Queens. On the day of the fight, a $20,000 bout, the Bloods arrived in five cars, including an old limousine with curtained windows, to meet Gunn and Bobby Jr. under the overpass. "They called me the 'Gunn man,'" Gunn recalls. "The limo door opens, and pot smoke comes out. I said, 'My boy's here in the truck. Can he come?' 'Yeah, Gunn man, no problem. Your boy's safe.'"

Surrounded by construction equipment, Gunn and Big Daddy squared off. Fresh from work, Gunn wore his usual attire, a black muscle shirt and jeans. His share of the prize money had been fronted by the Irish mob, who sometimes showed up to watch the bouts and other times simply backed them. Regardless, their arrangement with Gunn was always the same. If Gunn won, he would take home half the spoils—$10,000 for today's match. "It was a lot of money, my brother," Gunn says. "I needed it bad." As evidenced in photos of the fight that were later posted to the Internet, Big Daddy—a bearded hulk with a long braided dreadlock hanging down his back—wore gray sweatpants, a black tank, and a black skullcap. He towered over Gunn. "I was pretty nervous," says Bobby Jr., who was eleven at the time. "He was big."

The match was long by bare-knuckle standards, a five-minute bloody duel. "Head shots, body shots—he threw a fucking beautiful jab," Gunn says. In the end, however, Gunn dropped him. "He got up, bleeding from the mouth, and said, 'You good, man,

[Figure 4.6] [Figure 4.7] Fighting **Big Daddy Bang** (Photos courtesy of Bobby Gunn)

you good.'" On their way out, the Bloods tipped Bobby Jr. $100, patting him on the head. "The guys you wouldn't think, the bad fuckers, are the nicest guys in the world," Gunn says. "They were gentlemen."

The fight was a minor victory in a trash-strewn alley, an underworld bout witnessed by a handful of people, Gunn's prize a brown paper bag of illicit money. "It's a way to make a quick buck," Gunn says, walking to his truck as a car turns into the alley, sees us, and then slowly turns around.

After decades of fights like these, however, Gunn is ready to leave them all behind—and hopes his $100,000 bare-knuckle match with Ritch will allow him to do that. In fact, with that fight, he is hoping to accomplish something extraordinary, something that hasn't been done in the United States in over 120 years—something that will almost assuredly draw the ire of commissioners like Greg Sirb and may even land Gunn in jail for his lifetime of illegal brawls.

Gunn is planning to stage the bare-knuckle fight as a legal match.

"I come too far in life," he says, cradling Max and pulling out from the alley. "I know what it is to be in the gutter, and now I want to overcome it—bare-knuckle boxing is going to become the next big sport."

CHAPTER 5
THE BLOODY RISE OF AMERICA'S FIRST SPORT

Come by yourself.

My introduction to the underground came in the form of a text. For a year, I had been interviewing Gunn, meeting him in gyms and at work sites in New Jersey, when, one Thursday in June 2012, he suddenly sent an invitation to an upcoming match. I was told the fight would take place sometime over the weekend, somewhere in the "NY/NJ area," and then heard nothing until the following Tuesday. That morning, at 8:00 a.m., I received another text, stating it would occur in Delaware that afternoon. After taking off from my job in Manhattan and arriving by Amtrak to the designated city, I was then told the fight had been moved to another state due to their "being on the run" from authorities. I was given a cross street and informed that it would start in an hour. *Good luck.*

Driving a rental car through a gray rain, I arrived at the location, a run-down boxing gym in an inner-city neighborhood in a major coastal city. Across the street was a taxicab dispatcher. Around the corner, an undercover cop was arresting someone. In the parking lot, Gunn approached, carrying a wooden baseball bat slung across his shoulder. "I bring this to all the fights," he said, leaning into my car window, rain soaking his skintight black T-shirt. "Insurance policy."

That afternoon, I watched a Hell's Angel drop a marine to the floor in thirty seconds with a shot to the chin and learned my first lessons of the underground: that the fights themselves are often the tamest moments of the night, disgruntled crowd members and entourages sometimes breaking into brawls among themselves. I also learned the sport's most important rule, one that explains why this illicit world can exist across the USA in total secrecy: No one talks about the underground. "This is like betting on a dice game in an alleyway," says Guy Pagan, a boxing promoter and former army ranger who attends underground fights in Miami. "Bare knuckle is a high like I had in combat. This is our sport—this is real life."

The bare-knuckle circuit has existed for centuries, across the world, in almost every major city, but you will never hear so much as a whisper about it. Compared with most sports, it is small but deep, and the same can be said about organized crime and Travelers. These are societies of profound fraternal bonds, which don't open to outsiders, and nowhere is this more evident than in one of their favorite pastimes, bare-knuckle boxing. "I'm taking a risk just by talking to you," says Ed Simpson, a Traveler who has accompanied Gunn to fights for decades. "The circuit is illegal. You're in a warehouse in a bare-knuckle match that is organized by the mafia—it's called the underground for a reason."

The oldest bare-knuckle tradition, and one that still precedes every match, is the side bet between the two camps of fighters. Gunn, like most knucklers, cannot afford to stake $10,000, let alone $100,000, on a bout, so he raises money from local gangs or friends and family, always paying them back double their investment. "I ain't a rich person, but I know he's going to win, so I'll take a few grand and bet it on him," says Mike Normile, a Traveler who calls me from a fracking field in North Dakota. "And I've never lost." In the weeks before arriving at the venue for a bare-knuckle fight, Gunn and his opponent will pay "kick-in money," perhaps 20 percent of the total purse, to a trusted third party to hold—a deposit to demonstrate commitment. The day of the fight, he and his opponent will then give the rest of their stake money, typically a substantial amount in loose bills, to the house for safekeeping. To ensure that no one gets any ideas, one promoter says he carries a contraption called a "cage," a portable metal safe with holes drilled into its lining. Once he arrives at the venue, he opens the safe, screws it through its back onto joists in a wall or shoots it with bolts into a concrete floor, and then places the prize money inside it. "We need to provide a certain amount of security," he says. "But it's not as easy to rob these places as you would think. What are you going to do, stick up a hundred guys?"

After a match, the winner takes all while the loser must scrape together enough funds to repay his backers. "He's going to be paying them back with interest," Gunn says of one fighter who loses a match. "That's how this game goes."

Fragments of stories about the underground can be found everywhere. Lamon Brewster, a former world heavyweight boxing champion, tells me his onetime trainer in Indianapolis, Bill "Honey Boy" Brown, used to "hobo" around the south, fighting bare knuckle for cash in the 1920s. John "Pops" Arthur, a sixty-eight-year-old boxing trainer in Los Angeles, came up fighting in underground "death matches" throughout Asia and Africa in the 1960s, brawling with only his bare hands or a thin pair of kangaroo-skin driving gloves. And today, multiple fighters from Gunn to Ritch, to Danny Batchelder, a pro heavyweight boxer who used to train with Mike Tyson, compete in the underground for extra cash. "It's a different beast from boxing," Batchelder says. "It's more pure. The politics ain't in it; the crooked promoters and managers ain't in it; there's no corruption. It's just who's the better fighter that day."

No matter where they exist, bare-knuckle fight circuits tend to have one thing in common: organized crime. "I been to some in Japan," says Billy Blanks, a former world kickboxing champion. "I was shocked. They were run by the yakuza, guys with tattoos everywhere. They'd open up the door of a warehouse and you'd walk inside to see Bentleys, Ferraris, girls, and the rings. I've seen people's legs get twisted off—it's rough stuff."

Bare-knuckle boxing may be illegal now, but it has not always been so underground. It is perhaps the oldest organized sport in existence, dating back to the ancient Greeks, who staged it in their olympiads, believing that fighting embodied discipline, bravery, and grace. It crops up in the Mahabharata, an epic Sanskrit poem of ancient India, in which combatants fought with clenched fists, kicks, and head-butts to honor the gods and kings.[1] And during the Roman Empire, the sport was elevated to a national pastime, becoming bloodier, stranger, and more specialized as slaves, soldiers, and even wild animals fought to the death in the sand pits of the gladiators. "Next is a boxing bout," Virgil writes in the *Aeneid*. "From somewhere he produced the gloves of Eryx and tossed them into the ring all stiff and heavy, seven layers of hide, and insewn lead and iron ... You can still see the blood and a splash of brains that stained them long ago."[2]

By AD 500, Rome had banned all fight sports in the name of Christianity. Bare-knuckle boxing went into remission for centuries, later reemerging in England in the 1600s before crossing to America two hundred years later and producing the first US champion, Tom Molineaux, a 5'8", 200-pound slave from Virginia. There is no hard evidence of Molineaux's early years, and legend has likely seeped into the historic record, but he is said to have come from a family of fighting slaves including his father, a noted prize-fighter, and that from an early age, Molineaux competed in bouts on plantations for gambling masters. After winning $100,000[3] for his wealthy owner in a high-stakes match around 1804—a sum now valued at $1.6 million after adjusting for inflation—he was given $500 and set free.[4] He promptly moved to New York, where he worked on the docks of the East River—likely competing in illegal fights at Catherine Market—before moving to England at age twenty-five and squaring off against UK champion Tom Cribb, for 200 guineas, near London in 1810.[5] The English champ, a 5'10", 180-pound coal heaver, a bull of a man who reportedly trained by punching the bark off trees, was the 4-1 favorite. Molineaux, however, shocked the crowd, knocking Cribb unconscious with a shot to the throat in the ninth round before dirty tactics—at one point, spectators even swarmed the ring, possibly breaking one of the American's fingers—cost him the fight. While Cribb would remain a national hero, Molineaux descended into drink and dissolution, dying of liver failure at age thirty-four in a barracks in Galway.[6] His era of the sport was immortalized by a nineteenth-century journalist as "the sweet science of bruising."[7]

By the 1840s, bare knuckle had surpassed horse racing as one of the most popular pastimes in the United States. In fact, from 1840 to 1870, the New York press gave boxing and bare-knuckle fighting more coverage than any other sport except baseball.[8] The fights, though illegal, were nonetheless covered obsessively by the country's burgeoning newspapers, and the combatants' techniques were the same as Gunn uses today. "Pugilists harden their hands in different ways," states boxing writer Robert K. Turnbull in 1889. "Good hard rubbing is one of the best things in the world to harden the flesh and bones of the hand. Alcohol, lemon-juice, rock-salt, gunpowder, saltpeter dilute, tannin, and alum are some of the washes used. Jem Carney, the English light-weight champion, used to whet his hands over a smooth plank for hours a day during his training, slapping the backs of his hands back and forth over the wood as a man straps a razor."[9] Just as today, the fighters were cautious, mostly aiming for the body. "In fighting or boxing, the hands should be held loosely, half open, all the muscles and those of the forearms relaxed, till the moment of delivery, when the fist should be most tightly closed,"

Turnbull writes. "The pit of the stomach, called the 'mark,' was one [of the most vulnerable spots for blows], and a severe blow on this spot was very telling. Other points of attack were the butt of the ear or on the jugular vein; the temples, the eyes, the throat, just over the heart, and on the short ribs."[10]

During its heyday, bare knuckle's true capital, as it remains today, was New York. In the mid-nineteenth century, the city swelled with hundreds of thousands of Irish immigrants fleeing the potato famine—first-generation Americans who soon became the country's first real sports heroes. By day, these top hat–wearing toughs worked as tradesmen. By night, they fought in illicit matches, spilling blood with guns, knives, and fists in pursuit of their American dreams. These were the real-life incarnations of the characters in Martin Scorsese's 2002 film *Gangs of New York.*[*] James "Yankee" Sullivan was an Irish convict exiled to Australia, who escaped and remade himself in Manhattan as a champion prize-fighter and a saloon owner. John C. Heenan, the 6'2", 200-pound son of Irish immigrants, swung a sledgehammer for the Pacific Mail Steamship Company in San Francisco before becoming a top bare-knuckler. John Morrissey, a ruthless prizefighter known as "Old Smoke" for once searing his skin on a coal fire during a saloon brawl, even managed to transcend the ring, becoming a US senator and founding the Saratoga Race Course in Saratoga, New York—now the oldest racetrack in the United States. But no Irish immigrant would achieve more as a bare-knuckle fighter than John L. Sullivan—a plumber, a drunk, a womanizer, and a full-blown millionaire sports star by the end of the nineteenth century.

The son of Irish immigrants, Sullivan was born in Boston in

---

* Daniel Day Lewis's character was based on Bill "the Butcher" Poole, a nativist New Jersey butcher who fought Irish gangs like the Dead Rabbits, at one point gouging and biting an opponent's face—blood "streaming from ... both eyes" according to a contemporary account—before dying of a gunshot wound to the chest.

1858. As a teenager, he brawled in the streets of the Roxbury neighborhood, frequented saloons, and froze and scalded his hands on rusty pipes. One night, he passed a vaudeville house where a famed boxer was challenging all comers. On a whim, he stripped off his coat, donned thin gloves, and knocked the man out, sending him tumbling backward over a piano. Emboldened by the victory and eager to escape his ditch-digging father's footsteps, Sullivan decided to become a pro fighter. "At the age of nineteen," he wrote in his 1892 autobiography, *Reminiscences of a 19th Century Gladiator,* "I drifted into the occupation of a boxer."

[Figure 5.1] John L. Sullivan (Copyrighted by Richard K. Fox, New York. photo by Chickering, Boston, Mass. - Library of Congress Prints and Photographs Division)

From the beginning, the "Boston Strong Boy" was a celebrity. Standing 5'10" and weighing 200 pounds, with cast-iron biceps, dark eyes, and a meticulously curled mustache, Sullivan began his career in 1880, winning match after match on the strength of what newspapers described as his "bull-like rushes" and "sledgehammer right hand." This was a transitional time for prizefighting in America, with gloved boxing beginning to take hold, and "scientific exhibitions of skill" were legal if combatants refrained from heavy hitting—a ludicrous mandate that both Sullivan and the police ignored. A natural showman, Sullivan would don skintight gloves and offer $50 to any man who could enter the ring and last four rounds with him. He knocked out scores of opponents, dropping money on their prone bodies as if leaving a tip, while fighting in the backs of beer halls, on moonlit barges, and during short tours through cities like Buffalo, Pittsburgh, Louisville, and Chicago. He drew increasingly large crowds and joined them in saloons after his victories, buying rounds, fighting, and chasing women (despite his marriage to Annie Bates Bailey, a former prostitute) before returning to his hotel for his customary breakfast of six dozen clams and a whiskey. In 1882, at age twenty-three, he defeated reigning bare-knuckle champ Paddy Ryan for $5,000 in a makeshift ring in Mississippi City, a resort town on the Gulf Coast, becoming the most famous man in America.[11] "My name's John L. Sullivan," he would bellow, "and I can lick any son-of-a-bitch alive."

Following his bare-knuckle victory over Ryan, the Boston Strong Boy embarked on an endless "knocking-out tour," earning upward of $500 a night, sometimes fighting gloved, sometimes bare knuckle, across America, Australia, Ireland, and even on Baron de Rothschild's estate in France. He fought in circuses, surrounded by clowns, jugglers, and elephants. He fought in Buffalo Bill's Wild West show amid cowboys, Native Americans, and mustangs. He flexed his muscles for wax museums, acted in stage plays, endorsed beef broth, and was measured and photographed in the nude by a Harvard doctor infatuated with his "anthropometrical" profile.[12] The song "Let Me Shake the Hand that Shook the Hand of Sullivan" played on piano rolls across the nation.[13]

After five years of hard living, however, Sullivan had become the unimaginable—soft. He had bloated his body with heavy drinking, broken his left arm in a gloved match, and, most damningly, fought to a draw in a bare-knuckle bout in England—a result that brought his championship title under question. On the eve of his thirtieth birthday, bedridden with alcoholism, his career on the line, Sullivan decided to risk it all on one final bare-knuckle bout. Staking $20,000 on a super match against Jake Kilrain, a Boston mill worker turned champion fighter, Sullivan retreated from the press to recuperate and train in an isolated barn in upstate New York. Emerging two months later, he looked, according to eyewitnesses, stronger than he had in years, "a small protuberance in the lower belly" the only remnant of his former beer gut.[14]

The most famous bare-knuckle fight in American history, the Sullivan-Kilrain bout was also one of the wildest, most talked about sporting events of the nineteenth century—a match endlessly hyped by the press as a tabloid grudge match.

Years before, Sullivan had insulted Richard K. Fox, the publisher of the *National Police Gazette,* a popular national newspaper that was one of the first publications in the United States to print a sports section. While dining at a restaurant in New York, Fox had seen the Boston Strong Boy and invited him to visit his table. Sullivan, however, said the publisher should walk over to him instead—an insult resulting in a years-long public feud. Obsessed with humiliating Sullivan, Fox began insulting him in the *Gazette,* running slanderous cartoons and editorials about him while simultaneously backing fighters in a bid to defeat him. Over the years, Fox scoured the world for heavyweights to take down his nemesis, supporting Ryan, Tug Wilson from England, and even Herbert Slade from New Zealand. Sullivan, however, defeated everyone. Finally, in Kilrain, Fox thought he had found his man, a clean-living slugger who could topple the dissipated legend. For months, Fox ran stories and illustrations on the upcoming fight, whipping the nation into a frenzy, depicting the heroic Kilrain doing deeds like training and cradling babies while the villainous Sullivan abused dogs and drank in taverns. "Good and evil as typified and contrasted in the lives and habits of two famous American pugilists," stated the *National Police Gazette* on March 30, 1889. "The Boston Strong Boy and our hero Jake." Ultimately, by the day of the fight, the entire country was hanging on the outcome, readers taking sides and betting on their favorite brawlers while waiting on the results. "The city is fighting mad," stated the *New Orleans Picayune* as the Crescent City, the chosen staging ground, prepared to host the match. "Everybody has the fever and is talking Sullivan and Kilrain. Ladies discussed it in street cars, men talked and argued about it in places which had never heard pugilism mentioned before."[15]

Finally, at midnight on July 8, 1889, five thousand fans, reporters, and even the legendary gunslinger Bat Masterson loaded into special train cars in New Orleans, steaming a hundred miles north to a secret location—a thirty-thousand-acre lumber farm in Richburg, Mississippi—in an attempt to evade authorities. At 10:00 a.m., as temperatures soared over a hundred degrees, Kilrain stripped off his shirt and entered the ring.* Sullivan, wearing green tights and an American flag belted around his waist, followed. Surrounded by derby-wearing gamblers in rough-hewn bleachers, the two fighters put up their $20,000 purses—$10,000 apiece from their backers—made a thousand-dollar side bet, and shook hands. Fighting under the London Prize Ring Rules, the men could grab and throw. Rounds did not have time limits, so each would end when a fighter was knocked down. Overall, the match would continue until one man either quit or could no longer stand.[16] Sullivan, a steel-chested 215 pounds, who had shaved his signature mustache due to the grabbing rules, walked to the "scratch"—a line scratched out in the middle of the ring—and faced off against Kilrain, a chiseled 195 pounds. With sweat beading their foreheads, and pine pitch oozing from the stands, the men dug their spiked cleats into the ring and raised their fists.[17] The referee, a future mayor of New Orleans, looked at the fighters, then at the surrounding crowd, and raised his hand.

"Time!"

---

* Kilrain's great-great-grandson is Colin Kilrain, a former Navy SEAL who became head of the NATO Special Operations Command in 2016. Citing his bare-knuckle lineage, Admiral Harry Harris said the epic match proved "the Kilrain family is built tough."

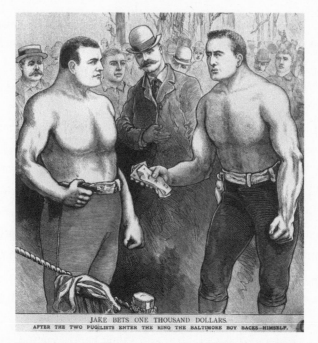

JAKE BETS ONE THOUSAND DOLLARS.
AFTER THE TWO PUGILISTS ENTER THE RING THE BALTIMORE BOY BACKS—HIMSELF.

[Figure 5.2] Sullivan versus Kilrain. (Photo courtesy of the National Police Gazette)

[Figure 5.3] The most famous fight of the 19th century (Photo courtesy of the Library of Congress)

The final bare-knuckle title fight of the sport's American heyday was also one of its longest, an epic two-hour, seventy-six round slugfest. Early on, Kilrain took the lead, toppling Sullivan with a wrestling move and drawing first blood. In the sixth round, the Boston Strong Boy responded with the fight's first knockdown, a thunderous right, at one point yelling to his ducking-and-weaving opponent, "Why don't you stand and fight like a man, you sonofabitch!"[18] As the crowd cheered, the two brawlers settled in. They battered each other mercilessly, stomping feet with spiked cleats, hammering necks and ribs, and slashing faces, their secondaries sucking blood from their eyeballs and spitting it out between rounds. Kilrain swigged whiskey. Sullivan, supposedly on the wagon, drank tea laced with whiskey and then vomited in the ring. At one point, a section of the newly built grandstand collapsed, the crowd descending into a massive pileup of bodies. Through it all, however, the two men continued fighting until the final round, when, their skin broiled and blistered by the sun, the match was clearly over.[19] At the start of the seventy-sixth round, a ringside doctor announced that Kilrain was near death. One of his cornermen, Mike Donovan, had seen two men die in bare-knuckle matches. Barely able to keep his head upright, Kilrain staggered toward the scratch, when Donovan threw a wet sponge into the ring.[20] Sullivan had won.

The Boston Strong Boy was now the most famous person in the world, his victory heralded from New York to London, to far-flung Tahiti. "Sullivan's colors were everywhere about [New York City]," declared a special telegram from Manhattan to the *Omaha Daily Bee* on July 10. "At almost all the picture stores, the windows were filled with his portraits."[21] "The bigger brute won," sniffed the *New York Times*. The celebration, however, was fleeting. Robert Lowry, the Mississippi governor who had been humiliated for his inability to stop the match, offered a $1,000 bounty for Sullivan, leading to his arrest in Nashville on his way back to New York. After a long trial, the Boston Strong Boy was found guilty of illegal fighting and sentenced to a year in jail. Eventually, the verdict was overturned and he paid a $500 fine. Kilrain was arrested and given a two-month jail sentence.[22] Disgusted with the whole ordeal, Sullivan vowed never to fight bare knuckle again, going on to popularize gloved fighting under the Marquess of Queensberry Rules, eventually leading to the sport's legalization in 1892 and creating modern boxing as we know it.

But bare knuckle never went away. After Sullivan's death, the sport went truly underground, thriving in the shadows of America, in illegal gambling dens, far from the headlines it once dominated. Along the way, one group would come to perfect it as a cultural tradition, ultimately giving rise to a hero who would one day claim the belt Sullivan left behind—a fighter from one of the most secret societies in America: Bobby Gunn.

CHAPTER 6

"I KNEW HE'D BE A GOOD BANGER"

On Christmas Day 1973, Jackie and Robert Williamson Gunn were driving south from Niagara Falls, Ontario, to Tampa, Florida, to work for the winter, in their red one-ton dual-rear-wheel pickup truck—all their possessions in a sixteen-foot metal caravan behind them—when Jackie's water broke somewhere in rural Appalachian Virginia. For years, the young couple had been trying to start a family, at one point enduring the stillbirth of a daughter. So, when Jackie finally went into labor in a roadside hospital on the occasion of Jesus' birth, it must have felt like a miracle, a sign from above that their fortunes were changing. Like their savior, Robert Williamson Gunn III was born in transit. Right away, Robert saw that his son was blessed. "He was a funny-built boy with long arms," he says. "I knew he'd be a good banger."

The Gunns were poor, constantly moving from motel rooms to trailer parks, to campsites, chasing work. Beginning in the fall, they lived with his father's clan in their home base of Niagara Falls, staying in roadside hooker haunts with names like the Tropicana, the Blue Moon, and the Three Diamond Inn, struggling through the onset of Ontario's bleak winters. "I remember sitting in motel rooms and it's thirty below outside, the wind blowing," Gunn says. "We'd put a towel under the door to keep the heat in, and I'm sleeping on an old mattress on the floor." Come December, for a few weeks, they traveled south for a respite, to be with his mother's people in Tampa, living in a swampy trailer park on the southern edge of town before returning to the frozen motor courts of Niagara Falls. Finally, every spring, they moved into their battered caravan to rove from campsite to campsite across Canada and the American heartland, the young Traveler kid forced to defend himself against rival clans and local rednecks. It was here, in these anonymous RV encampments, that Gunn first learned to fight. "We had a pretty rough lifestyle," Robert says. "That's why most of these gypsy kids are a little tougher than the average person—you had to be to survive."

Gunn's parents were Travelers, the nomadic tribe mostly found throughout Ireland and the UK but who also live across the United States in secretive, highly insular communities. Deeply religious, they segregate themselves according to Irish (Catholic) or Scottish (Protestant) origins, and they speak a language called Cant or Shelta, a mixture of Irish Gaelic, English, and a homegrown slang. In Traveler culture, the women are homemakers while the men toil as laborers—paving, roofing, painting—traveling with the seasons in search of work. And when they have downtime, they fight. "If you have Traveler blood in you, you start going to the boxing gym at five years old," says Mike Normile. "This is a tough life, so you need to get used to dealing with hard stuff."

According to Gunn family lore, the clan's first fight in the New World pitted Bobby's paternal great-grandfather, Robert "Black Bob" Williamson, against "Kicking Joe" Watson, a Traveler who earned his nickname for once kicking a lock off a stall to free a trapped stallion, and also for booting a man so hard, he died of internal bleeding. Named for his raven-black hair, Black Bob was the first member of his clan to cross the Atlantic, leaving the Scottish Highlands for Montreal in 1915. (Gunn is a mix of both Scottish Traveler on his father's side, and Irish Traveler on his mother's side.) At age nineteen, Black Bob settled in Toronto, going to work as a horse and mule trader while also continuing the other family tradition, fighting. "Black Bob was a sparring partner for the sparring partner of world heavyweight champion Jack Johnson," Gunn says. "Never beat in the street, either. Quite a man."

As generations of Gunns have told it, Black Bob fought Kicking Joe on a Sunday afternoon at a Traveler picnic in Toronto in 1917, the clans socializing on a meadow after church during their one day off. Watson, a renowned bully, got into an argument with one of Black Bob's brothers, a newly arrived minister, and poured lemonade on his head. Incensed, Black Bob stripped off his shirt to defend the family name, squaring off against the towering Traveler as a crowd encircled them. Watson made first contact, kicking Black Bob "near the stones" before the tables turned and Bob connected with a left hook, slamming Watson into a brick wall and laying into him repeatedly, knocking him unconscious. "My grandfather told me teeth come out his mouth from the impact," Gunn says. "You're not going to beat the Williamson boys."

In 1919, Gunn's grandfather, Robert Williamson, was born one of eight children to Black Bob and his wife in Toronto. Growing up in poverty during the Great Depression, Robert Senior learned to fend for himself, brawling for cash in alleyways. "My dad was a street kid," says his son, Robert Jr. "He grew up the hard way, having to fight for everything—best left hook I've seen in my life." Changing his surname to Gunn to avoid confusion with another family of Williamsons who were infamous scam artists, Robert senior married and began roaming a thousand-mile circuit in Ontario with his wife and two sons, working asphalt jobs while competing as an amateur boxer and bare-knuckle fighter. A devout man of God, he wore a button-down shirt and tie even while paving roads. "My grandfather never cursed," Gunn says. "But he also never lost a fight."

A hard-nosed disciplinarian and brawler, Robert senior ran his household like an army barracks. Once, on a snowy February day in the 1960s, a young Traveler arrived with two other men at Robert senior's caravan door, calling him out to fight over some grudge. When Robert senior's wife told the men to leave, they insulted her—a grave error. "They gave her some cheek," Gunn recalls. "So my grandfather just laughed." Taking off his tie, Robert senior walked into the snow to fight all three men. "The old man is punching, pulling, and swinging when one of them cuts his head with a big saddle ring," Gunn recalls. "So Grandpa hit him with three left hooks, split his face like a fish from his nose to his forehead. Knocked him unconscious."

Robert senior and the rest of his clan excelled at fighting, one of his nephews even becoming a Canadian middleweight champion, once knocking out Sugar Ray Leonard in a training camp. But no Gunn would take brawling to the level of his son, Robert William-son Gunn Jr., a hard-drinking bare-knuckle fighter who defied all Scottish Protestant Traveler law by marrying Jacqueline Marie Lindsay, a stunning dark-haired Irish Catholic Traveler from Tampa. "My grandfather was better with his hands," Gunn says. "But nobody messed with my dad—he was a bad motherfucker."

Born in Toronto in 1943, Robert had a traditional Traveler upbringing, leaving school after the fourth grade to roam with his parents and younger brother in a caravan throughout Canada and the United States. "I never really went to school," he says. "The old lady would put me in class, I'd get shit as the gypsy kid, and then the old man would move us." The little time Robert did spend in a classroom was torturous. "One time, a teacher stood me up in front of everybody and gave me the strap for three days,

BARE KNUCKLE | 71

whacking the fuck out of me," he says. "Everybody thinks we're the worst." At home, Robert didn't fare much better. Once, when he was twelve years old, he was severely beaten by an older bully and returned to his father with a broken nose. "I was all cut up, and the old man says, 'You didn't do so good. I can't have that. You better go back tomorrow and see the guy again,'" Robert says, laughing. "I wasn't getting no pity there."

After leaving home, Robert soon began drifting on his own, finding trouble along the way. "I loved rock 'n' roll, hot-rod cars, and fighting," he says. "I fought in bars and picked a lot of glass out of my head. What can you do, eh? It was fun. I enjoyed it." At 5'11" and 235 pounds, with wide-set eyes, thick black hair, and a sly grin, Robert would go on drinking binges for weeks at a time, working tirelessly on jobs and then thinking nothing of blowing everything in a single night, tipping a favorite musician $500 or buying rounds for the house as he held them rapt with stories. Not surprisingly, money was always tight. "Bobby's father was a free spirit," says Jimmy Ruml, a family friend and Traveler in Niagara Falls. "He lived for today. He liked to drink, liked to travel, people loved him. But he was not responsible in terms of looking to the future. Some people just can't make much money. It can be the booze, the lifestyle, whatever, but no matter what the hell they do, they just can't make it."

When it came to fighting, Robert developed a lethal style. As a young man in the 1960s, he performed in over a hundred shows on America's fledgling pro wrestling circuit, an early no-holds-barred version of the modern WWE. Touring as "Black Bart," a heel, Robert did high-flying stunts and body-slamming theatrics along-side other Ontario wrestlers like Tony "Cannonball" Parisi. The men traveled together in vans, sleeping in motels and eating at drive-ins while putting on wild, bloody shows in municipal gyms and arenas throughout North America. "Get the images of Hulk Hogan and spray tans out of your head," Gunn says. "My dad and them guys wasn't like the WWE today. Them guys was hard old bastards with cauliflower ears and broken necks flying thirty feet in the air, landing on the cement, and then going to the bars." On the wrestling circuit, Robert went up against legends like Bruno Sammartino, a head-pounding muscleman, and Fritz Von Erich, a merciless former college quarterback, once getting flung sixteen feet from the ring and breaking his ankle. "Yes, my dad and them guys were actors who knew who was going to win and who was going to lose," Gunn says. "But many a night, they would get a few drinks in them, decide not to cooperate, and begin wrestling for real, blood pouring out of them, breaking bones." Already seasoned from years of fighting on Traveler campgrounds, Robert became even deadlier from his time in the wrestling ring. "My old man didn't have any problems," Gunn says. "He destroyed everybody."

In 1969, Robert was traveling in Tampa for work when his life took a new turn, one even more tumultuous than the wrestling circuit: love. By chance, he noticed Jackie, a beautiful dark-haired Traveler, leaving the Hawaiian Village, a Polynesian-themed resort near the airport. Instantly smitten, he made an incredibly bold— and dumb—move, intentionally bumping his borrowed Pontiac convertible into the back of her car to meet her. He was soon brought home to meet her father. "He didn't worry about the dented bumper," Robert says, laughing. "The old fella knew I was after his daughter." In the strict tribal world of the Travelers, one defined by clan and religious affiliations, a Scottish Protestant like Robert marrying an Irish Catholic like Jackie was high treason— not as bad as marrying a non-Traveler, but still grounds for getting shunned. "According to Traveler ways, my mom was never meant to marry my father," Gunn says. "It's two different worlds, Catholic and Protestant, two different bloodlines." Despite their families' disapproval, Robert and Jackie were in love, determined to be together even if it meant total alienation.

[Figure 6.1] "Nobody messed with my dad."
(Photo courtesy of Bobby Gunn)

"I had to live with it," Robert says of their families' disapproval. "I couldn't fight the whole world over it. If they didn't like it, they could go jump in a lake. I loved her."

In 1969, within months of meeting each other, Robert, then twenty-six, and Jackie, twenty-four, were married. Although the union was not recognized by law—Robert never filed the paperwork—the couple were happy and in love, soon moving to Canada to begin working and traveling with the seasons. Pulling back from the wrestling circuit, Robert began living the more traditional life of his people, doing odd jobs from painting to paving to selling scrap while trying to start a family. In Nova Scotia, he chopped trees alongside lumberjacks and fishermen. On the outskirts of Toronto, he painted barns and laid asphalt. He even ventured into the States, buying trailers in Indiana and then driving them south to Monroe, Louisiana, to resell by the roadside. "A gypsy guy I knew used to build 'em," Robert recalls. "I'd pay three thousand for four of them and then sell them, making a couple grand a week—enough to have nice clothes."

Despite his best efforts, however, Robert, could never leave behind his other passions, drinking and fighting. Wherever they were, after work, Robert would inevitably head to the nearest bar, soon finding trouble. In Nova Scotia, he fought local toughs in alleyways for money. In Toronto, he took on Travelers in disputes over jobs. In Monroe, Louisiana, he once even started an all-out brawl in a bar, pouring a beer into a saxophone player's instrument and igniting a melee. Along the way, in every town, Jackie would remain in the caravan at night, managing the money, cooking the meals, and treating Robert's bruises when he returned home before dawn. "Dad would take locals out back of the bars and make bets, punching the piss out of them," Gunn recalls. "Then he'd come back to the KOA with bleeding knuckles, and my mom would ask, 'What was the accident?'" Gunn laughs. "No accident—he punched the fuck out of three people."

Of all his battles, however, there was one fight Robert could never win: the one against his disapproving family members. In Niagara Falls, his Scottish Protestant people may not have liked his Irish Catholic wife, Jackie, but they wouldn't dare fight him about it. The same, however, would not be true for her family. Soon after getting married, Robert arrived with his new bride for their first visit to her clan's campsite in Tampa—and immediately decided to go ahead and get any confrontations out of the way. Parking his caravan in the center of their community, he turned out his loudspeakers and blared "The Old Orange Flute," a traditional song about a Protestant who marries a "Papist" woman and goes to live with her family, only to have his flute refuse to play anything but British loyalist tunes like "Kick the Pope."[1] The song was a bald-faced challenge to the campsite's hundred Irish Catholic families, an opening salvo about as subtle as pissing on a doorstep. Every Traveler there wanted to dismember Robert. The honors, however, would go to only one clan, and soon they came calling.

Robert was sitting on his couch when he heard one of Jackie's relatives knock at the door and yell, "Get your fucking ass outside NOW!" Ready for the attack, Robert used an old wrestling move, charging the door and kicking it open with both feet, sending the man sprawling to the ground. "Dad kicks him in the chest, gets on top of him, and power-drives him with right hands to the head, knocking his teeth out," Gunn says, having heard the story from uncles since birth. "Then Dad jumps in the air, comes down and busts his leg. This happened in under a minute. Worst fucking mess you could ever imagine."

As the man lay unconscious, Robert began fighting his wife's other family members, the men punching him and the women hitting him with tent poles, the large brawl extending across the campsite. Finally, the cops arrived to find one of Jackie's relatives unconscious, toothless, and with a broken leg. Robert was arrested and spent the next thirty days in jail. Jackie, infuriated with her husband for nearly killing one of her family members, refused to post his bail. "I knew, sooner or later, I was gonna have trouble," Robert recalls about the fight. "But I still felt bad about it because I had to live with it all those years. I was married to their Jackie. You know what I mean?"

When Robert emerged from jail, he seemed to have passed some sort of test, the Lindsay clan grudgingly accepting him into their fold. He began working for Jackie's father, Joe Lindsay, a massive 6'1" Irish Traveler who walked with a limp after being shot by a sheriff in Indiana in 1920. In the 1980s, for several weeks every winter, Robert would travel with Joe and his sons to campsites from Tampa to West Virginia, to Ohio, paving roads by day and hitting bars by night. Once, at a saloon in Ohio, Robert walked into the bathroom to find his father-in-law punching a man in the Adam's apple for some transgression, blood all over the stall. Another time, in a dirt-floored bar in Kermit, West Virginia, Robert says Joe was trying to pick up a local coal miner's wife when her husband walked in and pulled a .22 pistol. Robert intervened, swatting the husband's hand away and taking a bullet through his foot. "I got a tetanus shot, and the doctor was some ol' guy chewing tobacco," Robert says, laughing. "West Virginia is not like being in the United States."

Even at the age of eighty, Gunn's grandfather, Joe, continued to fight. At one point, four young Travelers tried to rob him, stabbing him multiple times before he fought them off. Although he won the battle, Joe broke his fingers so badly, a doctor later had to surgically remove his gold saddle ring. When Gunn and his parents made the overnight drive to Florida and found Joe in the hospital, he told them to empty his pockets, which still contained a piece of an assailant's nose. "He told my dad to throw it in the garbage because he was worried about the cops," Gunn says. "Didn't take pain medication, because he thought the doctor would steal his money. Toughest man I've ever seen."

Gunn pauses. "I know all this fighting can sound sick and crazy to a normal person," he says. "But if you go into our culture and our way of thinking, winning a fight is what makes us proud. My father, my grandfathers, they were men amongst men. Where they walked, the ground shook. There was nothing more in life I wanted than to be like them."

CHAPTER 7
BLOOD ON THE CAMPGROUNDS

From the beginning, Gunn had it hard. His father may have won the respect of his wife's family, but the truce was uneasy. As a result, Gunn's mixed Protestant and Catholic heritage made him an outcast, shunned by both sides of his family. "It's like being a half-breed," says Jimmy Ruml. "He had no friends." When wealthier cousins and uncles visited, they would insult Gunn and his parents. When children in campgrounds had parties, he was never admitted.

"I was invited to a birthday party, so my mother put a suit and tie on me," Gunn recalls. "I go up to their RV trailer and give them a card and they hand me a paper plate outside. They wouldn't let me in." He pauses. "That's heartbreaking."

Like his father and grandfather before him, Gunn hardly attended school, showing up to classes whenever the family was in Niagara Falls and then abruptly departing again. In the second grade, a teacher accused him of cheating on a test, which Gunn denied, and rapped his knuckles with a ruler. Gunn shoved the teacher, leading to more abuse. The next morning, Gunn's father came to school, grabbed the man by the tie, and threatened him. Gunn never entered a classroom again. He was eight years old.

"Mom tried to homeschool me, but it didn't take," he says. "From then on, I was in the work truck with my father, out painting barn roofs, working hard and training." Gunn pauses. "You know, I never had time to be a kid. I was a man before I was a man."

Gunn learned to lay asphalt, paint houses, and work construction. As a child, he would tie a rope around his waist and climb hundred-foot-tall grain silos, dangling in the air as he painted their steel hulls, his father shouting directions from below. Sometimes, he would climb atop giant barns, helping his father spray silver coating on sloped metal roofs, while staring out across the endless Canadian prairie. "It seemed like we were on top of the world," Gunn recalls. "My dad would be silver like the Tin Man. He would say, 'Be brave, work hard.'" Afterward, Gunn and his father would strip down and wash the paint from their bodies, eating sandwiches brought by local farmers. For big jobs, Robert would hire Mohawk Indians from a nearby reservation to help them for the day. One of Gunn's earliest memories is of the Native Americans catching trout for their lunch, slicing open the silver bellies, inserting lemons, and then covering the fish with mud to bake in a riverside fire. Wherever they went, Gunn, who had no friends, worked with one goal in mind: to win his father's approval. "Once, my dad gave me fifty dollars for a day's pay, saying, 'Good boy, I'm proud of you,'" Gunn recalls. "I was a wee boy but so proud of myself. I was helping him."

Yet no matter Gunn's efforts, his childhood remained a struggle. His parents would sometimes have terrible fights, Robert disappearing for days at a stretch. Once, after his father had walked out, Gunn, just a boy, put a telephone book in the driver's seat of the family work truck, driving around town to find jobs to support his mother. "They had a real bad argument and separated," Gunn recalls. "So I had to be a man. Sometimes, we had to put water on our cereal because we didn't have no milk. It was hard times."

Even when Robert did stick around, the money was tight. Some of his clan in Niagara Falls did well working construction, even owning their own asphalt businesses, but they never gave Robert a hand, likely because of his marriage to Jackie. "I had a lot of family that made good money in construction," Gunn recalls. "Doing really regular. Kids had nice clothes. But they wouldn't take us with them. Wouldn't offer no help." As a result, Gunn grew up both penniless and ostracized. He idolized Travelers who boxed, but they discouraged him from entering the ring. He tried to befriend cousins, but they would take him to restaurants and then belittle him for not being able to afford anything to eat. Sometimes, Robert would defend his son, once threatening two family members who had insulted Gunn for being poor. But, for the most part, Gunn was left to survive on his own. "They treated me like dog shit," he says of his extended family. "They hurt me real bad, hurt my heart. I would get so embarrassed that I would just go silent. There's only a handful of people that were good to me when I was a kid."

Yet there was one comfort Gunn could find, and he poured his soul into it—fighting. "I took the loneliness and turned it into creative things in my mind by mimicking fight moves," he says. "It bothered me that I didn't have things that other kids had. But I knew that in order to have that stuff, I would have to go out and get it. I'd have to be a hustler. No one was giving me nothing."

From a young age, Gunn had one ambition: to become a world-champion boxer. He idolized Travelers like the Hilton brothers, five Montreal siblings who used their fists to transcend the campgrounds, becoming wealthy and famous as professional boxers in Canada. "The fighting Hiltons were my heroes," he says. "They were Travelers and so popular, they were like guys you'd see on a Wheaties box. They were fucking superheroes." With no education or prospects, Gunn turned to fighting as his only way to a better life, soon devising a plan. He would win an Olympic medal followed by a world-title belt, launching his own spectacular career. "I wanted to be a world champion," Gunn says. "I wanted to show all my family who said I could never have anything. Fighting was the only thing I had."

Gunn first began brawling in the trailer parks. Each year, when the weather warmed, Robert would hitch the family's rickety caravan to his truck and drive west through the plains, the Rockies, and sometimes clear to the Pacific Northwest, knocking on farmers' doors for work, the family sleeping together in parks on the edges of towns. "It was a little tiny RV trailer, no heat or electricity," Gunn says. "I'd walk to a water faucet and brush my teeth and wash myself outside." During the summer, the campgrounds swarmed with Scottish, Irish, and English Travelers from across North America, everyone on the road, trying to make money. Far from the campfire idylls romanticized in myth, these parks were war zones—desolate, dangerous, trash-strewn patches of broken glass, inhabited by squatters and feral dogs.

"They were all gravel, no grass," Ruml says. "Working-class types who didn't like strangers. It was a hard life, especially for kids." The locals didn't like the Travelers, and the Travelers fought among themselves along clan lines. As a young boy, Gunn was once almost abducted by a child molester, his grandfather jumping in to save him at the last moment, pummeling the man and calling the police.

"These gypsy camps were rough," Gunn says. "You hear that expression 'trailer trash'? Them places would be Holiday Inns compared to where I was raised."

Sometimes, the Gunns would roam with different Scottish Traveler families, trading tips on jobs and pooling resources, setting up coalitions to defend themselves within the campgrounds. More often than not, however, the family survived on its own. And as Gunn would soon learn from his mother, weakness was not an option.

Jacqueline Gunn was a drop-dead brunette, a devoted mother and wife, and perhaps the toughest member of the family. "She was a lioness," says Ruml. As an Irish Catholic Traveler who had turned her back on her people for Robert, moving north to live among his openly hostile Scottish Protestant clan, she had to fight every day just to raise her family.

"A lot of people wasn't nice to her," Gunn says. "They would ask my dad, 'Why did you marry an Irish girl, a Papist? You shouldn't have done that.'"

Sometimes, Jackie would try to make peace, inviting her husband's family into their home. "One time, my father's cousins and uncles come and visit in their big shiny cars and trucks, the smell of cologne off them," Gunn recalls. "My poor mom, she's a proud gypsy woman, but we weren't doing so good, and we looked it. But she was nice and said to one of the young boys, 'Oh, you're so handsome, what a beautiful sweater that is. We should buy one for Bobby. Where did you get it?' And the man said, 'Darling, you couldn't afford that. Take him down to Goodwill and get him something.'" Gunn pauses. "After they left, my mother started to cry. And she looked at me and said, 'Don't ever forget this day as long as you live. You will have it all.'"

Although Robert would sometimes disappear on drinking binges for weeks at a time, Jackie remained sober. She attended mass, read Old Testament stories about Israelites fighting Philistines to her young son, and stared down every last son of a bitch who threatened her family. "She could be sweet, but God help the person that came after her little boy," Ruml says. "Man or woman—she wasn't afraid of nobody."

As a child, Gunn remembers his mother often going to battle in the campgrounds. "Today, the Traveler girls don't fight," Gunn says. "But my mom wouldn't think twice. She'd put her hair in a bandanna, put Vaseline on her face, and punch your fucking head off." In a faded family photo that Gunn keeps of his mother, Jackie is looking intensely at the camera, her brown eyes hard, hair in a towering beehive, hands holding up her infant son's fists in a fight pose. Once, in a spat, she even knocked her own husband unconscious. "She said, 'Come on, you bitch!' and knocked my dad back three feet," Gunn says. "The old girl was game."

In the early 1980s, while the Gunn family was camping in rural Ontario, an older English Traveler teenager started a fight with Gunn, then about eight years old. Despite the difference in age and size, Gunn managed to pin the teen to the ground and was beating him when the boy's mother suddenly stepped in, slapping Gunn across the face and sending him home. After examining her son's welt, Jackie marched to the English Travelers' trailer and confronted the woman, who stepped outside with her three sisters. Seeing she was outnumbered, Jackie returned home, wrapped two

[Figure 7.1] Gunn's mother holds up his fists
(Photo courtesy of Bobby Gunn)

rolls of pennies in two of her husband's work socks, clenched the coins in her fists, and returned to the English Travelers' caravan. Calling the sisters outside, Jackie soon went to work. "She fucking leveled 'em," Gunn says. "Whack! I mean, they started to run. I remember the last one she hit, the boy's mother, the fucking sock tore and pennies scattered everywhere. Mom grabbed her by the hair, and the woman's blouse ripped off and mom was smacking the fuck out of her. 'Stop it!' I yelled. Oh, God, she was tough."

Sometimes, the entire Gunn family would fight alongside each other. At ten years old, while camped in the dense forests of northern Saskatchewan, Gunn was playing with his BB gun when three teenage English Traveler brothers jumped him, breaking his gun and beating him with it. "They whacked me, punched me, jumped on me, kicked me, and laughed at me," Gunn recalls. "I got up, went home, and Mom made me some lunch. She said, 'What happened to you?' 'Nothing, nothing, nothing.' 'Where's your gun?' 'It's broke.' 'What do you mean it's broke?'" Enraged, Jackie grabbed Gunn by the hand, went straight to the English Travelers' trailer, found the teenagers' mom, and called her out. "She said, 'Now, listen here, you dirty cockney bastard, your boys beat my wee boy,'" Gunn recalls. "'Come out here and apologize.' The woman said, 'Nah, he was looking for it.' So my mom grabbed her right out the trailer and began punching the fucking head off her." When one of the English Traveler teens stepped in, taking a swing at Jackie, she threw him to the ground. Seeing his mom in trouble, Gunn picked up a bat and whacked the teen in the leg. With a crowd beginning to form, Jackie pulled her son back. "As we were walking away, Mom yelled, 'Wait till my husband gets home,'" Gunn recalls.

At seven, Robert returned to the campsite, heard the story, looked over his son's bruises, and simply said, "All right." He marched to the English Travelers' trailer, pulled the father outside, and began beating him. Then, when the teenage sons came out, he leveled them as well. "He beat the fuck out of all of them," Gunn says. "My mom was standing right there." Afterward, the Gunns returned home, but the fight was far from over. In the middle of the night, the English Traveler father banged on the Gunns' caravan door, brandishing a shotgun. Sneaking out through a side window, Robert crept inside his work truck, gunned the engine, and rammed his extended-cab dually straight through the English Traveler family's trailer. "My dad yelled, 'You cocksuckers, now we're going to fucking war!'" Gunn recalls. Not wanting to continue the feud, the English Travelers abandoned the site with the other members of their clan. Soon, the police arrived. Robert told them his clutch had gotten stuck and that he had accidentally driven through the trailer, assuring them he would sort it out with the family when they returned. "He squared the whole thing away," Gunn says. "And then went back to work the next morning."

In the family, Robert was the last line of defense—and only Jackie could soothe him once he turned blind with rage. In the mornings, Gunn would often awaken to find his mother spraying blood off the concrete slab next to their trailer—the remains of his father's brawls from the night before, caked and dried on the asphalt. "I remember bloody handprints on the side of our RV trailer," he says. "Mom outside the next day washing it off."

Once, in the early 1980s, the family was eating dinner on a campsite in North Bay, Ontario, when they were interrupted by a man pounding on their door—a Traveler who had come to challenge Robert over something related to a job. Leaving his soup on the table, Robert walked out and immediately began fighting the man, trading blows until he threw him to the ground, straddling him. "Instead of choking him, my father put his hands in his mouth, took his two fingers on each side of his cheeks, and started ripping," Gunn recalls. "My mother come out screaming, 'Stop it, you're gonna kill him!' The man was lying on the ground, the blood pouring out of him, and Dad just stood up and walked away." In the trailer, Robert sat back down at the table. "He's all blood," Gunn recalls. "So he combs his hair, puts on aftershave, and goes back to his soup. Twenty minutes later, the old man asks,

'Is he gone yet?' And Mom's just looking at him. She knew the man had come looking for it, knew my dad had to go fight him. She was a proper gypsy woman. But she stopped him because she knew he was going to kill him." Gunn pauses. "I'll never forget the poor bastard outside, who finally somehow got up and drove away, bleeding all over his truck, as my old man watched TV. Dad was a hard fucking man."

Sometimes, feuds between Traveler families would last for years, passed down through the generations like a birthright, their causes long forgotten but the animosity lingering. One of Gunn's earliest memories is of his father standing in a telephone booth, relaying the news of a victory over another Traveler to Gunn's grandparents. The man Robert had defeated was the son of a man whom his own father had fought and beaten decades before, this the latest win in a generations-long feud between the clans. "My Grannie got on the phone and asked, 'Did your daddy put it to him good?'" Gunn recalls. "'Oh, yeah, unbelievable, Grannie.' 'Good job. All right, my darling. We love you.'" Gunn pauses. "It's unreal, my family."

Gunn's childhood was a montage of Traveler campsite brawls, a never-ending battle for survival. But there was one fight that stood out for its brutality, one in which he began to make his own reputation among his people, and it occurred in, of all places, Disney World. For Travelers, the Magic Kingdom is a special place. The spired castles, plush dolls, and carnival rides constitute a neutral ground, a sort of theme-park Switzerland where warring tribes can mingle in peace. One summer, while working as a teenager with his mother's people in Tampa, Gunn took the day off to visit the park with thirty other young Travelers. Wearing a blue suit and leather shoes for the occasion, he spent the day strolling the grounds and enjoying the rides, the trouble arising only late in the afternoon, when he and the other teens returned to the parking lot. There, amid the sun-beaten vehicles, stood a 6'2," 200-pound Irish Traveler in his early twenties—an older, bigger known brawler who was shirtless and greased in Vaseline. "It was even all through his hair," Gunn recalls. The man walked up to Gunn—then a rising fighter in his own right—and challenged him. Gunn declined. Due to his mixed heritage, he had never been truly accepted by his people. Yet without them, he had no tribe to call his own. "I don't want to fight you, pal," Gunn said.

Ignoring him, the Irishman charged. Gunn hit him with two jabs and then threw him face-first into the side of a pickup truck. Bleeding, the man stood and came again at Gunn, who hit him with a straight right hand, dropping him to the asphalt. Then something strange happened.

[Figure 7.2] Training as a teen
(Photo courtesy of Bobby Gunn)

The Irishman began crying, moving as if to hug Gunn around the waist—and sank his teeth into Gunn's upper thigh. "He was trying to bite my dick off," Gunn says. "I fixed my hand in his curly hair, pulled back his head, and bit the top of his ear off. I gave him two left hooks—bang, bang!—and his teeth fell out like Chiclets and he dropped to the ground." The Irishman's people wrapped him in painter drop cloths and took him to a hospital. Gunn, his suit bloodied and torn, returned home. He would soon leave the Traveler battlegrounds forever.

"It was a hard, lonely life, the good ol' Traveler country," Gunn says. "It wasn't right and it wasn't wrong—but it wasn't normal."

CHAPTER 8
SECRETS OF THE SUMMER WALKERS

From Genghis Khan's thirteenth-century Mongols to the Comanche of America's southern plains, to Bobby Gunn's roving family of today, nomadic people have always been fighters. Never conforming to law, never trusting outsiders, never settling down, they have historically been divided into two groups: foraging or herding wanderers in search of food (e.g., Australian Aborigines, the San of southern Africa, the Sami of the Arctic); and roving tradesmen in search of work (the Tuareg Berbers of the Sahara, the Travelers). While Western society has often romanticized the open-road lifestyle of the nomad, in reality, these groups—living hand to mouth, facing persecution at every turn—endure brutal existences. Nomadism is "that most deeply biting of all social disciplines," wrote T. E. Lawrence, the famed British archaeologist, officer, and diplomat known as Lawrence of Arabia, who lived among the Bedouin during World War I. "A life too hard, too empty, too denying for all but the strongest and most determined men."[1]

For nomads, a people without permanent dwelling, the only constant in their lives is their culture, and none still fight to defend theirs like the Travelers. To outsiders, their origins are murky. For starters, the term "Traveler" can broadly refer to any number of modern nomadic tribes in Europe and North America, from the Romanies to Irish Travelers, to circus workers, the fairground-traveling families also known as "carnies." Yet aside from their nomadic or seminomadic ways of life, these groups have little in common. Even the Roma, who once used covered wagons like the Travelers, are a completely different ethnic group, originating in northwest India, speaking a derivative of Hindi, and living mostly in Eastern Europe. The term "gypsy," which both Roma and Travelers find offensive, derives from "Egyptian," based on Europeans' initial misconception that the Romani people were Muslims from the Middle East. In truth, the Roma were *fleeing* Islamic armies who invaded India in the thirteenth century—and they have wandered ever since.[2]

Travelers, by contrast, are of English and Celtic origin. Descended from clans including medieval pre-Celtic tribes, farmers displaced by Oliver Cromwell in the 1650s, and tenants evicted during the 1840s Irish famine, the Travelers are outsiders who, over time, melded to form a distinct culture, one with its own rites, language, and customs apart from the "settled people" who cast them aside. The most prevalent group is the Irish Travelers, but Scottish, Welsh, and English Travelers all share similar traits. Largely illiterate for centuries, they have maintained an oral history without written record, shunning outsiders while preserving their culture of family, religion, and fighting. Difficult to penetrate and long ignored by researchers, they remain one of the most mysterious tribes in the world. According to the 2022 national census, Ireland has over thirty-two thousand Travelers.[3] In the United States, since they are not recognized as an ethnicity, there are no official numbers, though their population is often estimated to be at least ten thousand Travelers. "Comparatively little is known about them," wrote an Irish

Folklore Commission director in 1952. "No serious attempt has hitherto been made to collect information about them . . . in a systematic way."[4]

During the eighteenth and nineteenth centuries, Travelers roamed the UK in covered wagons, working as horse traders, tinsmiths, bards, beggars, trinket sellers, palm readers, day laborers—whatever it took to survive. Living in squatters' homes during the winter and traveling in the spring, families visited the same villages on a yearly schedule, camping on the outskirts of town, providing essential services in an era when travel was difficult. While most Travelers were honest tradesmen, some occasionally stole chickens or overcharged farmers on horse deals—transgressions that, over time, linked their name as a people with thievery, scams, and begging. Beginning in the late nineteenth century, UK society began to invoke them as bogeymen who snatched children—likely due to the hushed practice of young unwed mothers who often gave up their newborns to the Travelers—and targeted them with statutes on vagrancy.* By the early twentieth century, Travelers were openly despised. "In Scotland, they'd throw stones at the wagon and go, 'Gypsy, gypsy, live in a tent, because he can't afford to pay the rent,'" Gunn says. "They'd have to keep moving."

Gunn can trace his own history back to a paternal

[Figure 8.1] Irish Travelers on the move.
Public domain.

---

* For their part, Travelers were equally suspicious of the settled people, telling campfire tales of the "burkers," medical students in tall hats who drove black coaches through the countryside at night, stealing children to dissect.

great-great-grandfather, Robert James Williamson, the patri-
arch of a large clan near Inverness, Scotland, in the late 1800s.
Known as the Summer Walkers, the Highland Travelers roamed
upland villages from May through September, working as horse
traders, tinsmiths, and pearl fishermen, practicing the ancient
(and now illegal) art of digging through riverbeds to pry jewels
from hundred-year-old mussels.[5] During the summer months,
Williamson, his wife, and their ten children would have led a
procession of carts, horses, dogs, and chickens through Scotland's windswept mountains, the family working tirelessly while
camping in a barrel-top wagon or tent made of bowed hazel sticks
and canvas.[6] Robert James, his wife, and two of their daughters,
their hair thick with campfire smoke and fish scales, would likely
have shared a thin mattress, their bodies lined like matchsticks,
while the rest of the children huddled on the floor. The family
would have lived off potatoes, stew, and stale loaves of bread,
occasionally enjoying rabbit or trout. At night, they would have
gathered around a campfire, telling tales of banshees, ghosts, and
Celtic kings or singing folk songs, Robert playing the mouth harp
while his children took turns dancing atop a small wooden board.

But of all the Williamsons' rituals and arts, only bare-knuckle
boxing would have held an almost sacred significance. "Traveling men fight," writes former British bare-knuckle boxing
champion Bartley Gorman in his 2002 memoir *King of the
Gypsies.* "Not all of them and not all the time, but many, and
often. They would rather settle a row with knuckles than resort
to the courts or call the police."[7]

Living on the sides of roads, working backbreaking jobs
without guarantee of pay, Travelers have led a brutal existence—
according to a recent survey, fewer than 3 percent live to age
sixty-five.[8] For the stigmatized Travelers, fighting is almost a form
of currency, a means of establishing dominance and order and

respect among clans in a hostile world. Travelers fight to cement status, to defend their families, to settle disputes. They fight for wages when stiffed for a job, for pride when slandered on a campsite, or for fun when attending weddings and funerals. They fight so often and in so many situations—women and children included—the act of pugilism is almost as routine as the weekly trip to church. Overall, the Travelers have produced a large number of professional boxers, including, most recently, Tyson Fury, the 2016 world heavyweight champion, who sleeps according to tradition, in a double-wide trailer behind his mansion in Lancaster.[9]

"It's bred into us; it's who we are," Gunn says. "We're not like normal people—we're the pit bulls of the earth."

Travelers first began prizefighting during the golden age of the sport in the UK. In the 1820s, "Gypsy" Jack Cooper, a 5'5", 140-pound bare-knuckler, became famous for his "slashing" punches.[10] "The Gypsy peeled uncommonly well," wrote contemporary journalist Pierce Egan, referring to Cooper's physical appearance after he had "peeled" off his shirt. "In fact, these sort of wandering coves are always in training, and have a better chance of winning a turn-up than most other men."[11] In late-1800s England, "Gypsy" Jem Mace, an itinerant fiddler, rose to become a national champion, owning a saloon, meeting both Charles Dickens and Queen Victoria, and touring the world.[12] Uriah Burton became king of the "mountain fighters," a subset of miners and Travelers in Wales who fought for money in craggy "blood hollow" mines.[13] And in Scotland in the late nineteenth century, Gunn's

---

* The bare-knuckle mountain fighters would have a formative hand in American boxing. In 1914, former knuckler Dai Dollings left Wales for New York City, where he trained twenty world boxing champions. Every day, he walked five miles in a suit and tie from his apartment on East 14th Street to Grupp's Gym on West 116th Street, eventually passing his knowledge to legendary trainer Ray Arcel, who went on to mold champions including Roberto Duran and Larry Holmes.

great-great-grandfather, Robert James Williamson—an athlete who threw the fifty-six-pound weight in the Highland Games— fought strangers for cash in boxing booths, the wooden arenas that once traveled in fairs throughout the UK. "They'd fight bare knuckle in a little square booth no bigger than the hood of this truck," says Gunn's father, Robert. "People would bet on them. And my great-grandfather went around beating everybody—same as his father before him."

Yet of all Traveler fighters, none is more legendary than Bartley Gorman. A 6'1", 210-pound fiery-haired English-man, Gorman reigned as the bare-knuckle "King of the Gypsies" from 1972 to 1992, earning his title, as he put it, in "blood, snot, sweat and gore."[14] In Traveler culture, being "king" is perhaps the highest accolade a Traveler can achieve. He is the one knuckler whom no other

[Figure 8.2] Bartley Gorman, the "King of the Gypsies" (Photo courtesy of Milo Books)

Traveler can defeat. The king may fight *gorgio,* pronounced "gorger," the Cant (secret Traveler language) term for non-Travelers, who are also known as "country people." He may even don gloves to fight in the pros. But it is only his underground bare-knuckle bouts against his own people that will truly count.

Born in a trailer in Nottingham in 1945, Gorman grew up in the traditional lifestyle, hunting rabbits with greyhounds, riding horse-drawn wagons, and fighting for sport. At age ten, his father—a brutal disciplinarian who once gashed Gorman's head with a drain rod—hit him regularly and forced him to fight fifteen-year-old boys in order to toughen up, "crying as I was fighting," he wrote, but never backing down. Gorman eventually decided to continue the family tradition, setting out on his own at age eighteen. "Knuckle fighting is so strongly a part of the gypsy heritage—so tied up with family pride and honor—that I felt I had to do it."[15]

During his twenty-year career, Gorman fought in mine tunnels, stone quarries, and army-base saloons and at horse fairs. He learned to hit with his middle knuckles, the joints where the fingers bend, to extend his reach, and became renowned for his specialties, the "middle knuckle shot between the lip and the nose—agony," and the "hook under the floating rib—turns his lips blue."[16] He broke numerous bones, was arrested, and once even nearly got killed by a mob of rival Travelers in Doncaster, but he never lost a match, becoming famed for his ability to survive. "The boundaries of a prizefight are fluid," he wrote about fighting a roadway contractor in a rock quarry in 1972. "You can cover a lot of ground, moving, jumping, tripping over things, banging up against buildings, with the crowd all the time melting and reassembling around you in a swarm. We scuffled around, the mud up to our ankles, as the Kidds shouted, '*Muller* him,' which means 'kill him' in Romany, and our Sam shouted, '*Carib*,' which means the same thing in Irish Cant."[17]

For Gorman and other Travelers, fighting was more than just sport. The ritual gave a deeper meaning and validation to a lifetime of barn painting, road paving, and general poverty. It was a link to one's family and culture, a means to test one's worth where few other opportunities existed. It was why Travelers identified with other minorities, particularly the Black community. In the early twentieth century, Gorman's grandfather would stay up "all night singing *camorlias*" before the matches of Jack Johnson, the first Black heavyweight boxing champion, "because, like them, he was an outsider."[18]

In 2002, when Gorman died of liver cancer at the age of fifty-seven, his coffin was carried on a horse-drawn cart through the village of Uttoxeter in East Staffordshire, where hundreds of Travelers attended his funeral.[19] In the years since, several Travelers would go on to claim the title of king, most famously James Quinn McDonagh, who was featured in the 2011 documentary *Knuckle*. Yet only one fighter would take Gorman's legacy and elevate it to a legal arena, the new champion hailing from one of the least likely tribes, all but unknown to the outside world: the Travelers of America.

CHAPTER 9
"HIT HIM IN THE LIVER AND HE SHUTS RIGHT DOWN"

One night in the winter of 1984, in a run-down motel on the western fringe of Niagara Falls, Bobby Gunn awoke to headlights and voices. His breath plumed in the cold air. Stale cigarette smoke seeped from the shag carpet. He looked at the clock: 2:00. Lying on his sleeping pad on the floor, Gunn, then eleven years old, looked to his mother, Jackie, who remained still as a corpse in the room's queen-size bed. Gunn's father, Robert, was gone, but that wasn't unusual. He sometimes went on drinking sprees for weeks on end, disappearing each night to the bars along Lundy's Lane, returning home at closing time, and getting up a few hours later to go to work. Yet tonight was different. For the first time, Robert had brought someone back from the bar, and it sounded like a crowd. The door burst open. "Wake up, boy," Robert said, his cigarette glowing red in the dark. "There's somebody I need you to fight."

Situated on the Niagara Escarpment, Niagara Falls, Ontario, is famous as a tourist attraction. This is the 170-foot waterfall where Houdini swam the rapids, where little white boats with tourists putter back and forth all day under its boom and mist. But walk a few blocks beyond the boardwalk attractions, and you find another reality. Like Tijuana or Juárez, Niagara Falls is a border town, a major conduit between the USA and Canada for illicit drugs, guns, and humans. In 2023, over 17 million people and over 9 million vehicles crossed the border in southern Ontario, resulting in nearly 3,000 pounds of illicit drugs seized and over 350 prohibited-weapons seizures.[1] For four months every year, the border town was also where the Gunns called home. "It was like the Wild West back then," Gunn says. "A very tough town with a lot of bad people. Even the cops didn't care. So we were forced to live on both sides of the law."

From December through March, when the weather turned too cold to travel the northern plains in search of work, the Gunn family would park their one-ton truck and sixteen-foot caravan behind one of the motels lining the four-lane highway on the western edge of Niagara Falls. Surrounded by strip clubs, liquor stores, and jails, these motor courts were brutal places, no-man's-lands of drifters and drug dealers and prostitutes. At night, the Gunns had to check their caravan regularly, protecting it from thieves. By day, they scrounged for jobs in the stinging twenty-below winters. "You'd get a lot of rough white trash and gangsters in those rooms," Gunn recalls. "Sometimes, they would ransack our trailer, but nobody ever fucked with us to our face—they knew we were gypsies."

That night, staring at his father in the doorway, Gunn threw off his blanket and stood, naked except for a pair of jogging pants. Far from the hulking 200-pound brawler he is today, he was then just a skinny freckled kid, "an Opie-looking motherfucker," as he puts it. Shivering, he walked to his father. Robert told him to go to the bathroom, get dressed, and wipe Vaseline on his eyebrows—an old street-fighter trick. In the dark, nobody could see the grease, but it would make his opponent's punches slip. Gunn was walking to the bathroom when, from the bed, his mother called out. "Please don't do this," she said.

Ignoring his wife, Robert stared at his son. "I've got a real mouthy wee bum here," he said, nodding outside. "A real cocky wee cunt. I want you to put the head right off him, you understand?"

Gunn nodded.

"Okay."

Walking outside, wearing a T-shirt, jeans, and sneakers, Gunn squared off against a larger man in his midtwenties. Under the neon lights of the motel sign, surrounded by cars and bar patrons and a few prostitutes who had wandered out to see the show, Gunn put up his fists. His opponent just looked at him. "Is this him?" the man asked. "That's a fucking *kid*."

Gunn hit the man squarely in the nose, following it with a combination to his eyes, starting him bleeding. Suddenly attuned, the man began swinging, his vision blurry, the crowd growing louder. "This guy was throwing punches a mile away," Gunn recalls. "A real hillbilly. I mean, useless as two tits on a bull." Gunn quickly picked the man apart, dropping him to the snow-covered ground. "I punched the head right off him." Afterward, the crowd gone, Robert, a wad of newly won cash in his pocket, looked at his son, checking his face for bruises. He smiled.

"That's my boy."

* * * * *

Since birth, Gunn was trained to fight everywhere from gyms to boxing rings, to the campgrounds of America, honing his skills mostly against Travelers. By the time he was eleven, on the cusp of manhood, he had already begun his final, most important lesson: fighting for money. Under Robert's watchful gaze, Gunn would train around the clock in three separate prizefight disciplines: boxing, bare knuckle, and rough-and-tumble brawling. All his winnings would go to his father, who would stash the cash in money belts, under mattresses, and in a secret box welded to the undercarriage of his truck. Robert didn't believe in banks—or mercy. "My old man don't care about money," Gunn says. "He cared about fists. Dad was more of a rough-and-tumble guy than a straight-up bare-knuckle guy. He didn't fuck around."

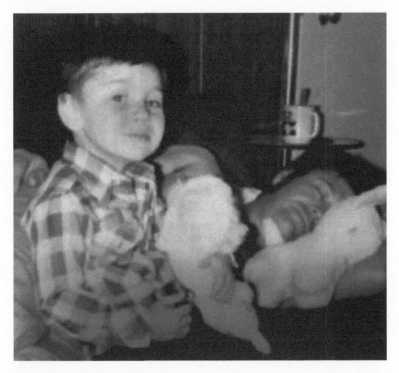

[Figure 9.1] "Dad took all them methods and applied it to street fighting." (Photo courtesy of Bobby Gunn)

Honed with a distinct style from his years on the wrestling circuit, Robert excelled at bare-knuckle fighting and trained his son in its vicious techniques. "When my father quit wrestling and married my mother, going back to work because he couldn't make money in the game, he took all them methods and applied it to street fighting," Gunn says. "He would say, 'There's no street-fighting rule book. You take a man down and you bite his fucking nose right off his head, because he'll do it to you.'"

Robert taught Gunn to push his fist deeper into a man's throat if he tried to bite his fingers, making him choke. He taught him the most efficient angle to break a man's arm, snap a leg, or rip out an eyeball with your thumb. He taught him always to turn the lights off before answering the front door, in case he needed to get a jump on someone. He taught him to put kerosene on his cuts, believing that it would heal them more quickly, and how to pull his own broken teeth out with pliers, resulting in *summer teeth*—"some are in and some are not." "He would work with me on the floor," Gunn recalls. "He would grab me and act like he was gonna bite me, and then show me how to take my two thumbs and spread them inside a man's mouth, ripping his cheeks open—he brought me up to be a street fighter." But most importantly, Robert taught his son never to waste time—a lesson he had long since learned for himself. Once, on a rainy night in Toronto in the mid 1970s, Robert fought a biker in a gravel lot outside a motorcycle bar for $100.

"The other guy started jumping up and down, saying, 'I'm gonna rip your head off!'" recalls Jimmy Ruml. "And Bob just looked at him and said, 'Okay, you ready?' 'Yeah.' Boom. And down he went. Bob said, 'See? I told you he had a glass jaw,' and went inside and finished his drink."

As a child, Gunn was first schooled in traditional boxing. At age five, coached by his father, he began working the bags at the Shamrock Boxing Club, a Spartan facility in Niagara Falls, soon making a name for himself with his hard punch and devotion to the sport. After training sessions, Robert would take him back to the motel room to watch black-and-white recordings of Rocky Marciano and Sugar Ray Robinson on VHS, telling his son to mimic their moves on a makeshift bag. "I lived it, breathed it, slept it," Gunn says. "It'd be twenty-five below at night, and we'd push the bed back and train in a six-foot space in the corner of the room. I'd be watching these films, my father telling me to feint and walk away, feint and walk away, the sweat pumping off me while I'm practicing there for hours, just standing there, *whack, whack, whack.*" He pauses. "I was obsessed with the fight game."

At six years old, Gunn began gaining a reputation as an amateur boxer, competing in one-minute rounds in Peewee fights in Ontario. By the age of ten, he was competing in events across Canada. His parents splurged their meager savings on boxing equipment, making sure he maintained his training, keeping their son in prime fighting condition. "I bought enough Vaseline and hand wraps to go to California and back six times," Robert says. Gunn's plan was to spend years building up his amateur rankings and then turn pro. "As a kid, I was going for the Olympics," he says.

In Traveler circles, Gunn was on the rise, his confidence growing along with his reputation as a fighter, leading to hopes he might one day elevate his family with his winnings. Yet, once again, he ran up against the same battle: his own uncles and cousins still refusing to recognize him. "I'm fighting championship amateur fights, and they wouldn't pay ten dollars to come see me in the ring," Gunn recalls about his extended family. "They wouldn't acknowledge it. It would be in the paper, and they wouldn't say nothing. They wouldn't turn their heads." He pauses. "That's why I fight. Not to spend money and throw it down the toilet, but to give my kids all them fancy sweaters— because they said I never could have it."

Channeling his anger during Canada's long winters, Gunn would wake before dawn, shovel people's driveways for cash, eat breakfast, and then head out for the day's barn or asphalt job. In the evenings, he and Robert would go to the boxing gym, Gunn jogging home afterward alongside the work truck, in army boots while carrying buckets of paint, his father yelling out the window at him. "I'd go two to three miles, faster and faster, harder and harder," Gunn says. "I trained like a racehorse." When Robert would disappear on drinking binges, Gunn would go to the gym on his own, a quiet skinny boy with oversize gloves, in a Batman T-shirt, pacing the canvas. "I remember the little seven-year-old kid in a boxing ring," says Mike Normile. "He was a bit of a loner and wasn't getting on with different groups—he had the weight of the world on his shoulders."

Gunn was a loyal soldier, never questioning his father's demands, and claims that the physical punishments, the long hours, the total isolation didn't bother him. Yet, when pressed, he will admit to one scar. "He never showed the right affec-

[Figure 9.2] Training as an amateur (Photo courtesy of Bobby Gunn)

tions, never gave me praise," Gunn says. "He was hard and could have done a lot better by me." No matter what Gunn did, no matter how many men he defeated or how long he kept pace with the truck, it was never enough for Robert, who often withheld his love, ignoring his son's accomplishments and compounding his sense of solitude. According to friends, Robert did this for the same reason he put kerosene on the boy's cuts: to create the perfect fighting machine. "He made me a trained assassin," Gunn says. But it didn't make it any easier.

"His father, in those days, wouldn't give approval, because he wanted Bobby to be better, tougher, stronger, meaner," Ruml says. "He was a bastard."

When asked about it further, Gunn just shrugs. "If there was twenty-five men outside with baseball bats and guns, my dad would say, 'Sit back, boy, I'm going first.' Was he going to buy me a teddy bear for Christmas? No. He'd buy a pair of boxing gloves. That's where his love was."

Away from the ring, away from the eyes of the world, Robert soon began training his son for another, more brutal arena: bare knuckle. His stone-age training techniques repelled even other Travelers. "It was barbaric," Ruml says. "I didn't want to see it. I didn't have the stomach for it." Robert, however, had been brought up this way. He knew the vicious world his son would encounter, and knew he could handle it.

"A fighter is shaped from the inside out," Robert says. "And Bobby was tough enough. He was breaking heavy bags in the gym. A lot of referees in the boxing ring didn't like him for roughing, for using the elbow, but he was perfect for brawling. I wanted to make him tougher for the times to come."

Robert expected his only son to uphold the family legacy. "He was harder than coffin nails," Gunn says. "The old man would take you to the ground, bite your nose off, your ear off, your face off. You might lose your eyeball. So, because of that, not too many people wanted to fuck with him." He pauses. "My upbringing sounds cruel, but it gave me the will to never quit. He knew I needed to be an animal to survive."

Gunn learned to control the tempo, keep his hands up high, and see the other guy's mistakes before he makes them. He learned where to aim his shots. "Hit right underneath the heart and he drops to his knees," Gunn says. "Hit him in the liver and he shuts right down." He learned to control pain, honing his body with leather belts, baseball bats, and bouts on wooden floors, transforming his soft childhood skin into armor. And he learned to show no mercy, to draw first blood, to disorient a man and break his spirit, finishing him as quickly as possible. Unlike boxing, in which fighters go the distance and are awarded points for finesse, bare-knuckle matches are fast and efficient—all that matters is the knockout.

"You're not getting paid by the hour," Robert says. "Give a jab, then swing to the right and come with an overhand to break the nose. Get 'em bleeding and cut the eyes—that takes the fight out of most people."

From age eleven to sixteen, Gunn sharpened his techniques in the street fights his father would organize. Most of the time, he ended the matches in just three or four shots, the men drunk and off-balance and wildly outmatched, as his father heckled from the sidelines. "The verbal tongue-lashing the old man gave these guys was even worse than their beatings," Gunn says. "I laid out one man and my dad looked at him and said, 'Jeez, are you okay? You can't fight at all. You told me you could fight.' And then Dad took him and bought the man breakfast!"

Robert, knowing the ringer he had honed from the cradle, once bet $1,000 on his son. "They were perfect victims," he says of the drunks he brought home. "They weren't no world-class fighters, but they would give Bobby a good workout, two or three minutes in the street. I'd aggravate them and say, 'Shit, you guys can't fight. You can't even beat this fucking kid.' And they'd get all pissed off and one would say to Bobby, 'Go sit down, you little punk fucker.' And Bobby—*Wack!*—the man's nose would be bleeding or his eye would be cut and he'd put them out. It give Bobby experience, you see—I was preparing him for what's to come."

For Gunn, most of the motel fighters are a blur, a montage of towering bleary-eyed hulks. Yet he does remember one muscled bald man, about thirty-five, who claimed to be a fighter, the man standing out for his spectacular downfall. About thirty seconds into the fight, Gunn hit him with a combination, a right hand to the body knocking the man back so hard, he fell and jammed his body between the wheel and fender of Robert's truck. As the man lay there, his body at a funny angle, Gunn, his father, and the entire motor court stood in silence, fearing the worst. "And then, finally, the guy said one single word," Gunn recalls, laughing. "*Fu-u-u-uck.*"

Gunn can joke about it now, but privately, he often felt pain and fear in those motor-court parking lots. "At the end of the day, I was still a little boy fighting men," he says. "It was stressful." Pushed to the limits by his father and mean-spirited relatives, he put all his heart into the fight game.

"Bobby became inward," Ruml says. "When he was younger, he was tortured by outsiders, tortured by family, and his father was hard on him. I mean, he took a mental and physical beating every week, and he was just a kid." Ruml pauses. "I'm surprised the way he is today, to tell you the truth. Most people would be seeing a psychiatrist for life. But Bobby's got no hatred in him. Not a bit."

Gunn doesn't like to dwell on the past. Yet he believes these fights made him the champion brawler he is today. Even more importantly, they were some of the only times he won his father's affection. "It's just what it was," Gunn says. "As sick as it sounds to a normal person. *'That's my boy.'* That little word of encouragement from my dad made it all right. It was a tough life. Yes, it sounds insane. It *was* crazy. But everything happened for a reason. And all them things made me the man I am today. And that's where I shine in fighting: on the street."

* * * *

Gunn excelled at boxing and bare knuckle. By his own admission, however, he was probably best suited to his father's third fight discipline, the most vicious craft of them all: rough-and-tumble. In the underground, rough-and-tumble, or "all-in," anything-goes fighting, is a closely kept secret, the combat equivalent of a snuff film—a sport so violent, few even want to discuss it. "Most fighters will never speak about them," a Canadian bare-knuckle fighter tells me. "They are a very different sort of storm. I have only seen two in my life and both were violent to the extreme, a far cry from a normal bare-knuckle fight and not for the faint of heart. Bobby was in one of those. He was outweighed a good eighty pounds, if not more, but won. And let's just say the other man will never need a tissue again."

Paul Tyler, an underground promoter and referee in Delaware who has seen Gunn compete in countless bare-knuckle fights, underscores the distinction between standard bare knuckle and rough-and-tumble. "When you're in a rough-and-tumble fight, it's usually out of disrespect," he says. "So it's more serious. Like, if you send your guy 'fair play' [meaning, to fight in a typical bare-knuckle bout] and the other guy says, 'rough-and-tumble,' that's like saying, 'Nah, this is personal.' Like 'You're a piece of shit.' And I've seen the other guy then say, 'No, I want fair play.' And right there you know he's got a little less heart. He's scared."

For Gunn, rough-and-tumble was a natural extension of the campground brawls he'd known since birth, the free-for-alls involving bats and battering-ram trucks and penny-roll fist-loads. Growing up, he had watched his parents stand up to rival clans, rednecks, and even farmers who tried to stiff them. Once, in the early 1980s, Gunn was driving with his father in rural Ontario when a man in a truck pulled behind them, flashing his lights and honking his horn. "What's this dirty fool doing?" Robert said, pulling over. Gunn and Robert had spent the day painting a barn. They were one of perhaps several Traveler families working the region, and maybe the farmer was upset over a poor job on his property. To this day, Gunn doesn't know why they were targeted. But he does know he and his father had never worked for the man—he had the wrong Traveler. The man approached. "He's a big young farmer in coveralls, about six-four and two-fifty pounds, the kind of guy who picks up sixty-pound bales of hay all day," Gunn recalls. "He rips off his hat and is giving my father abuse, screaming at him, and then pushes him. So my dad jumped up in the air and kicked this man in the chest with his two feet. Boom! The bum is lying on his back. My father rolled back like a wrestler and then jumped on top of him like a cobra. And I mean, it was bad. Blood was pouring out the man's mouth. I yelled 'Dad, stop!'" Gunn's father stood, removed the water cooler from the back of their one-ton truck, and poured it over the man's head. "The man wakes up, all blood, gets in his truck and drives away," Gunn says. "We get back in our truck, and Dad looks at me and says, 'Your old man still got it, don't he?'"

In 1988, at age fifteen, Gunn had his first rough-and-tumble bout, a vicious match in a dance club in Buffalo, New York. On a Saturday evening, Gunn and three of his Traveler friends crossed the border for a rare night out, winding up in a predominantly Black club where they didn't know anyone. "We were in the back, standing there like nerds, listening to stuff like Run DMC and 'Pump Up the Volume,'" Gunn recalls. "When this big, big Black guy in his midtwenties in a jogging suit walks up and pushes me." Gunn is not sure what happened, whether one of his friends—all of whom were Traveler boxers—had called the man out, or Gunn was simply being targeted. For whatever reason, he suddenly found himself in a fight. Gunn tried to demur, but the crowd encircled them, the man taking off his tracksuit top. "I said, 'Oh, shit,'" Gunn recalls. "He was all muscle."

[Figure 9.3] "We were in the back, listening to stuff like Run-DMC and *Pump Up the Volume.*" (Photo courtesy of Bobby Gunn)

The man grabbed Gunn in a bear hug, hoisting him aloft and head-butting and biting him in the face. Robert had taught Gunn to watch out for knives in a street fight, to try to cover all bases, but now the young Traveler found himself simply trying to survive.

"He was squeezing me and I couldn't breathe," Gunn recalls. "So I took my left hand, wriggled it down under his pants, grabbed hold of his ball sack, and ripped it off. He grabbed his butt, fell to the ground, and I knocked him out cold." As people screamed, Gunn and the other Travelers escaped to their car, driving straight for the border. "I was covered in blood," Gunn says. "So my friend Tommy takes off his shirt and gives it to me and he puts his winter coat back on. My coat's all fucked and I got an old sweatshirt and I remember driving across the border and we're shitting ourselves as we go through customs. 'Oh, yes, we just did a little shopping today.' 'Oh, yeah, everything good?' 'Oh, yeah.' The guy not knowing I'm sitting here covered in blood. I didn't feel safe until we were back across the border."

Gunn would go on to fight countless rough-and-tumble matches, taking the bouts to increasing extremes. "Nobody talks about it, but I'm better at rough-and-tumble than fair and square," he says. "Many times, there's a man down, I smash his head open, rip his ball sack off, if he had a ring in his balls, rip it out. Gut him, smash him, take your finger, put it in his eye, bite his ear and nose off. Christ, I've done that many a time." He pauses. "I know that sounds graphic, but I'm doing it to some animal who's trying to do it to me. That's a gunslinger fight, you know?"

Once, after winning a bare-knuckle match in Chicago in the late nineties, Gunn turned his back on his defeated opponent only to have the man jump him, the bout then turning rough-and-tumble. "He tried to bite my back," Gunn says. "So I took my thumb and stuck it in his eye. You know that warm, wet, slimy feeling around your tongue? That's exactly what it feels like. I stuck it in, turned it to the side, and ripped it. I *heard* it rip. And it got a squeal out of him and he let loose and he fell on the ground with his hands over his head and I could've given him the boots." Gunn is quiet a moment, speaking with detachment. "But I didn't."

"It didn't feel good," he says about the fight. "It was terrible. See, as bad as Bobby Gunn is, I'm not that bad. I was a nice wee boy. If you were nice to me, I gave you the best wee conversation in the world. I would never bully anyone. But this was one hard, dirty seasoned bastard—and that's what happens if you try to bite me."

Gunn shrugs. "I was trained to fight like an animal."

CHAPTER 10
JESUS WAS A FIGHTER

As a child, Gunn fought for the same reasons he fights today: money, family, and religion. "Jesus Christ and his disciples were warriors," Gunn says. "These were rough, manly men that went to wars, took abuse. If we don't have a godly foundation as humans, we will become animals. Fighting has been here since biblical times."

Remarkably, even now Gunn and the other Travelers of North America still center their lives on the same principles as their wagon-roaming nineteenth-century forebears. But unlike their contemporary UK cousins, whose fighting and customs have been portrayed in endless documentaries, TV shows, books, and films—most famously as Brad Pitt's mumbling knuckler in *Snatch*—the Travelers of North America are completely unknown. They are ghosts, a fabled society, a mysterious clan who shun all outsiders.[1] "We haven't done any research on them here," says George Gmelch, an anthropology professor at the University of San Francisco who specializes in Travelers of Ireland. "There just isn't very much."

This is by design. In seven years of reporting, I have yet

to meet Gunn's wife, Rose, or see the inside of their apartment. Gunn has never allowed me to record his people's secret language. "My wife doesn't want to talk, because she doesn't want to be persecuted by other Travelers for speaking to outsiders," Gunn says. "And if I weren't in the public eye, I wouldn't be allowed to socialize with country people, either. I would be shunned."

Only one man, John Stygles, a Catholic priest in Memphis, has been able to gain access to their closed-off culture. And what he has discovered is amazing—a hidden society maintaining Old World traditions of arranged marriages, traveling trades, mystical religion, and bare-knuckle fighting, all in the twenty-first-century American heartland. "They don't speak to outsiders, because they've been criticized and attacked," Stygles says. "The joke is, they call their language Cant because 'You can't understand us.'"

During the turn of the twentieth century, when Gunn's paternal ancestors were sailing from Scotland to Canada, his mother's people, the Lindsays, were arriving in the United States. According to Irish Traveler lore and backed by Stygles's research, the first eight families listing their trades as "tinker" in America arrived in New York alongside a broader wave of European immigrants in the mid-nineteenth century. Working as horse and mule traders, these Travelers settled mostly in livestock auction hubs throughout the south, where the three largest groups of descendants still live in tight-knit enclaves of double-wide trailers and subdivisions—the "Mississippi Travelers" in the Memphis area; the "Georgia Travelers" just across the state line in Murphy Village, South Carolina; and the "Texas Travelers" in Fort Worth. [2] In addition, smaller Traveler communities spread across the USA from Wilmington, Delaware, to St. Augustine, Florida, to Dayton, Ohio, to Los Angeles.

[Figure 10.1] A 1913 illustration of an "Irish-Gypsy camp in the South"
Public domain.

Occasionally mentioned in nineteenth- and twentieth-century newspapers as "Irish horse traders," "pedlars," or "the walking people," the first US Travelers were surprisingly wealthy. They were shrewd traders who bought malnourished mules and horses, tended them back to health, and then sold them for profit. They also bought investment properties across the country, the land doubling as camping grounds on their tours. According to newspaper accounts in the south in 1901 and 1908, the "straightforward, hard-working . . . studiously law-abiding" clans roved in groups of fifty in carts resembling "circus wagons," regularly attending church with their "neatly dressed" children.[3] Every spring, the Travelers would convene to mingle and to bury their dead in appointed plots in Atlanta and Nashville, the women wearing "jeweled crucifixes and rosaries" for the communal wakes, the men flashing diamond rings.[4] "Wandering homeless through the south, yet doing an annual cash business of hundreds of thousands of dollars; living in tents like gypsy nomads yet the owners of many city lots and valuable town property," states a newspaper in Springfield, Illinois, in 1913. "Such is the strange life of the Irish clan."[5]

Today, an estimated ten thousand Travelers live in the United States, working mostly construction jobs and continuing to live a seminomadic life, traveling for work nine months of the year and roosting during the winter.[6] Although undocumented by the US Census Bureau, they self-identify as an ethnic group, basing membership on descent. Suspicious of *gorgio,* they marry almost exclusively within their tribe, banish those who leave it, and routinely pull their children from school by the eighth grade so they don't assimilate with mainstream culture. "University will ruin them," Jimmy Ruml says. "Traveling is freedom. Once you stop, they've got you."

Travelers have good reason to be wary of outsiders—they've got a bad reputation. As Gunn will acknowledge, sometimes it's warranted. Google "Irish Travelers" and you'll get a litany of newspaper clips regarding petty scams. Travelers have been known to target neighborhoods and the elderly, offering to fix roofs, paint houses, or resurface driveways, only to use thin mixtures that quickly wear away.[7] Or they'll claim to be traveling salesmen, selling shoddy equipment or tools at a premium price, then, when they break, charging the customers an exorbitant rate to fix them.[8] Errant Travelers have even popped up in murder investigations and, in a high-profile case in 2014, were on the front end of a black-market deal involving moving taxidermy rhino horns from Texas to illicit buyers in China.[9] In another dustup in 2016, the FBI raided the Traveler community of Murphy Village, South Carolina, eventually getting twenty-one guilty pleas on racketeering charges stemming from fraud under the federal RICO act, meaning that the US government now legally regards the Irish Travelers as a criminal enterprise on par with the mob.[10]

Gunn is quick to point out that the Travelers' rep is over-blown. "Out of a hundred Travelers, ninety-five have done good for themselves in life," he says. "Did you know my people just repaved the White House drive?" Yes, as Gunn will attest, there are cliques of Travelers who run systematic scams. But the notion that as a people, they are running a nationwide criminal network to bilk other Americans is outrageous, if not outright bigoted. Stygles agrees. "They're good people," he says. "Most Irish Travelers just work real hard in a profession that a lot of people complain about—home repairs and that kind of thing. They really aren't what you think they are. You can't stereotype them."

For Gunn, as for most US Travelers, the three simple values of family, religion, and fighting mean everything. In Traveler culture, lineages are learned from birth. The elderly are taken care of. Children are raised surrounded by parents, aunts, uncles, and cousins. The family structures are nineteenth-century severe—men do the work while women tend the home. Work—constant, grueling, physical—begins at a young age. Corporate day jobs are unheard of. In fact, they're looked down upon. Working for a *gorgio* is considered degrading. Instead, often after leaving school by the age of fifteen, boys apprentice with their fathers, learning a trade and living at home until they can provide an income and hence find a bride. The Travelers are not as sequestered as the Amish— they work with *gorgio* when necessary, own cell phones, and watch TV—but they also don't invite outsiders back to the trailer park. "It's just easier to hang out with other Travelers," Bobby Jr. says. "You don't have to explain so much."

Perhaps the greatest tell of Gunn's outsider status is his voice. As an isolated tribe with a secret language, Travelers are famous for their unusual accents. In 2012, for his part as the villain Bane in *The Dark Knight Rises,* actor Tom Hardy based his voice on champion bare-knuckle boxer Bartley Gorman, knowing that the Traveler's accent would add to his character's mystique. The "accent was very specific . . . a Gypsy accent," Hardy said in a 2012 interview. "That's why it was difficult to understand."[11] In his 1946 novel *Nightmare Alley*, author William Lindsay Gresham describes the placeless accents of American carnival workers, a people often lumped in with Travelers. "[Their speech] was a composite of all the sprawling regions of the country," Gresham writes. "A language which sounded Southern to Southerners and Western to Westerners. It was the talk of the soil . . . a soothing, illiterate, earthy language."[12]

As a Traveler, Gunn, too, possesses an unusual voice. His accent and speech are both placeless and timeless, a Scottish-Canadian lilt combined with a 1940s street-tough vocabulary that sounds as if he had just emerged from a bunker after being cut off from mainstream society for decades. He calls boxers "pal," and female tollbooth operators "darling" or "my angel" and signs off texts with "my brother." A favorite phrase is "fair play to you," Traveler slang for best wishes on a good, clean fight. Often, he and his children abandon English altogether, lowering their voices and slipping in and out of Cant, the Travelers' secret language, in front of *gorgio* and *muskers,* the latter their term for police.* "It's our own code," Gunn says. "Sometimes I'll say, '*Fakem shem.*' '*Fake*' means 'beat him up' and '*shem*' means 'real bad.' My boy was sparring and this old trainer walked up and said, 'His name is Bobby?' And I said, 'Yeah.' He said, 'That's funny, I thought it was Fakensham.'"

Yet while Gunn adheres to many long-held customs regarding family, he, like other modern Travelers, has made some modern concessions. As a northern Traveler, he doesn't practice arranged marriage—"it's a redneck thing"—and has left behind the roving encampments of his youth, instead raising his family in an apartment. He refuses to allow his son to bare-knuckle fight. And his

---

* At one point, after calling someone's great-great-grandfather an insulting name in Cant—a term for a street person, dating back to Medieval times—Gunn later asked me to strike it from the record. He was worried that the man's descendants would take it as an "insult to the bloodline," starting a blood feud.

daughter, Charlene, will not get married at sixteen. "She's my little girl," he says. "Not until eighteen or twenty."

Gunn still clings to some customs, however. He pulled Bobby Jr. from school after seventh grade and began homeschooling him, also bringing him into the asphalt business. Despite working long hours to put her through private school, Gunn says Charlene will also not attend classes at her school past fifth grade. "She has all her little friends right now, but they will start to drift apart," he says. "If a Traveler girl goes to school with country people, she might not marry a Traveler boy." Instead, Charlene will likely spend her days learning how to manage the family finances—the traditional role of women in the Traveler household.

Alone with Bobby Jr. at one point, I ask whether he ever wanted to be part of the outside world, whether he feels as if he is missing out on something. "Nah," he says. "You've seen the movie *300*, right? Their culture was training, fighting, making war. People questioned it, but they were the greatest military in the world. For Travelers, it's just our way. We were born to do it."

Ultimately, Gunn will not budge on the two most central traits of Traveler heritage: religion and fighting. Whether Catholic or Protestant, Travelers practice a devout mix of Christianity and Irish Druidism, an almost medieval belief system in which God's literal word is sacred and saints and demons walk among us. For many of them, the Bible is the only book they will ever read. "It's very much an Old World outlook," Stygles says. "You would see the same type of thing in the north end of Boston, the old Italian widows who wear black and play with their rosary beads. The Travelers believe God will protect them. It's a traditional way of doing things."* Some Travelers believe they are the descen-

* Stygles says modern Travelers essentially practice Christianity as it was done in Ireland in the nineteenth century, and it's the same with many aspects of their lives. "If you go back to Ireland when the Irish were converted to Catholicism, they were

dants of Cain, banished by God in the Old Testament for killing Abel—"a fugitive and a vagabond shalt thou be in the earth."[13] Others say they hail from the blacksmith who forged the nails for Jesus's cross, his progeny forever flung to the wild.[14] Traveler men carry rosaries, wear decade rings with bumps on the shank for counting prayers, and hang crosses from their rearview mirrors, while women decorate their homes with artifacts and icons.

Gunn does not drink, but he is unusual—alcohol and tobacco are not forbidden. "That's just us," Gunn says, nodding at Bobby Jr. "Travelers love to drink—the beer factory couldn't fill them."

Perhaps the most biblical-era aspect of Traveler society is the practice of shunning. When a Traveler breaks a rule within the tribe, he must attend church and beg forgiveness as penance, the clan collectively shunning him. "If you go back to the biblical times, it was a shame-or-honor society," Stygles says. "Well, that's how it works in this community too." At one point, Gunn tells a story of a Traveler who cheated him on money. Gunn could easily have beaten up the man, but it would have been an unfair match. So instead, he humiliated him in the most demeaning way possible. Gunn walked up to the man while he was eating dinner with his family in his home, called him outside to fight and settle the issue, and then stood over him as he didn't move, forcing him to endure the mark of a coward. "He never even looked at me," Gunn says. "And his children will never look at him the same way again."

Each night before going to bed, Gunn lies fully prostrate

---

initially Druid or pagan and believed in a lot of magical things," he says. "The story is, they used the shamrock to explain the Trinity, the triumvirate of god, but the whole concept in Roman Catholicism of taking a piece of bread and some wine and changing that into the literal body and blood of Jesus Christ is magical. The same is true for other denominations—the transubstantiation of Jesus Christ. So that fascination with the priest is almost a magical magician type. Praying to saints and the different blessings and rites is very ritualistic. It all plays back into the Druidism, the core Irish cultural stuff."

on the floor, praying to keep his faith strong, to keep his family safe from sin. When he's not training at Ike's, he lifts weights with chain-smoking Polish priests at a Polish gym in Jersey City, absorbing their tales of modern-day exorcisms in country villages. They tell of strange incidents where eighty-pound girls snap the necks of horses and speak in tongues, of the weeklong process it can take to banish the "roughy"—Travelers won't even say the devil's name out loud—from their hearts. "If you don't believe," Gunn says, "then you can get taken out."

[Figure 10.2] Praying before a fight (Photo by author)

Only once has Gunn lost his faith. In the summer of 1999, while traveling the Midwest with his family, knocking door-to-door to drum up asphalt jobs, money tight at every turn, he stopped attending church. "I just wasn't walking with God," he says.

One night while sleeping at a Candlewood Suites in Ohio, Gunn suddenly awoke to an immense pressure on his chest, a weight smothering him. He looked up. He says a pale face with red eyes and a black body hovered over him, lingering before receding into the darkness. Gunn lay still, shaking. He looked at the bedside clock: 3:16. He ran to the cot on the floor, checked on Bobby Jr., only two years old at the time, and returned to bed ten minutes later. The clock still glowed 3:16. Gunn let out a cry. His wife, Rose, asked what was wrong. "It was a message," Gunn says. "John 3:16: *For God so loved the world that he gave his one and only son.*"

For Travelers raised on the Old Testament and its eye-for-an-eye worldview, violence is a natural part of life. In the swamps of Florida, they unleash pit bulls on feral hogs, hunting and then stabbing the four-hundred-pound animals through the armpits with six-inch blades. In northern Oklahoma, they race quarter horses in dried-out riverbeds in illegal competitions near Indian reservations, gambling and drinking on the windswept plains. At night, in the bayous of Gulf Coast Texas, they hunt gar with compound bows, from flat-bottom boats, spotlighting the prehistoric-looking fish before impaling them with double-barbed carbon-shaft arrows.

But of all blood sports, nothing is more revered, more devout a calling, than fighting. Gunn lives an ascetic life, treating his body as a temple, staying fit because, as scripture states, hardship is to be expected—and overcome only with might. "My mother used to read the Bible to me at night," he says. "Jesus Christ was not the poor wee skinny little man you see on the cross. He was a rough man, a carpenter who worked with big giant logs and stones.

When he flipped over them marble tables in that marketplace, them tables were estimated to weigh twelve hundred pounds. And he took a beating that nobody took."

Gunn pauses.

"Fighting has always been a part of mankind. I think it's no sin at all if you have no hatred toward the man. But if you're a bullying bastard, then you're not of God. Then you pay the price."

CHAPTER 11
THE SKINHEADS BRING IN A FARM BOY

In December 1989, in the final bout of his childhood, Gunn drove alone to fight the skinheads. Heading north out of town, into the hills, he played his new favorite song, U2's "With or Without You," on repeat on his cassette deck, his boots laced tight, his face coated in Vaseline. To the east, across the Niagara River, he could see the US side with all its promise, the land of his mother's people, the land where he dreamed of someday making it as a pro boxer. On this side of the border, however, was Gunn's reality: a cold Ontario scrap yard with towers of rusted cars, and twenty neo-Nazis waiting for him in a gravel lot.

Gunn parked his red Dodge Dakota pickup truck, nuzzled his beloved pit bull, Duran, and stared at the crowd—a mass of suspenders, Doc Martens, and swastika tattoos. He had not told anyone where he was going—not his mother, not his father, not any other Travelers. Now, on the threshold of manhood, he felt it was his time to finally prove himself, to go out alone and defend his family, to take the fight.

But first, he took a deep breath.

"I'll admit it. I was scared," Gunn later says. "At a moment like this, you don't know if you're going to get ten-timed.* And you don't know, even if you win, if you're going to be squared away, because these people, the skinheads, don't really have any honor. But they had been threatening my family, and I wanted to get this problem sorted out. So I rolled the windows up, stepped outside, and left Duran barking like crazy."

For Gunn, in many respects, the fight had been inevitable. Growing up, he had heard the generational stories of his family: of Black Bob taking down Kicking Joe; of his grandfather, Robert senior, once, in Toronto, defeating an Olympic boxing hopeful who had made fun of the Travelers; of his own father, Robert Jr., taking on an entire campsite for refusing to recognize his love for his wife. Yes, Gunn was trained to fight for defense and money. But more than that, he was taught to put up his fists to defend the family name. Now, in his most formative match, a bout against a gang of neo-Nazis threatening to burn his parents out of their motel room, he would finally be forced to step up and earn his rightful place in that saga of family stories, the same way as every Gunn before him: by taking the fight.

"You understand why I thank God for my upbringing, my hard times?" Gunn says. "In life, you got to prepare for the worst. There's always some dirty fool. And that's what my grandfather and father taught me, walking me through the parks as a baby, holding me and doing boxing moves on my hands." He pauses. "It goes so deep into the heart of this family. It's something in the blood. The fights never bothered me so much—my only real fear has been to disappoint them."

Gunn's trouble with the skinheads had begun a few weeks earlier, in a motel bar on the western edge of Niagara Falls. On

---

* By getting "ten-timed," Gunn means he was worried about a gang of ten or more of the neo-Nazis attacking him at once.

December 7, 1989, he had wanted to watch the historic third matchup between middleweight pro boxing champions Sugar Ray Leonard and Roberto Duran—a heavily hyped duel to be aired before a worldwide television audience at the newly opened Mirage Hotel in Las Vegas. Gunn was desperate to see the match, but his family's motel-room TV was on the fritz. So, on a frigid cold night, Christmas lights dangling over the trash-strewn snow along Lundy's Lane, he walked down the highway to Doc Magilligan's, an Irish pub next to a Best Western. Legally, Gunn, then sixteen, should not have been in the pub. But the bartenders, like everyone else in Niagara Falls, knew the young fighter, knew he would stand politely in the corner without so much as asking for a water, just wanting to watch the fight. The bouncer, however, was a skinhead and didn't much care for Travelers. So midway through the fight, he grabbed Gunn by the arm, yanking him to the door. When they got there, Gunn, incensed and embarrassed, retaliated—leveling the man with a right uppercut. "The whole tip of his tongue come right off and fell to the ground," Gunn says. "Blood pours everywhere, and I just walked away."

Soon after, the skinheads began calling Gunn's motel room, threatening to destroy his father's work truck and rattling his mother, who was then in the early stages of a mysterious illness. "My mom was upset," Gunn says. "They called saying, 'We're going to do damage to your boy; we're going to destroy your husband's equipment.' I knew I had to square everything out." Gunn's father, Robert, had once gotten in a fight with local mobsters, beating up a couple of connected guys at a bar. "Beat the fuck right out of them," Gunn recalls. A few nights later, Gunn says his mom happened to be across the street getting milk when she saw two men kick down the door of their motel room. She knew that the room was empty; Gunn and his father were at work. Still, although Travelers rarely call the police, Jackie was so upset that she contacted them. The cops told her the two mobsters were likely looking for her husband, their preferred retaliation method being to throw battery acid in the face. "So Dad had to get on the phone and make peace," Gunn recalls. "He did that to get out of a couple of them situations."

Thinking back to his father, Gunn picked up the phone and talked with the skinhead leader, agreeing to a meeting. The next morning, Gunn traveled to a building downtown, where the head neo-Nazi gave him an ultimatum: take the fight, or his family suffers. "He was a skinny guy, kinda young," Gunn recalls. "A little prick. He gave me an area and told me to come meet them on Friday, that I'm going to fight a guy they're bringing in from Toronto. And that if I didn't come, they're going to do damage to me and my parents with baseball bats and knives and burn down my dad's truck, our only source of money." Gunn nodded, shook hands with the skinhead leader, and returned home. "I tells my mom it's all square, I took care of it," he recalls. "She thought it was done." A few days later, Gunn left the motel at eleven in the morning, not telling anyone where he was headed.

Walking toward the group of twenty skinheads, Gunn tried to block out Duran, his pit bull, barking and clawing at the rolled-up window in his pickup truck, which was parked behind him, the engine turned on, the heater still going. Gunn has always loved dogs, and the stray—named for Roberto Duran, the Panamanian world champion boxer whose devastating punches earned him the nickname "Hands of Stone"—went everywhere with him, even to fights. "I called him, 'Paws of Stone,'" Gunn says. "I loved him."

Gunn's mind then turned to his parents, to the possibility that he might not walk out of this gravel pit. "I was more scared for my mom or dad if something happened and I wasn't around," he said. "I'm not Superman. I've been involved with so many deals. Baseball bats to the head. I've been stabbed. I've been shot at. I was waiting on that with this guy. I didn't think I was going to get fair play."

In the end, though, wearing only a T-shirt and jeans, Gunn did as he always did before a fight, clearing his mind, focusing on the one man before him. "Right when I get ready to fight, there's, like, this sound that comes on me," Gunn says, making a guttural *wwwwhhhhiiiiiiiirrrrrrrr* noise from deep in his diaphragm. "And I get right into it. And the world's boxed out. This sounds weird, but I'm more calmer in the middle of a fight than I am in church on Sunday. That may sound sick. But it's true."

Gunn landed the first blow, peeling the man's eyebrow from his face. Surrounded by neo-Nazis, Gunn stepped back, sizing up the skinhead they had brought in from Toronto. He was a 240-pound bruiser in jeans and a sleeveless shirt—not muscle-bound, but large, a farm boy. Right away, Gunn knew that it would be a one-way affair. "He left himself open," Gunn says. "At most, maybe he had a dozen fights on the street, but *they* thought he was tough and was going to do me in. And that's all that counts."

As blood streamed into his opponent's eyes, Gunn glanced at the crowd, expecting to be jumped. The skinheads, however, just stood there, so he went to work. Despite the flap of bloody skin hanging off his forehead, the Toronto farm boy managed to get in a few shots, lasting two or three minutes. In the end, though, Gunn hit him with two left hooks and a right corkscrew and the man went down. "Bang, bang, bang, bang," Gunn says. "Buzzed him. That's it—he quit." Gunn turned to the crowd, his adrenaline surging, his breath pluming in the cold air, his dog Duran barking like mad in the truck. "'We're sorted out?'" Gunn recalls asking them. "They were just like, 'Go on, it's over.' And I never had a problem with them again."

As the sun was setting, Gunn pulled back into the Tropicana Motel parking lot, his clothes soaked in blood. "It was all over me," he says. "Dried blood. Not red, but black." He walked in the door and his mother began crying, asking what had happened, while his father came to inspect his cuts. Gunn showed him his right hand, which was swollen. He thought it was broken.

"What happened? The fucking skinheads?" Robert asked.

"Yeah, I sorted it out," Gunn replied.

"And how'd you take him out?" his father asked.

Gunn gave them the story.

"Good man, good man. Let me see your hand."

Gunn watched as his father tended his cuts. The old man never showed affection, never said he loved him, hardly talked about anything at all. Now, however, Gunn had his attention. "'Oh, we got to fix his hand. Jackie, move away,'" Gunn recalls his father saying. "'Come in here, the champ's here, put his hand in water. It's not broken, just a sprain. Oh, what a *gadgie*, what a *gadgie*.' (That means 'What a man.') 'Jackie, put away the cooking. A steak dinner right now for him.'"

Gunn pauses. "I know it sounds weird, but that was like his son winning a college football game," he says. "It's love, but it's a strange love. It's like our family saying, 'Where the Gunns walk, the ground shakes.' It was a weight on my shoulders, but I wouldn't have it any other way."

At the time, Gunn had no idea, but he was about to leave the back streets of Niagara Falls and the campgrounds of his childhood forever. The young fighter was entering a new arena, one his father and family could never have imagined.

CHAPTER 12
BUSTED SPLEENS AND BROKEN DREAMS

Tijuana, Mexico, 1992

Gunn flinched as another beer bottle shattered against the chain-link fence. The crowd had spat on him as he walked to the ring, thrown cans and bottles at him during the fight, and howled when he knocked out Sergio García with a left hook to the chin in the first round. Now they wanted his blood. "I'm covered in beer and glass and they're trying to kick down the fence," Gunn says about being besieged in a makeshift dressing room after the fight. "It was scary."

He had seen worse over the years, but the fight in Mexico was a different sort of arena: the world of professional boxing. On March 24, 1992, Gunn fought super middleweight García in a pro boxing match at Agua Caliente, a run-down casino in the smog-choked heart of Tijuana. For Gunn, the fight was a turning point, a make-or-break scenario as he tried to accomplish what few Traveler fighters have ever done: make the transition from bare knuckle to pro boxing. While Travelers often fight for honor and money among themselves, only a few venture into the "country people's" world of professional ringed bouts. Growing up, Travelers don't have the traditional support systems of most aspiring pro boxers. Instead of a home gym and trainer, they often hone their skills on the road, grabbing snippets of workout time while laying asphalt. To succeed requires not just dedicating oneself to the sport—a different craft from bare-knuckle boxing—but also overcoming the hardships of being an outsider in an outsiders' sport. And Gunn was trying to do it under unimaginable pressure. Not only was he fighting to become a middleweight champion, but he also needed the prize money to pay the medical bills of his mother, Jackie, who had contracted a deadly blood-borne disease and was struggling to stay alive in a motel room off the Las Vegas Strip. "When I wasn't sparring, I was going to work every day in my little red truck," he says. "Every dollar went to her."

From the beginning, Gunn had been worried about the fight. Separated from San Diego County by the world's busiest border crossing, the Agua Caliente casino, dubbed "Satan's Playground" by California pastors in the 1920s, had once been a five-star resort. Hosting the likes of Charlie Chaplin, Bing Crosby, and Al Capone, it was a south-of-the-border getaway with a private airport, where wealthy Americans could drink and gamble beneath palm fronds swaying in the breeze.[1] By the time Gunn arrived, however, the old resort had long since burned to the ground, and the casino was a dilapidated relic of its former glory. The horse track had been replaced by a greyhound track, the baccarat tables by peso slots, the film stars by drug gangs. "This was not a nice place," Gunn says.

For Gunn, the fight was about revenge. The previous August, he had suffered his first career professional boxing loss against García in a Top Rank match in Las Vegas, trying to fight with a fractured right arm that cracked in two in the second round. "I got punched in the arm, and the bone was nearly sticking out of the skin," Gunn says. "The referee went 'Oh, my God!' and stopped the fight." Seven months later, famed trainer Johnny Tocco, who helped shape everyone from Sonny Liston to Mike Tyson in a gym next to a Las Vegas tire-repair shop, helped set up a rematch.[2] Gunn saw the fight as a crucial step to redeeming his loss and maybe, finally, proving to promoter Don King's camp that he was ready for the big time. Although only eighteen years old, Gunn had already been boxing professionally for three years. "I couldn't get the proper respect that I really wanted," he says. "I was just a sparring partner for all the top guys in the world."

Kenny "The Emerald City Assassin" Ellis, a former pro middleweight and fellow sparring partner with Gunn, remembers his friend's struggles.[3] "Bobby had the face of a choirboy and the left hook of a hell boy," Ellis recalls. "He worked with Don King. We came into town with eyes full of hope and left in broken spirits with our pants tied with rope."

Mike Hopper, sixty, a professional boxing trainer from Memphis who worked Gunn's corner during the nineties, chalks Gunn's inability to break through during this time up to management. "Back then, Gunn was a smaller guy, a middleweight, a gaudy-style fighter, a crowd pleaser," Hopper recalls. "If he had had good people back then, he probably could have gone on and done what he needed to do in the boxing world. But sometimes you get a bad-apple manager that's not looking out for your best interests—he's looking out for his pockets."

Gunn had been promised stardom, but by the time he got to Tijuana, he was starting to question everything. Despite his hard work, despite his talent, despite assurances he was being groomed for the main stage by promoter Carl King (the stepson of Don King, who was widely said to have truly run the show), Gunn had been given fights only in dead-end outposts like Phoenix, Juárez, and Baja California.* For the most part, he had been used as a sparring partner,

---

* According to some of his past fighters, King would often make his boxers enlist Carl King as their manager. Carl would then take half their earnings. "I don't blame him for anything that happened," said former pro welterweight boxer Saoul Mamby in 1992, according to the book *The Life and Crimes of Don King*, by Emmy-winning journalist Jack Newfield. "He just did what his daddy told him. I don't think he ever kept any of my money. I think he gave it all to

that most dispensable of underlings, who fights the A-list roster to keep them in shape, sacrificing his own health to help the superstars shine. In fact, according to Gunn, the whole reason he lost that first fight against García was because he had suffered a hairline fracture during a sparring session three days earlier against one of Don King's top talents, middleweight world champion Mike McCallum. Gunn's camp didn't want to postpone the fight, so he entered the ring with a damaged arm, ultimately breaking the fracture clean during his match. "They didn't want to lose money on the fight," Gunn says. "So they shot me with something like Novocain and sent me out."[*] Seven months later in Tijuana, Gunn, back to health, dropped García in minutes. "I does what I shoulda done the first time," he says.

Maybe García, a southern California native, was a local favorite. Maybe the crowd had bet against the gringo. Or maybe they were just drunk and upset the fight had ended so abruptly. Whatever the reason, they decided to take it out on the person responsible. The place erupted.

Gunn had time to remove only one glove as the chain-link dressing room was getting kicked down. Still in his trunks, he escaped through a back door, jumped in the back of a waiting car, and was escorted by police across the border.

The driver, an old boxer who worked for Johnny Tocco, lit up a joint and cranked the radio. Marijuana smoke and music filled the Lincoln Continental as he drove them north through the desert, Gunn staring out the window. Gunn had won the

---

his daddy." (Carl King did not respond to numerous requests for an interview.)

    * Boxers often nurse lifelong injuries and are used to entering the ring despite the handicaps. The trick is to pass the medical inspection beforehand. According to pro trainer Mike Hopper, some commissions are less stringent than others. "Boxers get injured in all kinds of ways," he says. "Torn rotator cuffs, torn back muscles. Some states do rigorous physicals before shows and some don't. If an injured guy wanted to get his record billed, we'd just run him down to South Carolina, Indianapolis, or Nashville. Hell, Memphis would approve a ham sandwich to fight down there."

fight, but the conditions had been terrible. Rubbing his knuckles, he wondered about his future with King, how he could possibly make it as a fighter with a damaged arm, how he would be able to continue supporting his mother. He felt nowhere near realizing the dreams of his savage childhood.

* * * * *

History is littered with the stories of Travelers transcending bare knuckle only to flame out in spectacular fashion afterward. In the eighteenth century, Benjamin Boswell, a highway robber and boxer, drew large crowds to London before quitting the sport and likely returning to a life of crime.[4] In England in the 1970s, "Gypsy Johnny" Frankham, a Romany Gypsy who chain-smoked, drank, and gambled away his winnings, managed to win the British title before fading out and getting convicted of fraud.[5] In Montreal in the 1980s, five Scottish Traveler brothers known as the "fighting Hiltons" grew up sharing a single bed in a trailer with their parents, attending barroom brawls with their father, Dave, and becoming one of the most successful boxing families in history before collapsing under a staggering rap sheet of over a hundred criminal cases. These included rape, firing a revolver in a hotel lobby, and the armed robbery of a Dunkin' Donuts for $160.[6] In 2012, Irish Traveler John Joe Nevin even won a silver medal at the Olympics, only to have both legs broken soon thereafter by a family member with a golf club. The attack left his right tibia protruding from the skin, and his career soon fell into an alcohol-soaked slump.[7]

Of all Traveler pro boxers, however, none would fall as spectacularly as Tyson Fury, a 6'9" slugger who won the world heavyweight championship belt in 2015—a higher achievement than any Traveler in history—only to firebomb his career in a cocaine-fueled fall so epic, it stripped him of his titles and nearly ended his life.

[Figure 12.1] Tyson Fury becomes the heavyweight champion of the world in Dusseldorf, Germany, in 2015 (Photo by Marianne Mueller/Imago/Icon Sportswire)

Descended from a long line of bare-knuckle fighters, Fury grew up in a trailer in Manchester, England. His father, "Gypsy" John, was a champion bare-knuckler once sentenced to eleven years in prison for gouging out an opponent's eye in a street brawl.[8] His uncle, Pete, was a street fighter who rose to become a crime boss in Manchester during the 1980s, importing amphetamines from Belgium and distributing them across northwest England. In 1995, after a life of Ferraris and turf wars, Pete was jailed for ten years. Released in 2008, he was then charged with money laundering.[9] "I was regarded as dangerous, so I was locked up with IRA members and lifers," he said in 2013. "I found fighting a release."[10] When Tyson's father, John, went to prison for street fighting, Pete, after serving his time, took over the training of the clan's prodigy, Tyson. The former crime boss then guided his nephew all the way to his upset victory over Wladimir Klitschko in 2015, Fury winning the WBA (Super), IBF, WBO, IBO, and *Ring* magazine heavyweight belts. "Nothing can ever, ever mean more to my family, my history of people, than winning those titles," Fury says. "We are bare-knuckle champions, boxing champions—all that matters to us is fighting."

From the moment he won the world title, when he grabbed the mic, turned away from the stone-face Ukrainian, thanked God, and then, weeping, belted out Aerosmith's "I Don't Want to Miss a Thing" to his wife, Paris, it was clear that Fury would be no ordinary world champion.[11] Within weeks, the Gypsy King's sexist, homophobic, and downright bizarre remarks—at one point, he asserted that the apocalypse was nigh and Klitschko was a devil worshipper—led to a petition to remove his name from the BBC Sports Personality of the Year Award.[12] A rematch with Klitschko was postponed again and again, with Fury missing press conferences, claiming his car had broken down, and, at one point, showing up in full Batman costume.

Nothing, however, compared with the story that dropped in

September 2016, when ESPN reported that Fury had failed a drug test for cocaine. In lieu of an official statement, the world heavyweight champion answered the charges by taking to Twitter, where he posted a series of strange tweets, including a Photoshopped image of himself sitting behind a *Scarface*-worthy mountain of coke, an announcement of his retirement, and then an immediate retraction of the announcement, all of which made worldwide headlines. In the end, he admitted to the charges and was stripped of all titles and hospitalized for suicidal bipolar disorder, claiming that endless bigoted taunts online had pushed him over the edge. "I used to love boxing as a kid and always thought once I got to the top it would all change," Fury said, referencing his proclaimed bouts with depression and racism. "But deep down, I knew it never would."

Soon thereafter, however, Fury would achieve a storybook comeback, becoming the lineal and WBC heavyweight champion of the world—and providing a guiding light for Travelers like Gunn.

* * * * *

Bobby Gunn was determined to break the Traveler curse, to become a world champion pro boxer without getting stripped of his titles or his sanity. As a young man, he seemed poised to do so. In 1988, at age fifteen, he was a rising amateur star who had trained with the Gatti brothers in Jersey City, exhibited for famed trainer Slim Robinson in Philadelphia, and even flown to Texas to spar for an oil heiress, Josephine Abercrombie, in her fledgling (and ultimately doomed) Houston Boxing Association.[13] Living in shabby motels in Niagara Falls, Gunn could have signed with any number of promoters but ultimately decided to go with the top name in the world: Don King. A wild-haired legend of the sport, who had backed everyone from Muhammad Ali to Oscar De La Hoya, to Mike Tyson, King, according to Gunn and his father, offered Gunn a noncontract job as a sparring partner—a low-level position for entry-level boxers to prepare them for prime time. "Bobby was hanging out with Don King's crew, sparring with all the big names," Hopper recalls. "He was a youngster taking on the big-timers." Gunn would make $500 a week, enough to cover the family bills and help save for an operation needed by his mother, who had recently become gravely ill. Amazed at the chance to work with King, Gunn agreed to the terms. "I was the youngest fighter they had," he says. His childhood friend, Mike Normile, puts it another way: "They threw him to the wolves." (King did not respond to numerous requests for interviews.)

Gunn may never have become a pro boxer had it not been for his mother. The year before he began fighting for King, Jackie had walked out of a coffee shop at night and fallen on a patch of black ice, cracking her head on the pavement and lying unconscious until a worker found her frigid body stuck to the ice. "Her hip was busted," Gunn says. "Twisted behind her back." In the emergency room, doctors performed hip surgery, giving her a blood transfusion. A year later, she said she wasn't feeling well. After undergoing blood tests, Jackie learned that she had been infected with hepatitis C, which was already ravaging her liver, and would die within months.* Then she was given even worse news. "The doctor said, 'We can't even give you a liver transplant, because your citizenship ain't right,'" Gunn says. Jackie and Robert had never gotten proper paperwork for their unlicensed Traveler marriage, so she, as an American citizen, did not qualify for Canada's health care.† "What did we have to do?" Gunn asks. "Go to America."

---

* In what became known as the Tainted Blood Tragedy, over a thousand Canadians were infected with HIV, and up to twenty thousand with hepatitis C, through blood transfusions before testing was introduced in 1990. Since then, over seven hundred of the people who contracted HIV, and an unknown number who got hepatitis C, have died. It remains one of the worst public health disasters in Canadian history.

† Born in the United States to a Canadian father and an American mother, Gunn has dual citizenship.

In 1988, the Gunns moved to Las Vegas, the fight capital of the world, for Gunn to earn enough money in the ring to pay Jackie's hospital bills. Making the rounds with his father, meeting promoters, Gunn lied about his age, claiming to be eighteen, the minimum age to fight professionally in Nevada. The family lived in a run-down apartment on Koval Lane, just off the Strip, Jackie remaining laid up without insurance. Her only chance was a liver transplant, which, without insurance, would cost at least $23,000. Overwhelmed by his wife's sickness and their financial straits, Robert sank into depression, drinking for days on end and doing nothing except focusing on a last-ditch effort to save his family's fortunes—selling Bobby as a superstar fighter. "The best trainers in the world said Bobby could hit three times as hard as any man," Robert recalls. "He done it all, seen it all."

Touting his son as the second coming of Ali, Robert made the rounds, meeting potential managers and promoters in gyms and hotel suites along the Strip, once even sitting down with actor Gene Hackman, who had just made the boxing film *Split Decisions* and loved the sport, racing cars with Panamanian lightweight champion Alexis Argüello and helping start a foundation for impoverished former fighters.[14] "He wanted a piece of me," Gunn recalls. "He owned a piece of the Ruelas brothers.* Gene Hackman was a man's man. I liked him." Yet of all his meetings, Robert was most impressed by Don King, the most famous and ruthless promoter in the world. At the time, King was at the height of his reign, a powerful overlord with Troll Doll hair, who had pitted Muhammad Ali against George Foreman in the 1974 "Rumble in the Jungle" in Zaire, and who now oversaw fighters

---

* Gene Hackman's stand-in for lighting shots on film sets was Greg Goossen, a former Mets catcher who helped run Ten Goose Boxing, a promotion company in Van Nuys, California. Goossen's most famous fighters were Gabriel and Rafael Ruelas, two brothers who one day entered his gym selling candy and were soon groomed to become world-champion boxers.

including superstars Julio César Chávez and Mike Tyson. His control of boxing was absolute. King worked as a promoter while his stepson, Carl King, acted as manager for all their fighters, receiving at least 33 percent of the purses.[15] Although often cited as a conflict of interest—managers are supposed to see that their fighters get treated fairly by promoters—the setup was not illegal.

In fact, King was often able to control both fighters in the same match, ensuring that he would win no matter the outcome. "In this corner, a Don King fighter," wrote Michael Katz in the *New York Times* in 1983. "In that corner, a Don King fighter. Frequently, they are both managed by the promoter's adopted son, Carl . . . To an increasing number of angry and envious rivals, this common matchup is an introduction to monopoly."[16]

Meeting King in his room at the top of the Mirage hotel and casino, Robert says he was offered a road map for his son to become a champion. "Julian Jackson was the super welterweight champion of the world, and he wanted too much money from Don King," Robert says, referring to one of King's fighters at the time, a 5'11" pro boxer from the US Virgin Islands. "Also, his eyesight was going. They wanted to get rid of him. So they were going to program Bobby, a white boy, to come up and knock him out, making him the new champion."

Backed by his father and King's camp, Gunn, at sixteen, donned boxing gloves and entered the rings of Sin City, chasing

[Figure 12.2] Turning pro at 16 (Photo courtesy of Bobby Gunn)

his own desperate version of the American dream. He was fighting literally to save his mother's life. "The money we had didn't cut it," he says. "I had to go out and turn pro, earn my scars, earn my battles the hard way in life. I killed myself working and fighting to help my mom."

Gunn thought he'd hit the big time in Vegas. But instead, he was soon shipped to King's training compound in Orwell, Ohio—a desolate facility of wooden buildings and giant stone statues of gods and boxers, on a four-hundred-acre farm in the middle of Amish country—to work endlessly as a sparring partner.[17] "Horrible," Gunn says about the center. "It looked like a concentration camp." He sparred twice daily, once in the morning and once in the afternoon, boxing champions nearly twice his age and up to a hundred pounds heavier—seasoned killers who worked the young fighter for his speed while pummeling him mercilessly. At night, Gunn pissed blood from the kidney shots. He broke his arm, continuing to spar while wearing a cast. He woke up one Christmas morning, his pillow soaked in blood, his eardrum ruptured by a blow from Julian Jackson, the thirty-one-year-old middleweight champion he was supposedly being groomed to overtake—a fighter now considered one of the hardest punchers in pro boxing history. "I goes to the hospital, they put a needle in my ear and suck out the fluid," Gunn says. "I lost forty percent of my hearing."

Gunn became lonely, despondent, depressed. In his off time, he did nothing but watch TV or walk to a nearby Dairy Queen, where he would sit and stare out the window. "They could have been locked up for the beatings I got in that gym," he says. "I just knew it was a bad deal."

Even when Gunn did get his own fight, it was always in some rinky-dink venue like Tijuana, and the money was never what he'd been promised. Instead of Don King, Gunn mostly dealt with Carl, glimpsing Don only when he showed up, hair unteased and matted, to watch the boxers run early in the morning in Las Vegas. Finally, after being underpaid thousands of dollars on several fights, Gunn decided to confront King at the Mirage in 1992. King did not take it well.

"I was promised five thousand for the second match against Sergio García but only got sixteen hundred," Gunn says. "They were bleeding me. But Don just put his hands up: 'Don't talk down to me, you punch-drunk motherfucker. What's the matter with you? Can't you count? You take a nickel. That's two cents for me and that's two cents for my son. And out of your one cent, you got to pay for living accommodations, training expenses, and travel expenses.'" Gunn never questioned King again.

Gunn was stuck. He wasn't sure where else to turn—he was already with the supposed top manager. And even if he could have left, he needed the money. So he continued to spar King's fighters, shuttling back and forth between Ohio and Las Vegas, occasionally glimpsing the decadence surrounding the champions he battled in the gyms. Once, in August 1991, on the night before his first match against Sergio García at the now demolished Hacienda Hotel in Las Vegas, Gunn says he was pacing the lobby, unable to sleep, when Carl King told him to check on one of King's top heavyweights on the penthouse floor. Using a special key, Gunn ascended to the top of the Hacienda and stepped out into a haze of marijuana smoke, pulsing rap, and wall-to-wall partygoers—a world apart from the spartan existence he lived. "I was looking around in shock," Gunn recalls. "I just wanted to get away from it all. A bunch of bums. Not my kind of people."

Far from the glitz of the penthouses, Gunn had his own life. When not in the ring, he helped care for his mother. He took odd jobs: roofing, painting, laying asphalt—anything to make a dollar. Gunn's father occasionally made it out to meet with King's people, but he was so laid up by alcohol and depression, he mostly just looked after their savings. Robert and Jackie hid their son's earnings in money belts they wore strapped to their bodies at all times, or in the metal cash box the old man had bolted to the undercarriage of his truck. Jackie remained bedridden. Some nights, the family would stay up, making each other laugh while watching TV. Most nights, however, Jackie would lie awake, crying out in pain, causing Gunn to go sleep outside in his truck. "It ripped my heart out," he says. "The disease was eating her alive. It was like living under a death sentence."

[Figure 12.3] With a friend in Las Vegas
(Photo courtesy of Bobby Gunn)

Gunn found solace in the friendships with his fellow low-level boxers, fringe contenders like Mike "the Bounty" Hunter, an LA fighter who was later shot to death by police on Sunset Boulevard in 2005, and Ellis, the Seattle middleweight, who now works as a caregiver for special-needs people in Phoenix.[18] "We were both green as pool tables," Ellis remembers, laughing. "Bobby was pretty much the only white guy, but he ain't white. He was a gypsy and understood some of the tribulations that we go through. Bobby was one of us." Gunn would often bring fighters back to his family's apartment, where his mother would rouse herself for a few hours to cook Irish stew while his father would sit in the corner, the smell of alcohol rolling off him like a fog. "His mom was one of God's handpicked angels," Ellis says. "But his dad was a gritty, tough old man—Papa didn't take no mess."

Finally, after years of sparring, Gunn saved up the $23,000 they needed for his mother's operation. The family found a clinic in Pittsburgh. Gunn says he walked into a room, met a hospital representative sitting alongside a lawyer, and handed them the entire sum in cash. "These are professional cons," Gunn says. "The medical profession is all about making money."

While waiting for the operation, Gunn went to work the bags in a boxing gym in a rough neighborhood in Pittsburgh, where he got an offer that would change his life forever. After a session, the manager approached him, asking if he wanted to make a little money. "The guy said, 'There's an underground bare-knuckle fight happening here,'" Gunn recalls. "'You want in?'" The stakes were stiff—$3,000. Gunn didn't have the money, having given all his earnings for his mother's operation. He knew he might be killed if he showed up, lost the bout, and then couldn't pay. But he also knew he couldn't turn the opportunity down. "I needed it, needed it, needed it," Gunn says. "I was nervous, by myself, but my mom was dying. I needed the money."

The next night, Gunn drove his father's white Dodge van to the gym, left his pit bull, Duran, in the front seat, and went inside to find a crowd of a hundred, mostly bikers waiting for a show. His opponent stood in the ring—6'2", 200-plus pounds, and heavily tattooed in jeans and boots. Gunn took off his shirt, wearing only acid-wash jeans and black Reeboks. The bikers were not impressed. "The guy started laughing at me, calling me a little kid," Gunn recalls. "His team was yelling, 'Don't kill this punk!'"

The manager rang the bell, and the fight began. It didn't last long. The biker rushed Gunn, who spun and clipped him a few times in the midsection. Angry, the man began swinging wild shots as the young gypsy picked him apart. "He's on his knees, blood pouring out of him, and the manager come and raise my hand," Gunn says. "And you know what I was thinking about?

In the van, I had my mother's Doulton dolls and Dresden plates, the old gypsy woman's pride and joy. Probably worth about ten grand, and I was going to sell them to a pawn shop to get money."

Gunn pauses.

"I wasn't worried about the fight," he says. "I was worried about someone stealing those dolls."

* * * * *

The end came fast.

Jackie underwent a liver transplant and seemed to be doing well. Then, one night, Gunn and his father were called to the hospital from their nearby motel. According to Gunn, a hospital trainee attempting to perform a liver biopsy had opened up Jackie's stitches on the internal organ, causing it to rupture and, in the shock and pain, her heart to fail. "She had a massive heart attack while squealing in pain with a tube down her throat," he says, crying. "My mom never had no easy go."

Gunn and his father wanted to take Jackie back to Canada, but they also wanted to respect her family's wishes. So, in the winter of 1993, they buried her on her family's plot in Baltimore. With Jackie's Irish Traveler clan in attendance, there was both a Catholic and a Protestant service. The mood was tense. "It was a big, big funeral," Gunn says. "Must have been a thousand gypsies there." With his last $300, Gunn bought a boxing belt and had it inscribed "Champion of the Universe, My Old Mom: The Toughest Fighter I Ever Knew." He placed it atop the casket as the bagpipes played "Amazing Grace." Some of the Linsday clan objected to the belt, saying it was disrespectful, nearly starting a brawl right there at the funeral. "Dad said, 'You cocksuckers, walk now or you're going to be in there with her,'" Gunn recalls. "He flipped out, the old man. This was his wee wife, the love of his life."

After the service, Gunn borrowed some money from one of his uncles, collected his heartbroken dad and the dog in his pickup truck, and drove south. The last two years had shattered Gunn, so he was headed with his remaining family for a remote Traveler outpost in Florida, a place of palm trees and sand and bright, thoughtless sun—a place where he could remake his life. "King wanted me to fight a guy and told me, 'It's your breakthrough fight; it'll put you on top of the world,'" he says. "But I just got a dirty, rotten, disgusted feeling with the whole game when I buried Mom."

Everything Gunn owned was in his pickup truck. He had clothes, his boxing gear, and a small piece of paper he'd received from the gym manager in Pittsburgh: the number of a man who could get him more underground fights—bigger fights—if he was interested.

Gunn didn't enter a boxing ring for another eleven years.

PART II
CHAMPION OF THE UNDERWORLD

CHAPTER 13
LOVERS AND BIKERS IN ALLIGATOR ALLEY

Bobby Gunn promised his wife he was through with fighting.

In the winter of 1993, shell-shocked by the death of his mother and the sudden collapse of his boxing career, Gunn had moved to Fort Lauderdale, Florida, and fallen in love. Once, while boxing in Las Vegas, he had met Rose Keith, a beautiful blond Scottish Traveler, and she had never left his mind. Glamorous and outgoing, Rose came from a wealthy real-estate family. Her father, Hugh, owned twenty mobile-home parks and was doing so well, they had settled down. "All the Traveler kids were out visiting in Vegas," Gunn recalls of his first meeting Rose. "I just remember she was so beautiful. But she was the elite. She didn't go to T.J. Maxx. She went to Neiman Marcus. I didn't think I'd have a shot." Rose had grown up with everything Gunn had not—money, security, a fixed address, unconditional love, even box seats at the Dolphins games—and would seem an unlikely match. But Hugh, a 6'5" hard-nosed businessman, had once been a knuckler himself, and Gunn's reputation as a fighter added weight.

"In the Traveler community, sometimes that means more than money," says Ruml.

For Gunn, Rose was a lifeline. In Florida, with neither boxing nor Jackie to unite them, he and his father had grown further apart, with depression hanging like a fog in their tiny apartment on the northern fringe of town. Occasionally, Gunn and Robert would venture out to the local gym, shadowboxing or working the pads, trying to regain some sense of normality. But not even training—the one communion they had always shared—could snap them out of their funk. "Dad was bad," Gunn recalls. "And I just broke away from boxing."

Turning his back on the fight world, Gunn decided to chase a new prize: love. "I never even had a girlfriend before Rose," he says. "To me, she was a princess." As with so many aspects of Traveler culture, Gunn's courtship of Rose was torn straight from medieval times—he may as well have arrived with a lute beneath her balcony. Travelers don't date, and they certainly don't have premarital sex. Instead, teenagers must socialize within group settings on weekends. So, one night at a Benihana, after just two months of quick conversations amid the crowd, Gunn took Rose aside to ask for her hand. "That Elvis song 'Only Fools Rush In' was playing," Gunn recalls.* "I just said, 'I think you're beautiful and want to marry you. I'll be good to you.' She said, 'I know you will,' shook my hand on it, and gave me a kiss."

To confirm the engagement, Gunn next went to meet Rose's parents, inviting them to breakfast at a Denny's. "Her folks pull up in a big Mercedes 500, wearing Rolex watches," Gunn recalls. "I get out of my work truck in an old leather jacket and says, 'I'm Bobby Gunn.' And her dad just says, 'I know who you are.'" In the tight-knit Traveler world, Gunn knew that Rose's parents would

* For Gunn, the Elvis song held special significance. According to Traveler lore, Presley's mother, Gladys, was a Romany Gypsy. Other celebrities with supposed Roma or Traveler roots include Charlie Chaplin, Rita Hayworth, Yul Brynner, and President Bill Clinton, but no one is revered like the king. "The song played twice in a row on the radio," Gunn recalls. "It was a sign from God."

have heard about his years as a pro boxer and about his courtship, knew that they were weighing his family background and intentions. Nervous but resolved, he laid down his story over eggs and pancakes. "They're looking at me and thinking, 'This is a fighter and he don't have nothing. Is he going to be a deadbeat? Is he going to torture my girl?'" Gunn recalls. "So I says, 'I'll be straight with you. I love your girl and I swear to God I'll never lay a hand on her. My mom just died. I don't have much. But I'll make a go at it in life.'" Gunn sat back, silent, staring at Rose's

[Figure 13.1] With Rose (Photo courtesy of Bobby Gunn)

parents across the Formica tabletop. Finally, after a few moments, her father, Hugh, spoke. "He just says, 'Gamest words I've ever heard any young man say,'" Gunn recalls. "And he shook my hand." Gunn smiles. "They respected me."

Finally, after six weeks of fervent hand-holding while chaperoned by family members, Gunn, then twenty-one, was about to marry Rose, nineteen. His boldness had paid off. Yet one final hurdle remained. In the final days before the ceremony, Rose approached Gunn, telling him she had one last condition: he had to give up the gloves. "She never wanted to see me fight," Gunn says. "It bothered her." Gunn's prestige as a fighter had won him her family's respect, but it would not win her. So, already burned out with boxing and deeply in love, he agreed to quit the fight game. "I thought she was too good for me," he says. "I was tickled to death. I just said, 'Let's give it a go.'"

For the first time in his life, Gunn felt at peace. "I never had no brothers or sisters," he says. "Compassion, for me, was only from my mom. So having someone like Rose opened a different part of my heart that I was hoping I could find. I could trust her. She was a Godsend."

After a brief honeymoon at Disney World, he and Rose moved into an apartment at Sawgrass Mills Mall, settling into a suburban routine amid Florida's sunshine, ocean spray, and orchids. Following Traveler custom, he went to work at his father's trade, laying asphalt along vine-draped, alligator-ridden roads, while Rose tended the home and oversaw their finances. Coming home at night, he would often surprise her with a new dress bought at a local boutique. On weekends, he took Rose to Orlando or went hunting with his father-in-law in the Everglades, where he once shot a giant tusked boar only to have an even bigger alligator come along and eat his trophy. In the subtropics, a world apart from the cold and chaos of his childhood, Gunn finally started to move past the death of his mother and loss of his career, finding unexpected fulfillment in a stable home. "It changed his life," says Ed Simpson, a Traveler and family friend. "He finally found love and a normal life."

The marriage also freed Gunn from his father. A month after the ceremony, Robert came to him with surprising news: he was returning home to Niagara Falls. "After my wife died, I had to be alone for a while," Robert recalls. "I couldn't train Bobby, and everything had gone wrong."

For Gunn, the departure was unexpected. "When I got married, Dad told me 'Good man' and shook my hand," he recalls. "Then I come back to see him and he said, 'You're a man now. You made your bed and you gotta lay in it.' He even took my dog, Duran."

Gunn felt mixed emotions about his father leaving. Robert was his only remaining close family. In the end, however, weary from years of prizefighting and from his mother's illness—and also, perhaps, from his father's drinking and sinking spells—Gunn decided that it was time to go out on his own. "Me and

Rose just made a go of it," he says. "Movies on Fridays, no work on Saturdays, and church on Sundays. Life was fun."

Yet something still gnawed at him. He came from a line of fighters, had brawled his entire life, and couldn't help missing the ring. Also, he felt an obligation to make more money, to give Rose the kind of life she'd given up—even if it meant breaking their wedding-night promise. "My wife kept the fire under my ass," he says. "I couldn't just be a normal guy, because she was used to having high things."

So one day in 1994, when a Traveler asked whether he was interested in making some money in an underground bare-knuckle fight, Gunn didn't hesitate—not even when told he'd have to take on two guys in a row. "I said, 'We'll have a little bit of fun,'" he recalls.

The next night, after telling Rose he was going to the gym, Gunn drove to a run-down warehouse in South Beach, Miami, to square off against the two local fighters. With none of its modern revitalized gleam, South Beach in the early 1990s was a wasteland, a saltwater melting pot of drifters and immigrant Cubans eking out a living amid seedy hotels, boarded-up warehouses, and dilap-idated Art Deco buildings. In the darkened warehouse, with the smell of sea and sweat in the night air, Gunn faced off against the men in consecutive bouts in a small ring in front of a large crowd of Cubans, other Latinos, and bikers. "We fought right off the ocean," Gunn says. "Broken windows and glass was everywhere." Right away, his years sparring the world's top boxing champions became apparent. "They were dumplings," he says of his oppo-nents. "Out cold. Bang-bang." He walked away with $1,500 cash.

Gunn didn't realize it at the time, but he had just stepped into what would become his true calling, a world he had first glimpsed a few months earlier at the biker fight in Pittsburgh as his mother lay dying—a world he would now enter full-time: the underground. "That's the first time I really seen the circuit," he says, "but it was here long before I was born."

A patchwork of regional promoters and fighters as varied as the states themselves, the underground is a dark mirror of America. Whether it's with gangbangers in Los Angeles, ranchers in Texas, Native Americans in Arizona, or good ol' boys in Mississippi, fights can differ wildly in feel and custom and crowd. Yet one fact remains constant. The more populous East Coast has the most bouts—and its mecca is New York, where the top fighters contend for more money more often than anywhere else. "All the best fighters go to New York," Gunn says. "Manhattan, Queens, Brooklyn, the Bronx—the underground circuit brings them all there."

Gunn had stumbled onto the other end of the East Coast bare-knuckle spectrum, Gotham's raw, steamy shadow world. In the underworld, Florida is a sort of proving ground, a major feeder system where fighters come up brawling year-round in backyard bouts, making a reputation that will take them across the country.

"South Florida is kinda like the old days in New York," says Guy Pagan, fifty-eight, a boxing promoter and former army ranger who attends underground fights in Miami. "You got a lot of immigrants. But instead of the Irish, it's Mexicans, Puerto Ricans, and Dominicans. Every now and then, you'll get a guy flies in from somewhere that wants to test the waters. Like some tough guy that just ran over everybody in Mississippi. Big white dude who gets out the car and you're like 'Holy shiiittt, look at this dude!' And he wants to scrap. And some of these guys are like white supremacists, thugs, and they put it out there in black and white: 'Let's go down there and fuck with these niggers.'"

In Florida's underground scene, no one oversees more bare-knuckle fights than Dhafir Harris, a former corrections officer known as Dada 5000. Harris, thirty-nine, has long staged bare-knuckle bouts in his grandmother's backyard in south Miami, transforming local gang leaders into paid brawlers. "People get robbed and killed here every day," Harris says. "These guys are amateur boxers, football players, brawlers, and wannabes, all just fighting for a way out." Florida's most famous bare-knuckle export is Kevin Ferguson, better known as Kimbo Slice. A 6'2", 230-pound Bahamian-born fighter raised in South Miami, Slice briefly played linebacker on the Miami Dolphins practice squad before becoming homeless, living in his car, and eventually gaining fame for his bare-knuckle bouts on YouTube. These bloody brawls include a thirteen-minute fight against a Boston cop, which ultimately earned him a contract with the Ultimate Fighting Championship (UFC). In 2016, at age forty-two, Slice died of heart failure. Yet in his final months, the aging street champ had been planning to return to his roots in a bare-knuckle match against Gunn, back on his home turf. "All fighters love Florida," says Harris. "But we didn't invent this—it's been around since the gladiator days."

In 1994, soon after his double knockout in Miami, Gunn began making his own name in the Sunshine State. By day, he would lay asphalt and paint buildings. By night, he would scrounge for local fights, usually taking on a bout every few months. A melting pot of Cubans, Blacks, Puerto Ricans, and whites, south Florida was awash in international drug money, and the traffickers and dealers backed dogfights, cockfights, and, when possible, bare-knucklers. Gunn fought in backyards, abandoned swimming pools, and warehouses. He fought in bars and nightclubs and private homes. He fought alone and on cards with other fighters, in bouts held midday and at night. All the while, he kept his growing reputation in the underworld a secret from Rose, coming home with gifts and dresses while telling her he was sparring in gyms to keep in shape. "I'd come back with a little black eye and she'd ask, 'What happened?'" he says. "'Tough workout.'"

Of all Gunn's early fights in the underground, none would compare with one of his first major money matches, a bout against a biker, in a parking lot behind a bar off I-75 in west Fort Lauderdale—a section of highway known as Alligator Alley. The fight was held in the afternoon. About seventy-five people crowded the lot, the air thick with the smell of sweat and warm beer. "I'd been painting roofs and was wearing my painter's shorts," Gunn says. "The back of the place was like a wrecker's yard of cars and trucks." As usual, Gunn arrived with no idea of his opponent's identity. All he knew was the sum of the prize money—$10,000. After being contacted by his opponent's backers, he had paid his initial security deposit of $2,000, the 20 percent "kick-in" money, to a third party and now walked in with the rest in a bag, flanked by two Travelers. Entering the lot, he saw his opponent—a muscle-bound 6'2", 225-pound biker backed by twenty-five of his friends, a roving militia of tattoos and leather vests.

"We were like, 'Oh, shit, where's the exit?'" recalls Ed Simpson, one of the Travelers who was with Gunn that day. "It must've been a hundred degrees, the sweat running off you. And I was terrified: 'Man, if Bobby puts this guy to the ground, are we getting out of here alive? Or are these guys going to kill us?' Because there was a lot of money on the line. But it never bothered Bobby. He was like, 'All right, bring it on.'"

The biker came out swinging, the crowd cheering. "They thought they had it in the bag," Simpson says. "We're talking about a big dude, brother—a lot bigger than Bobby." To the crowd's surprise, Gunn sidestepped the biker's shots, each one a potential knockout blow, while waiting, watching, getting a feel for his opponent. The two men traded a couple more hits, Gunn's punches seemingly having no effect, and then came the shot that put the crowd into a frenzy. The biker punched Gunn with three jabs in a row, nearly toppling him. "They were really good shots," Simpson says. "Kinda shook Bobby a little bit."

Gunn embraced the biker, the two men hanging on to each other for fifteen seconds, catching their breath, and then they separated. Now looking for the kill, the biker came in for another possible knockout punch—and made his fatal mistake. Gunn sidestepped his hook and hit him with a quick combination: a left to the body—stunning his opponent, making him drop his arms—and then a right to the temple. The biker went down. "It went from yelling and cheering to dead silence," Simpson says. "Weirdest thing you ever seen in your life." Without hesitating, Gunn grabbed the money and left. "Stick around too long," he says, "and they'll get buyer's remorse."

For a couple of years following his victory in Alligator Alley, Gunn continued to take on fights throughout Florida, with no one detecting his background. "At first, I could throw my hat in the mix and get in fights anywhere," he says. "They didn't know who I was, so I could slip in like a pool shark and take you to school." He shrugs. "It was nice for me. Young guy, married, come home with ten thousand in my pocket. It made my marriage a lot nicer. And Rose was thinking I was out working."

Gunn's years as a ghost were numbered, however. "I had started making waves in the bare-knuckle world," he says. "And then it become challenge fights—people calling me out because of my name."

CHAPTER 14
AMERICAN UNDERGROUND

In February 1998, Gunn risked his life in a last-minute fight for one reason: to take his infant son to Disney World. "I didn't have the money to go on vacation, but couldn't tell my wife," Gunn recalls. "So on the day before we were supposed to leave, I took on the fight, bluffing my way in with no money—sometimes you gotta roll the dice."

A year before, in November 1996, Gunn and Rose's son, Robert Williamson Gunn, had been born in a hospital room in Fort Lauderdale. "It was nerve racking," Gunn recalls. "I was just holding Rose's hand—I didn't even want to think the word 'miscarriage.'" During the entirety of Rose's pregnancy, Gunn had been haunted by the death of his older sister, Vivianne Marie, whose stillbirth had devastated his family. So, determined to keep Rose healthy, he had put her through a daily training regimen, overseeing her diet and exercise until the delivery date.

"I was like a physical therapist," Gunn says. "Real protective." In the end, however, Bobby Jr.—technically a third but called "Junior"—had been born a healthy eight pounds. Just seconds after his birth, Gunn, like his father before him, had first looked at the boy's hands. "They were in little fists," Gunn recalls. "I said, 'What a right wee man. He's a champ.'" Sneaking out to a pay phone, he had immediately called his father, Robert, in Niagara Falls. "Dad said, 'The prophecy has been fulfilled,'" Gunn recalls. "'He'll be king of all gypsies.'"

For Gunn, the birth of Bobby Jr. changed everything. During the initial years of his marriage, he had worked to spoil Rose, buying her a used Mustang and expensive clothes while also splurging on himself for the first time in his life. He had even spent $4,000 on a Majesties of the Seas cruise, the couple staying a week on white-sand beaches in Cozumel, Mexico, and Grand Cayman. Soon, however, Bobby Jr. was born, and once again everything shifted. "I was fed with a wooden spoon," Gunn says, "but I was going to make sure my son got silver."

By early 1997, Gunn was working double-time, taking asphalt jobs and tarring roofs and painting even more houses in the relentless sun. It was difficult, struggling for money while his in-laws prospered just down the road. But Gunn refused to ask for help or a job. "My father-in-law owned twenty mobile-home parks at one time," he says. "Worth millions. And I never seen none of it."

Gunn wanted to give his son a stable home, and his wife a measure of the comfort she had once known. Yet no matter how many hours he stayed out in his work truck, it never seemed enough. "I had bills up my asshole," he says. "I had to push to give my family a nice life, to put them first. But I was struggling."

At least Gunn had the underground.

In February 1998, on the day before he was scheduled to take his family on a promised trip to Disney World, Gunn had only $1,000 to his name—hardly enough to cover a long weekend at the resort. He was wondering how to tell his wife when, out of nowhere, his beeper buzzed. It was an offer to fight in Miami. "It was a hard winter for work," Gunn recalls, "and then I got a call to fight for three thousand, winner take all, literally on the Thursday before we left. So off I went."

Gunn didn't have enough money to enter the fight. So he changed all his cash into twenties, wound the bills into tight rubber-banded rolls, and stuffed them in a gym bag, giving the appearance of a large stake. Walking into the same dilapidated warehouse where he'd first fought upon landing in Miami—broken windows, salty air, a run-down boxing ring—he handed over his money to the house, hoping they wouldn't count it. Gunn had seen men lose a fight and then not be able to pay. It never ended well. "They woulda taken me out back and given me a good going-over, maybe five or ten of them," he says. "But I was confident—I knew I was a good boxer."

Stepping into the ring, Gunn eyed his opponent, a "skinny hillbilly" in boxing trunks, with blond hair and tattoos. "He

[Figure 14.1] Family trip to Disney World
(Photo courtesy of Bobby Gunn)

was smoking a cigarette," Gunn recalls. "A tough little bastard." Surrounded by a crowd of Dominicans, Puerto Ricans, and a large contingent of the fighter's friends, the two men squared off. At first, the hillbilly came out swinging haymakers, trying to topple Gunn. Biding his time, Gunn waited, watched, and then finally began throwing jabs, breaking the man's nose. After about three minutes, his opponent wheezing, Gunn gave the finishing blow. "A left hook to the body put him right on the ground," he recalls. "He was done." The crowd went silent. "When there's silence, it's good for me," Gunn says. "But not for the other guy."

Gunn took his money, walked straight to his truck, and drove home. "I remember feeling like I had a million dollars," he says. "I had the money to take my little boy to Disney World. And I went there and I enjoyed it. That was a big thing for me."

As Gunn's reputation in the underground grew, he began to take on bigger bouts for better money, in Florida and beyond. Each spring, when the weather warmed, he would pack up his family in the truck and roam for months, searching for jobs in Pennsylvania, New Jersey, Arizona, and California. "I traveled all over America," Gunn says. "That'd be my rounds." In between sealing driveways and painting barns, Gunn would call Johnny Varelli—the national underground matchmaker whose number he'd been given in Pittsburgh—to set up local fights.

These were the pre-Internet days of the underground, back when the sport was truly unknown. Fights were arranged through matchmakers, beepers, and pay phones. Personal ads were placed in newspapers, the coded messages intended solely for their bare-knuckle audience. "The ad would be very vague," recalls Joe Mack, a former bare-knuckle fighter. "They would have a code word and say something like 'Lost Bracelet' or 'Lost Dog. His name is whatever. Call this number.' And you call and they don't say anything when they answer. So you say, 'Hey, man, I'm calling about the fights,' and they'd give you a location and date. And if someone said they were calling about the lost gold necklace or whatever, they'd say they already given it back to the owner."

For years, when Gunn's beeper buzzed, he would call back, get an address, and then leave Rose and Bobby Jr. behind in their motel room—he refused to take his family to trailer parks—and head to the match. Fearful that she would leave him, Gunn never told his wife about his matches, always claiming that the bruises on his face, arms, and chest, the welts and cuts on his eyes and nose, were from the boxing gyms he frequented on the road. He says she never asked about the extra money, which only kept growing. "Even though the technology wasn't so good, the underground thrived back then," Gunn says. "There were more fights than there are now. It was more freedom without the phones. And word of mouth went wild—the more famous I got, the more better the fights got. It all fell in place."

In these early years, in his initial forays out of Florida, Gunn began learning the national scope of the underground, its different tiers and fighters and nuances. He claims he didn't enjoy the fights, says it was only work, but that isn't exactly true. In bare knuckle, Gunn finally found what he had long sought in the ring: success. "People forgot I was a highly decorated boxer," he says. "I would leave my right hand open like a catcher's mitt and then turn that left hook into the eye, like a corkscrew. *Bang!* That's what separated me from all these other guys—my hands."

Along the way, Gunn would make allies. In Nova Scotia, he befriended Paul Thompson, a 5'10", 240-pound former tank gunner in the Canadian army, turned scrap-yard worker and bare-knuckle fighter.* Whenever Gunn was in the area, Thompson would go with him to regional bouts. He was impressed by the Traveler's ferocity and kindness. Once, Thompson saw Gunn defeating a much larger opponent who, in frustration, began head-butting him. "The small crowd was furious," Thompson recalls. "We wanted to kill this guy. But Bobby just said that if the motherfucker wanted a rough-and-tumble, then he could have one."

---

* "Paul Thompson" is a pseudonym. Since I first interviewed him, I have not been able to reach the fighter to confirm whether he is okay with printing his name. Before losing contact, however, he did tell me he was okay with my using his story, which Gunn could, in part, confirm.

Gunn unleashed on the man, retaliating with head butts, body blows, and rabbit punches—devastating shots to the base of the skull that can lead to spinal injury. Finally, in a last-ditch effort, the man grabbed Gunn in a bear hug and began to head-butt him again. "I shit you not when I tell you Bobby removed his nose, ending the fight with his teeth," Thompson recalls. Gunn, his face covered in blood, left with his money and soon met a homeless man on the streets and gave him part of his winnings. When the man dropped it, change scattering and bills blowing in the wind, Gunn helped him collect it off the ground. "So here was this fighter who only hours ago had removed a guy's nose, and now he was on his hands and knees helping this poor soul pick up money," Thompson says, laughing. "But that's Bobby."

In 1997, in the back of a Dominican grocery store in Wilmington, Delaware, Gunn took on a local Black Dominican street fighter known as "the Bull." Gunn, who was traveling for work with his wife and child and nearly broke at the time, quickly agreed to the $5,000 match when it arrived on his beeper. Entering the store through the alley, he walked past crowds, through puddles of blood sopped with newspaper from earlier fights, and past windows blacked out with butcher paper, to finally square off against his opponent, a seasoned amateur boxer in shorts, sneakers, and a green FUBU shirt. "It was the main event," says Paul Tyler, an underground promoter who was there that day. "But nobody knew who Bobby was."

The fight was over in three minutes. The Bull, fighting as if he wore gloves, threw jabs at Gunn's face. Seizing the opportunity, Gunn dropped his forehead, maimed his opponent's hand, and then quickly finished him with a left hook to the chin. Lying on the ground, unconscious, the Bull began convulsing, making choking noises. As the crowd panicked, Gunn knelt down and turned the man on his side to keep his throat clear of saliva or vomit. He then took his prize money and left. "It was the scariest sound—I thought the guy was dead," Tyler recalls. "But Bobby was relaxed. I was like, 'Who the fuck *is* this guy?'"

Gunn's reputation soon expanded across the country. J. C. Wilfork, a 6'9", 300-pound bare-knuckle fighter from Fort Pierce, Florida, began fighting during the late 1990s, traveling for bouts from Boston to Texas, to Tupelo. He says Gunn has long stood out for his pro boxing skills, his talent and science elevating him to the higher tiers of the underground. By contrast, Wilfork, a self-taught Black brawler, says he survived on the fringes, once even having to escape a hostile white crowd after defeating a hometown hero in an abandoned warehouse along the Mississippi River south of Memphis.

"Somebody threw a beer at me, the bottle exploding next to my head," Wilfork recalls. "And then someone fired a few shots in the air." Wilfork shakes his head. "Our circuits were different. Bobby's circuit was more organized. His style was better, more technical. Most of us guys were just street fighting. For us, it wasn't always legitimate promoters, but just a lot of guys betting money—pretty much like cockfights. It could be downright brutal. But Bobby's an actual boxer."

Gunn took on everyone from steel workers in Pennsylvania to oil-field hands in Texas, to farm boys in Ohio. "You meet all kinds," he says. "Sometimes tough guys, sometimes not. One time, I fought a guy, walked out, and saw his wife and poor wee kids waiting for him in the parking lot. It broke my heart, so I give him back his money."

At a bout in Albuquerque in the mid-1990s, staged by a Hispanic gang in a warehouse on the outskirts of town, Gunn met a fighter who would one day change his life. Gunn was working in Phoenix when his beeper buzzed with an offer. Agreeing to the match, he left Rose and the baby and drove the seven hours east through desert wasteland and mountains to New Mexico, entering a warehouse of gang members and fighters to compete as the headliner. "It was a Mexican fight," Gunn recalls. "I beat my guy, just your average bum, and left. Didn't think much of it."

Though Gunn was not impressed, another fighter he had met that night, one competing on the undercard, would remember the young Traveler for years, rising up through the ranks until he would face the bare-knuckle champ in an epic battle of West versus East Coast undergrounds—Shannon Ritch. "I saw Bobby fight several times," Ritch says. "We were in the same circuit, but I was out west: New Mexico, Texas, California, and all of Mexico. I never really did anything back east."

Like Gunn, Ritch—arguably the top modern bare-knuckle fighter in the West—first began fighting bullies. Born in 1970, he grew up "picking cotton, chopping cotton, and dragging tractors" on a twenty-acre ranch outside Coolidge, Arizona, a tiny farming town on the edge of the Gila River Indian Reservation in the Sonoran Desert. Small, skinny, and half Native American, half white, in a predominantly Hispanic region, he was mercilessly picked on. "Two or three guys at once throwing me into lockers or garbage cans in school," he says. "Horrible, man. I had low self-esteem." Ritch's parents, strict Church of the Nazarene parishioners who boarded horses, told him to turn the other cheek. But in high school, he began wrestling and studying kickboxing to defend himself, eventually using his newfound skills in the last place imaginable: art school. While studying advertising at a graphic-design trade school in Tempe, Ritch noticed a group of fellow students with black eyes. "Most art-school students aren't your typical badass jocks," he says. "But these guys were like, 'We go down to Mexico and fight in the bull rings. Come with us.'"

For the next few years, in the late eighties, Ritch, then nineteen, paid his way through college by bare-knuckle fighting in border-town bull arenas, earning $500 a night for wins in places like Nogales, Agua Prieta, Tijuana, Juárez, and Nuevo Laredo. "They'd have the chicken fights, the dogfights, and then us," he says. At his first bout, in Nogales, about seventy miles south of Tucson, he arrived at the ring at dusk, stripping down to his Spandex shorts and wrestling shoes in a livestock stall. "There was cow shit all over the floor—the ripe smell of hot manure," he recalls. "Hispanic music playing loud, and people selling beer and balloons—an all-age show."

When his time came, Ritch was pulled into the center of the four-hundred-seat arena, the crowd cheering as he stepped out amid "blood and feathers and crap." An emcee pointed to another stall, one holding the local fighters, and a man raised his hand, stepping into the dirt-floor arena. "Jeans, boots, and no shirt," Ritch says. "Big-time cowboy." There were no rules; anything went, so as his opponent came out swinging, Ritch dodged him and took him down with a wrestling move, ending the fight with a choke hold. Guaranteed no money, Ritch then walked the perimeter of the ring as if he had just slain a bull, the crowd's happy gamblers handing him pesos—a feat he would repeat countless times over the next few years. "I never lost," he says. "They quit paying me—that's why I eventually quit going."

Ritch dropped the underground after college, doing a stint in the army and then as a private contractor for Blackwater in Iraq, protecting US ambassadors from firefights, IEDs, and car bombs before finally settling down as a bouncer in Dallas in 1995. It was during this time, while wrangling drunks and trying to break into the fledgling UFC, that Ritch truly entered the circuit. He fought for businessmen in hotel ballrooms in Houston, for Hell's Angels at their camps near Phoenix and Las Vegas, and for crowds that included uniformed policemen in bouts in downtown LA warehouses. He fought in the backs of bars, in empty swimming pools, in apartment-complex courtyards. "Dude, I even fought in a playground one time," he says, laughing.

In perhaps his most spectacular bare-knuckle fight, he was once paid $10,000 to fly to Khabarovsk, Russia, on the far eastern edge of the taiga, past Mongolia and China, to fight (and eventually win) an eight-man tournament in a gym, surrounded by men and women eating at white-cloth tables. He has twice broken his hand, has ripped off a man's nipple with his teeth to keep from getting smothered, and has seen a man hit so precisely with one punch that his face opened up from his cheek to his ear, "like a razor blade cut him open . . . Sometimes the crowd is a hundred people; sometimes it's just four guys," he says of the underground. "You never know what you're getting into."

Of all Ritch's fights in the circuit, however, it is a cartel match in Mexico that still haunts him. In the late nineties, at dusk, he fought a "huge Mexican guy, a boxer" in a shopping mall in Matamoros, a Gulf Coast border town just south of Brownsville, Texas. After beating his opponent with a leg lock—the match was bare knuckle but open rules, meaning MMA moves were fair game—Ritch and his matchmaker, a fellow fighter from Dallas, were told they had to go meet "the boss" for their money. Seated in the back of a pickup truck alongside two "cowboy-type guys" holding rifles, Ritch and his friend were driven through the night, finally arriving at a run-down pinewood saloon ringed with Mercedeses and BMWs, in the middle of the desert. They were frisked and then entered the bar to find a "militia-type scenario"—vaqueros holding guns around a table of older, well-dressed men who looked to be in their sixties. When asked for the prize money, $2,500, one of the older men refused to pay, at which point Ritch's friend, the Dallas matchmaker, began to protest. "They tapped him on the shoulder and said, 'Hey, we'll bury you if you open your mouth again,'" Ritch recalls. "I said, 'Fuck it, man, just get me back across the border.'"

After a lifetime of bare-knuckle bouts across the world, Ritch eventually climbed to the top of the circuit. Yet there was always one man he wanted to defeat: Gunn. "I've never gotten the chance," Ritch says. "I would love to fight him."

According to everyone else in the underground, he will have one hell of a battle. "Gunn is a legend," says Thompson, the scrap-yard worker in Nova Scotia. "When you're dead and gone, when you don't have any money, you only have your name—and Bobby is without question the greatest bare-knuckle fighter I've ever seen."

* * * * *

In August 2000, Gunn was painting a metal roof on a twenty-foot-tall barn in rural Pennsylvania when he slipped while straddling its peak. Sliding headfirst down the roof, he grabbed on to a gutter, flipping his body in midair and landing on a concrete slab. "My left heel disintegrated and blew bones out my toenail," Gunn recalls. "I gets up and said, 'Ah, Jesus.' It was a squishy sound. Blood was coming out my boot."

After tying off his leg with a bungee cord from atop his truck, Gunn, covered head to toe in base paint, hobbled to the house of the landowner, who called in an ambulance. Trembling in shock and pain, Gunn was rushed to a nearby hospital in York, where the nurses struggled to remove paint from his skin while treating his foot as well as a broken elbow and a cracked vertebra. Finally, he was given a prognosis. "A doctor comes in and says it's so bad they can't operate," Gunn recalls. "And that if an infection starts, they're going to have to amputate my heel. As soon as he left the room, I turned to Rose and said, 'Get my clothes and a wheelchair.'"

Sneaking her husband out of the hospital, Rose drove him fifty miles south to Baltimore and checked him into Johns Hopkins, one of the premier hospitals in the United States. There, Gunn says a radiologist looked at his X-rays, saying he could treat him but also adding a warning—Gunn would need a cane for the rest of his life. After a three-hour surgery, Gunn emerged with bolts, plates, pins, and screws in his left foot and was told he would never be able to run again. He returned home to Fort Lauderdale.

Four months later, in December, he was back in the boxing gym. "I had to change my style of fighting," Gunn says. "I couldn't run like I used to. I couldn't move like I used to. I couldn't balance on my legs like I used to. I shoulda been dead, pal. But I adapt and come back. I come too far in life. I couldn't accept that."

Mike Hopper, the pro boxing trainer who worked Gunn's corner during this time, recalls Gunn's challenges. "It looked so bad, I asked him to get another operation," Hopper says. "After that, Bobby just had to work out and train in different ways, jumping rope while just standing on his toes. He is a beast for what he was able to do."

By early 2001, Gunn, now twenty-seven, was at a crossroads. Gone were the quick legs of his youth, the nimble footwork that had seen him through amateur championships, a brief pro career, and a rise to the top of the bare-knuckle circuit. Instead, he would now have to compete as a stand-and-bang fighter—ducking, weaving, trading blows while keeping his feet firmly planted. "After the fall, he couldn't move as much anymore," Hopper recalls. "So, he just became a total brawler. He was gonna get you out in four or die trying. Instead of fighting hard, he had to box smart. He'd use the jab to keep himself long. If a fighter rushed him like a bull, he'd turn, let the guy go by, and then crack him a couple on the way. Gunn was sneaky. He'd show you one hand and then crack you with the other."

In effect, the injury meant Gunn's days as a championship boxer—and the return to the ring he'd secretly longed for—were over. But he also knew he could still attain another title, one that would allow him to continue competing—king of the underworld. There was just one catch. Despite all his road victories, Gunn was rarely making more than $5,000 a night in bare-knuckle matches in the South and the American heartland. To really make it big, he would have to uproot his family and move to the sport's ultimate arena, New York. "All the guys want to go to the apple of the world," he says. "That's where you can go wildfire."

In truth, the move also made sense for his family. Increasingly, Gunn was finding more work during his months-long ramblings in the Northeast than at home in Fort Lauderdale. Relocating would mean settling down, offering his family a life of stability as opposed to the way he'd been brought up, on the road. "I heard guys were doing pretty decent for painting work, construction work," Gunn says of the Northeast. "Plus, I'd be in the heart of fighting—I always heard the big fights were there."

First, however, Gunn had to make a confession. After years of lying to Rose about his matches, he finally mustered the courage to tell her about his ambition, about the secret he had hidden from her since their wedding day. "She said, 'Yeah, you didn't think I knew you was Bobby Gunn the fighter when I married you?'" Gunn recalls. "'I know I'm not going to break you, but I can help you get back to the top.'" He laughs. "I just said, 'Wow.' She knew."

When asked how Rose could seem so casual about leaving her family behind in Florida and the years of lying, Gunn shrugs. "Yeah, she gets mad sometimes," he admits. "But what is worse? Someone hiding that they're going out and taking drugs and being an alcoholic bum? Or boxing? At the end of the day, I'm like Mr. Magoo. I drive thirty-five miles per hour and am home in my pajamas at nine thirty. I make up for things. She knows she married a fighter." Ultimately, Gunn's decision underscores a stark tenet of Traveler family structure. "I'm the man of the house," he says. "I go to work. She's my wife. She follows my lead." (Rose refused requests for an interview.)

In 2001, Gunn and his family moved north, settling in an apartment just across the Hudson River, in New Jersey. "That's when it really started snowballing for me," he says. "I was going to become the king of New York."

CHAPTER 15
THE MOBSTER'S MOUNTAIN LION

Gunn did not expect the mountain lion. The Porsches and Lamborghinis and Bentleys, yes. The hundred people surrounding the makeshift ring behind the Boston mansion, yes. Even the owner of the house, a mysterious character in his fifties, wearing a smoking jacket and Elvis sunglasses and flanked by two goons holding shotguns, yes.

After all, this was the Irish mob. But the caged mountain lion in the corner?

"Fucking crazy," Gunn says.

In 2001, soon after landing in New York, he had entered the true heart of the underground. According to Gunn and other brawlers, New York, with its density of fighters and organized crime, hosts more big-money bare-knuckle bouts than anywhere else in the United States. Typically, the fights come together in one of three different ways. Brawlers can call an underground promoter like Johnny Varelli and request a match. "A week later, he'd call back and have every detail ready," Gunn says. Or fighters can set up bouts directly with each other, staking their own money in small-time promotions, as Gunn often does through Ike's gym in Paterson. Or fighters can take on matches for organized crime, often brawling at private parties as entertainment. "It's a sport for them," Gunn says. "It's like fighting dogs and roosters. They bring in the baddest guys they can find to represent their families— Who's going to beat Bobby Gunn?"

Gunn had first met the Irish mob at one of his fights in Miami in 1998.* "They came right down from New York to the warehouse in South Beach," he recalls. "I liked them a lot. Game guys. Proper guys." Gunn reconnected with them in New York and soon struck an informal arrangement: The Irish would back him in certain matches, supplying fight locations and muscle in case something went wrong. In exchange, Gunn would be their sole representative in the underground—their personal prizefighter to stake against other families in big-money bouts. "I represent the Irish," Gunn says. "And they're game to support me, making side bets and backing me up."

According to Paul Tyler, an underground promoter, Gunn soon became their top breadwinner. "They're fairly well organized," he says. "And they respect Bobby heavily."

Early on, Gunn learned the importance of having connected friends—high-stakes underworld matches can go dangerously off course. In a bout overseen by a faction of the Irish mob at a suburban mansion outside Boston, Gunn arrived in the late afternoon to find a waiting crowd, a ring, and the caged mountain lion. "I had been told by my guys in New York it was okay to go," Gunn says. "And it was a very nice area. But the guy, a millionaire, turned out to be a sick nutcase with some kind of mountain lion or leopard with a chain around its neck. I felt very uncomfortable. I didn't feel safe."

---

* The Irish mob has several different factions in New York. Gunn has requested that the specific group that backs him remain anonymous.

The man in Elvis glasses, the owner of the mansion, walked the party with his gun-toting entourage, mingling with members from various Boston gangs, all convened for the illicit fights. "Latino gangs, Russian, Irish," Gunn recalls. "All of them Boston." According to Gunn and Paul Tyler, who brought two combatants for the event, Elvis acted like the house of a casino. Upon arrival, the fighters and their gangland backers gave him their agreed-upon prize money for safekeeping, presumably in a safe somewhere. After the bouts, which were overseen by a referee, Elvis would then see that the winner was paid. In addition, the crowd would make ongoing side bets throughout the day, with liquor, marijuana smoke, and hundred-dollar bills changing hands as blood flew in the lush backyard. "Elvis was the 'fair play' guy," Gunn says. "He handled the money, so he had those two Frankensteins with guns standing by him at all times."

After several bare-knuckle matches, Gunn was finally summoned to the ring, a thirty-foot-square platform surrounded by a chain-link fence. Wearing his trademark black shirt and jeans, he squared off against his opponent, a 6'2", 240-pound "foreign guy" in trunks and boxing shoes. The man came out swinging haymakers, trying to topple Gunn. But in just two minutes, Gunn ended the match with a quick combination of jabs and a hook. "Cut him up, split him open, good night," he says.

But the real trouble had only just begun. As Gunn started to leave the ring, a member of the Russian mob became upset with a member from another gang, pulling his gun and turning the backyard into chaos. "People started screaming," Gunn recalls. "It looked like a riot was about to take place." Tyler hit the ground. "They were trying to settle up a gambling dispute, and suddenly all these guns came flying out," he says. "I hid behind a chair." Finally, somehow, the argument was resolved, and the crowd quieted down. Gunn, however, had seen enough. He asked Elvis for his

$25,000 in prize money, was paid with small bills in a brown paper bag, and vanished, driving straight back to New Jersey. "It was time for me to go," he says. "I just wanted to get home to my family."

In New York, when not taking on underground fights for the mob, Gunn traveled the Tri-State area, finding better-paying jobs—including some commercial-property gigs—than he'd had in Florida. Yet with greater opportunity came greater expense. He was shocked to see how the New Jersey taxes and contractor fees ate away at his bottom line. So in the summer of 2001, he agreed to let Rose take Bobby Jr., then four, on "go-sees"—the industry term for auditions—for acting parts in Manhattan. "My little boy began doing commercials," Gunn says. "Campbell's Soup, McDonald's, Sprint—that was Bobby."

On the morning of September 11, 2001, Gunn was painting a house off Highway 46 near Hackensack, New Jersey, when the homeowner suddenly came outside, her face ashen. "She says, 'Come here; a plane hit the World Trade Center!'" Gunn recalls. "I went inside, she gave me an iced tea because it was warm, and we watched the second plane hit—and all I could think was how my wife and boy were supposed to be there." That morning, Rose had been scheduled to take Bobby Jr. for an audition in downtown Manhattan, meeting a producer outside the World Trade Center. Rattled, Gunn stared at the TV. Suddenly, his cell phone rang. Expecting the worst, he picked it up—and heard his wife's voice. "She said they had been on their way to the audition when the agent called and canceled," Gunn says. "I couldn't believe it. We were saved. After that, the woman at the house says, 'Go home, my son.' So I wrapped up the job and went back to our apartment, driving through complete chaos."

Needing to make more money, Gunn now began diving even deeper into the underground. These were the interim years of the sport, when bare knuckle was first beginning to emerge from the shadows. Gone were the beepers and pay phones and coded personal ads in newspapers. In their place, digital cameras, cell phones, and the Internet—not to mention the fact that the UFC had yet to take off—were skyrocketing the sport to sudden popularity online, beaming bare knuckle to millions of new viewers in suburban dens across the world.

In 2003, Kimbo Slice, the gold-chained Miami bodyguard, defeated a neighborhood tough known as Big D in a bloody palm-tree-ringed brawl to win $3,000 and Internet fame.[1] The taped fight led to a contract with the UFC, and even the cover of *ESPN the Magazine.* Controversial DVD series of street brawls, such as *Felony Fights* and *Ghetto Fights,* emerged.[2] Yet despite all the increased interest, celebrities like Slice were still the outliers. Most underground fighters remained in the shadows.

"Kimbo got a videotape," says former bare-knuckle fighter J. C. Wilfork. "But we didn't want anyone taping ours—this was a hood thing."

Ed Simpson, a Traveler who accompanied Gunn to fights for years, was shocked to see the sport online. "There is no video cameras allowed," he says. "It's underground for a reason—you can get charged with assault. So when Kimbo started posting those videos, we were blown away: 'Wow, you gotta be kidding me.'"

By January 2002, Gunn had replaced his beeper with a cell phone—but he wasn't about to start letting anyone tape him. At this point, he still thought bare knuckle was beneath him, an almost shameful way to make cash, and didn't want his name publicly attached to it. "I just needed the money," he says. "I'm a bad bastard. I can take you to the deep water, but I don't really want it. My wife, God love her, her nerves ain't the best for this. You have to imagine me coming home with marks on me. Over the years, it's taken a toll on her."

In New York, Gunn's reputation only continued to grow, and

so did his purse sizes. He learned how to conduct himself, always to bring a few guys as backup, giving them a cut of his winnings. He learned never to stop fighting until the other man quit—a lesson from when he broke and then reset his own finger with his mouth during a match in Cherry Hill, New Jersey. "The other guy's eyes bulged with shock," he says. "So I hit him with my other hand, split the top of his head, and he went down." He learned never to judge a fighter by his looks, once going a savage seven minutes with a run-down forty-five-year-old chain-smoker in Scranton, Pennsylvania. "I said, 'Oh, my God, this is going to be an easy fight," Gunn recalls. "Then he turned out to be a wild bat from hell, throwing every punch in the book until I finally knocked him out with a right hand. After a minute, he got back up, lit another cigarette, and said, 'Hey, good fight, man.'" Gunn pauses. "I was in shock." And, most especially, Gunn learned to sometimes bring along his own connected guys. "In the underground, about sixty percent of the fights are good and square, in and out, no problem," he says. "But the other forty percent, you're getting guns pulled and looking over your shoulder—you're not in the clear until you're driving down the road."

Mob fights are often surprisingly civil affairs. A family or gang will play host, sometimes bringing in different fighters for their own amusement, sometimes inviting other organizations to bring their best men as challengers in high-stakes matches. These are parties on home turf, events where fighting is expected to happen only within the ring, and any outside violence—as happened with the mountain-lion match in Boston—is a serious act of disrespect. The fighters know there is an inherent integrity at play here, one on which the entire criminal world is based: one's word is the only real contract. The fighters know they will be paid the full amount so long as they fulfill their end of the bargain: showing up to rumble. And this, despite all the danger, is the appeal of the underground—the guarantee that no promoter or venue owner will try to hide behind the paperwork and wriggle out of paying them. The mob pays on time and in small, unmarked bills.

But even the good fights can still be harrowing. Gunn fought in the backs of Irish mob–owned bars in Midtown, walking through kitsch and crowds and flat-screen TVs to brawl in cramped storage rooms on Saturday nights. He fought at events for Nigerian gangs in Queens, entering the basements of brick houses on crime-ridden blocks to take on opponents who disrobed from traditional West African dashikis to brawl. He even took on fights at Pagan's motorcycle club rallies, wading through drugs and prostitutes and bikers in backwoods Maryland to walk away with $5,000. "It was Christmastime," he says, shrugging. "I needed the money."

Yet nothing compared to Gunn's match in Chinatown. One day, the Irish mob called with an offer. They were backing him against an Asian gang in an illegal gambling parlor in the insular Lower Manhattan neighborhood. Flanked by his mob managers, Gunn entered an anonymous-looking storefront, walking past rows of roasted ducks, cages of turtles and squawking chickens, down a flight of stairs, and through a blood-spattered butchering area to enter a smoke-filled basement. The room was filled with people gambling with both US and Chinese currency. Guns were openly displayed. "I could hear dogfights happening in a room down the hall," Gunn says. "I hated that. The poor wee animals. And the smoke, oh, my God. I remember one guy smoking two cigarettes at once. I couldn't breathe."

Standing in the center of the low-ceilinged room, Gunn faced off against his opponent, a 5'10", 240-pound Asian fighter. "Tough little bastard," Gunn recalls. "He didn't speak no English to me." Neither, Gunn claims, did their hosts. Just a few seconds into the fight, the Asian brawler grabbed Gunn in a martial-arts grappling move, causing him to back off and yell to the local overseers that this was against the rules. When they remained stone-faced, Gunn turned to his Irish mob counterparts. "I'm telling my handler, 'You can't do that! This is bare knuckle, not rough-and-tumble,'" Gunn recalls. "And he tells them and then they get upset. Never seen anything like it in my life."

After a few seconds, Gunn and his opponent squared off again. The smoke-filled room got quiet, the only sounds the fighters' breathing, the wet slap of punches, and the muffled noise of the dogfight raging next door. "The triads and yazuka don't make no noise at all," Paul Tyler says, "except to clap when something happens. It's kind of eerie."

Soon, Gunn began to win the match, picking his opponent apart with quick jabs to the liver and arms, and the martial-arts fighter slid back on his previous moves. "They forget when they get hurt," Gunn says, "so he resorted back to his grabs and locks, stepping on my toes." Finally, exasperated, Gunn ended the fight with a devastating blow, one that went against all his own rules— he punched his opponent with a right jab straight to the forehead, the hardest bone in the body. "It's not where you want to hit, but it happened," Gunn recalls. "I split his head right open like a watermelon. It looked like a cunt, God forgive me. He went straight down to the ground in pain, and all of them started jabbering." An Asian referee stood over the fallen fighter, counting him out. The match was over.

Gunn and the Irish mob walked away with $30,000.

CHAPTER 16
THE RETURN OF SUPERMAN

In 2004, at the height of his years in the underground, just when he thought he'd seen it all, Gunn faced one of the most terrifying matches of his life—watching his son compete in an amateur boxing league.

In keeping with family tradition, Gunn had begun training Bobby Jr. when he was in diapers, molding his baby hands into fists to teach him the mechanics of punching. "I remember coming back from work, and Bob would be waiting outside for me, wearing little overalls and going, 'Dada, Dada, Dada,'" Gunn recalls. "I used to pick him up, go to the mall, and buy him a toy. At two years old, he was shadowboxing. At five, he started working the pads—I never seen a boy so obsessed with boxing."

Upon moving to their apartment in New Jersey, Gunn increased the intensity of Bobby Jr.'s training, taking him to a gym in Mahwah that specialized in youth boxing. "This little coach there used to work on Bobby's sparring," Gunn says. "I trained him, too. He was just a baby, but he loved it." Whereas Gunn had been forced to jog alongside his father's work truck through the snow, he treated Bobby Jr. differently, letting him decide whether he wanted to continue boxing. "We was never hitting the pads like, 'Hit, hit, hit,'" Gunn says. "It was fun. It just naturally come out of him. He'd be giggling, throwing right jabs with perfect form. And I said, 'My God, he's good.'"

In 2004, Gunn heard about a boxing gym where only the toughest fighters could spar—a training ground in one of the most dangerous neighborhoods of New Jersey. Naturally, he decided to take along his eight-year-old son. "I went to Ike and Randy's and was blown away by the work ethic of the fighters that would come to that gym," Gunn recalls. "Lifting Jane Fonda weights will make you look good, but it ain't going to let you smash someone's head in. It was my kind of world. So I started taking Bobby Jr. there to train alongside me. Me sparring those monsters was a faster way

[Figure 16.1] [Figure 16.2] Training Bobby Jr. (Photo courtesy of Bobby Gunn)

for him to learn, because he could watch his dad fight. It became his natural environment. That boy was raised up fighting."

That same year, at one of Bobby Jr.'s first amateur fights, Gunn stepped to the ring as he had throughout his life—but this time as a cornerman. Amid a collection of parents and skinny kids in outsize headgear and mouthguards, in a run-down gym in Passaic, Gunn stood by, shouting out encouragement as his son, then eight, fought, and nervously wiping him down when he returned to the corner. "I kept him going, kept him moving," Gunn recalls. "Protected him: 'Take your time, my boy.'"

When Bobby Jr. won, Gunn yelped with joy, entering the ring to hug his son. He shook the hand of the other boy and his father, making sure Bobby Jr. did the same. Then it was back to the work truck, the Gunns driving home while reenacting the match the entire way, having the sort of father-son moment the aging boxer had longed for as a child when he fought grown men from the bar. "I was grooming my boy in ways I wasn't groomed," Gunn says. "Don't rush him. Let him spar the right guys—don't break him."

It was during these drives that an audacious new plan took hold. It was something Gunn had secretly longed for and that was reawakened by his son, who saw him as a champion: his own return to the ring. "My boy wrote something about me in school," Gunn recalls. "It said I was his hero, his Superman. So a lot of that comeback was for him."

By 2004, Gunn had risen to the top of the underground, commanding at least $10,000 to fight in exclusive matches for organized crime. But it wasn't how he wanted Bobby Jr. to see him. No, Gunn wanted his son to see the full picture, to know him as the man he should have been, the hero he had wanted to become back when he was a child—a legitimate world champion boxer. And he knew there was only one way to give that to his son. "I'd always known I was a champ," Gunn says. "I just never got my breaks. So I wanted to show my boy he should never take no, but go and get what he wants in life."

At first, the idea looked like a suicide mission. Gunn was thirty, the age at which most boxers begin to wash out. He hadn't fought a gloved match in years, couldn't afford to see a trainer or take time off to condition properly, and was struggling with a lifetime of injuries. On paper, he looked like a total washout. "I was beyond medically written off," Gunn says. "I couldn't even turn my right foot."

But all the naysayers forgot one thing: Gunn had been fighting the entire time. He had ruled the bare-knuckle circuit for years while also taking on the occasional "smoker" boxing match, unsanctioned bouts held for money in gyms, in which fighters wear light eight-ounce gloves. He had changed his fighting style to compensate for his injuries, moving his feet less while relying on his ability to duck and weave. And, most importantly, he still knew how to throw a pavement-crushing right jab, his ability to knock out an opponent at any moment making him dangerous. The world may have forgotten about Gunn, but he was ready.

"On any given night, I had a puncher's chance," he says. "I could bang. And you can never count a puncher out. In the last second of the last round, he can land that one haymaker and win the title."

Gunn had no money, no manager, and no real prospects. But he did have a part-time promoter, Joe "Mack" McEwen, a former male stripper from east Nashville, Tennessee. The son of a cop, Mack craved adrenaline, from boxing as a kid in the police athletic league, to running plays as a tailback in high school, to his improbable turn, in his twenties, as a dancer in an all-male revue. In the early 1980s, Mack toured the south from Nashville to Atlanta, to Panama City, Florida, as a member of the Heavenly Seven, performing in (and out of) his father's old metro cop uniform to Rick James's "Super Freak," until, he says, his manager went to prison for laundering drug money.

"I was stripping, driving a Firebird, fighting, and working a job at a health club," Mack says. "I had a long blond mullet and Velcro pants. We were doing ecstasy and cocaine and it was exciting and absolutely, totally insane. It was the eighties." Mack pauses. "But now the guys don't like to revisit it. Hell, one of us is a physician's assistant."

Mack, now a successful contractor in Murfreesboro, Tennessee, has long since lost the mullet and tear-away pants. He is fifty-two, bald, and married with two pet dogs, hardly so much as drinking a beer on Saturday night. But there is one thrill he can't shed, the one that helped him survive those east Nashville kids who taunted him for being a cop's son—the bond that ties him to Gunn like a brother: the fight game. "My favorite sport is fisticuffs," Mack says. "I even carry a mouthpiece in my pocket. But I fought at the small level—Bobby was in the big-time shit."

Mack first met Gunn at an underground fight in a warehouse in Tampa in the early nineties. At the time, Mack was selling satellite phones—those boxy precursors to cell phones—while bare-knuckle fighting in Gulf Coast bouts, when he shared a bill with Gunn. He walked away impressed. "Neck like Mike Tyson, legs like tree trunks, a back as wide as a '57 Buick," Mack says. "The guy is just super strong."

Over the next decade, Mack would continue to work office jobs in Florida while Gunn settled in New Jersey to work asphalt. But the pair stayed in touch, connecting at bare-knuckle bouts from Ohio to Chicago, to Philly. Finally, when Gunn decided to return to pro boxing, there was one friend he knew he could call for help. "Joe was my promoter," Gunn says. "Crazy as he goes on, he can be very intelligent when he wants to be."

With Mack overseeing his career, Gunn quickly scored a comeback pro boxing match set for December 2004 against Leon Hinnant, a thirty-two-year-old cruiserweight from Wilmington, North Carolina, with a 2-8 record. Hinnant had stepped inside a ring in the past eleven years, but that was about all the journey-man fighter had going for him—he had lost his last eight matches in a row. Still, Gunn treated the bout as if it were a prime-time title fight at Caesar's Palace, training around the clock at Ike's and at job sites, lifting fifty-pound buckets of asphalt sealant. Finally, he was ready. Bobby Jr. was in awe. "To me, my dad is the best man who's ever lived," he says. "When he came back, battling a lot of injuries and told he'd never walk again, it was amazing to see him in professional boxing—I have pride and respect for my dad."

Finally, on the eve of the match, Gunn had one last call to make. In the years since their split in Florida, he would periodically contact his father to see that he was getting by in his monthly-rate motel room in Niagara Falls. "I always called my old dad on the pay phone," Gunn recalls. "Or I'd send him a letter. I'd check on him."

Now sixty-one, Robert had returned to laying asphalt and painting barns, knocking on doors and hustling for rent money. He lived in the same motor court as his lifelong friend and fellow Traveler Jimmy Ruml, the two aging bachelors often reminiscing over old times at the local bars. "We go out for drinks and coffee," Ruml says. "Old Bob is crazy, but he's my best friend—we laugh all the time."

Racked with injuries from his decades of wrestling, brawling, and manual labor, Robert could no longer climb as high or coat as many driveways as he once had. His eyesight was beginning to fail, and according to Ruml, he was suffering with the first signs of arthritis. "He drinks a couple beers and still thinks he's Genghis Khan," Ruml says. "But he's had a rough life—it's starting to catch up with him."

Still grieving the death of his wife, Jackie, Robert had begun drinking more heavily, getting into bar fights and falling into dishevelment, his motel room a wasteland of empty bottles and dirty dishes. "It would bother me to think of the grave site," Robert says. "I remember me and Bobby burying his mom, and it made me kind of melancholy."

During these years, Gunn says his father obsessed over the death of his wife, perpetually mourning her. "About the fifth year after I was married, it really took its toll on Dad," he says. "He was getting sad and emotional, wearing black slacks and a black tie to represent her. He said to me once, 'You don't appreciate how much you love something till it's gone.'" Gunn pauses. "He was never the same—a shell of himself."

In the days before his return to the ring, Gunn used his cell phone to call his father at his motel room, hoping to hear some last-minute advice. Instead, he got an earful. "He told me, 'You could've been super middleweight champion of the world and now you're handicapped,'" Gunn recalls. "'You're okay fighting bare knuckle, because they can't lay a hand on you, but I don't want to see you back in the boxing ring—you're taking away from who you were.'"

For Robert, Gunn's return to the ring was a painful reminder of the death of his wife, of the bright future he could have achieved with his son, and he didn't want to face those feelings again. "Everything was going good until my wife died," Robert says. "We never thought she would die. It put a complete monkey wrench in the whole plans. That fucked things up. We had built a beautiful racing car and we couldn't get certain parts for the motor." Robert also worried about losing Gunn—now older and maimed—to the dangers of pro boxing, although he could never articulate that to his son.

"Old Bob had a hard time watching little Bob fight," Ruml recalls. "He'd be pacing at the bar. 'I don't want to see my boy hurt.' I said, 'You put him through this shit when he was young.' 'Yeah that was different. Today I don't want to see him hurt. He's older.' It really bothered him."

Gunn, of course, did not hear his father's concern, only his disapproval, his command to stay out of the ring. Once upon a time, Gunn would have obeyed him. Upon turning thirty, however, he had begun to assert himself. Perhaps it had to do with his own son, or maybe just his years of independence in Florida. Whatever the reason, something had fundamentally shifted within Gunn, leading to a broader change in the relationship between him and his aging father—the old man no longer had his hold. "When Bob passed thirty, old Bob stopped doing that kind of stuff," Ruml says, referring to Robert's days of domineering.

"Now Bob just looks at him. He don't have to say nothing—he's not that little kid he can push around anymore."

In the end, against his father's wishes, against his wife's wishes—she vowed never to see him in the ring—Gunn decided to go through with the match. Fighting was his one talent, and he wanted to show the world he could still bang. "I felt I better do it now or regret it the rest of my life," he says. "I wanted to prove everybody wrong."

Only one final hurdle remained: the state medical exam. In pro boxing, all fighters must undergo inspections to fight, and at the last moment, there was concern that Gunn's lifetime of injuries would keep him from getting a pass. But according to Mike Hopper, his cut man at the time, who once sewed up a fighter with two-pound-test fishing line, a debarbed hook, and Jack Daniels for antiseptic, Gunn managed to conceal his injuries from the doctors. "He had a screw poking out his heel so bad you could run your hand across it and feel the threads," Hopper recalls in his thick Tennessee accent. "But Bobby was able to conceal it—if you know the right doctor, you can pass, no problem."

Finally, eleven years after his last pro boxing match, eleven years after the death of his mother, Gunn returned to the ring as a cruiserweight on December 11, 2004. He fought Leon Hinnant, a southpaw, at a local venue in Greensboro, North Carolina. It was a cold night with a lackluster crowd, and Gunn was out of practice. Yet he walked straight up to Hinnant and dropped him with a combination right and left hook, winning the match in the first round. "A total bum," Mack says about Gunn's opponent. "But we were building Bobby's confidence."

The fight was a nonaffair, a match between has-beens, which nobody watched. But to Gunn, it was the victory of a lifetime—he was back. "You could slash me, rip my heart out, and I come back a better fighter," he says. "I'm good because I don't give a fuck—I believe in myself."

CHAPTER 17
BLOOD ON THE CANVAS

Following his victory in North Carolina, Gunn began a new phase of his career—using his bare-knuckle matches to subsidize a comeback in pro boxing. "Whether it's the underground or the bright lights of a casino, a fight's a fight," he says. "I take 'em all to the deep water and drown 'em."

By 2005, Gunn was commanding a challenge fee of $10,000 in the underground—often his minimum even to show up. Capitalizing on his spreading fame, he traveled increasingly afar for big-money matches, fighting in warehouses in downtown LA, in backyard bouts in Phoenix, or in empty lots in Tennessee, Ohio, Michigan. Sometimes, he took on bouts because he happened to be in the area, traveling for work. Other times, he drove or flew specifically for fights. "The guys who put on these fights all know who Bobby is," says Paul Tyler. "Could be a gym owner, a connected guy, a rich guy, a regular guy trying to put these on—but a lot of them can't afford Bobby."

Once, while traveling for work near the Mexican border, Gunn even fought on a ranch outside Corpus Christi, Texas, brawling in the late-afternoon sun amid the cactus and sagebrush.

Staged by a rancher and attended by a large crowd of local whites and Hispanics, Gunn was the main attraction. "The promoter was this cowboy I'd met at a bare-knuckle fight in Boston," says Tyler, who had flown out for the event with his own fighters. "They were looking to put on a big fight, and Bobby was out there working with the gypsies. The cowboy said he normally doesn't bring people out, they do their own thing out there, but, you know, everybody knows Bobby." Arriving with a crowd of Travelers who were moving through the lower Rio Grande Valley for work, Gunn faced off against his opponent. "I fought a cowboy guy, nice kid," Gunn recalls. "Dropped him in about thirty seconds. Just didn't have much in him."

When big-money bouts sometimes became rough-and-tumble, Gunn fought even harder. "Grab the tip of the ear and it rips right off," he says. "Take your thumb and stick it in someone's eye—done it many a times." Once, in a parking lot match in Camden, New Jersey, while suffocating in a headlock, Gunn reached down, ripped his opponent's balls, and then spun around to bite his ear and finish him with punches. In a warehouse fight in Brooklyn, he once threw a corkscrew punch so hard, he knocked a man's eyeball out of its socket, the organ "swelling out like an egg" before popping out to hang by a vein. Years later, Gunn happened to meet this man again, now wearing an eye patch as he filled Gunn's truck with gas at a roadside station near Hackensack, New Jersey. "I thought he was going to try to murder me," Gunn says. "But he was excited: 'Hey, Bobby!'"

But of all his rough-and-tumble matches, Gunn's most high-stakes bout was against a former NFL player in a match staged by several different Latino gangs in a Bronx warehouse in 2007. Arriving in the early evening wearing his trademark muscle shirt and acid-wash jeans, Gunn arrived to find about a hundred people drinking and gambling. The event was a social gathering, a night of tequila and bare-knuckle fights. Gunn was the headliner. "These guys were all blinged out," says underground promoter Paul Tyler, who was with Gunn that day. "A couple of pieces were flashed. There was cash out. Guys smoking weed. It looked like some type of Columbian cocaine thing."

Gunn took off his shirt and stepped inside the center of the crowd. His opponent was a 6'1", 220-pound Black man in shorts and a tank top. According to Tyler, the brawler was a former linebacker who had played two years in college, briefly competed in the NFL, and then tried to make it as a pro boxer. Perhaps he saw bare knuckle as a new opportunity. "I believe he'd had one pro boxing fight at that point," Tyler says. "He was there to win."

Gunn came out swinging but had trouble reaching the linebacker, who towered over him and had a longer reach. In response, the linebacker threw big, hard lumbering punches, trying to end the fight with a knockout. Gunn easily avoided them, the crowd becoming animated—this was going to be a good fight. For five minutes, the two men roamed the lot, jabbing and ducking, occasionally landing shots. The linebacker was damaging Gunn, connecting on hard shots. But Gunn was landing some of his own. Slowly, the linebacker began to tire—and the momentum turned. Finally, Gunn dropped him. "And that's when he bit him," Tyler says.

After being counted out, the linebacker stood, approaching Gunn with his arms out as if for a hug. Then the massive football player did something nobody was expecting. He craned his neck and bit into the meat of Gunn's neck. "He went, '*Harhn,*'" Gunn recalls, mimicking a chomping sound. "I went, 'Oh, you fucking cunt.'" Gunn gripped the linebacker, lifted him up, and bit a hole the size of a quarter in the man's cheek. Still holding on to him, Gunn then took the whole top of his ear off with his teeth.

"I mean, like a fucking animal," Tyler says. "It was gushing and there was mess on the ground and everybody just went 'Woah!'" Gunn spat out the man's ear, hit him with four punches, and dropped him to the ground. The linebacker's people yelled foul, but the organizers stepped in to resolve it, pointing out that their man had bitten first. Gunn walked out with a hole in his neck, and $20,000—his largest purse to date.

* * * * *

Flush with cash from his underground fights, Gunn could now subsidize his pro boxing comeback. Competing as a cruiserweight, hovering at a lean, ripped 190 pounds, he spent hours at Ike's gym, sparring and lifting and hobbling on the treadmill to maintain his fighting form. "Even though my leg was bad, I was in good shape," Gunn says. "I knew I could pull something off."

Following his initial win in Greensboro, North Carolina, Gunn quickly took on another confidence-building match in an undercard bout against Earl Kirkendall, a thirty-eight-year-old amateur champion with only one pro fight (a loss) to his name. In February 2005, at the 9,200-seat municipal auditorium in Nashville, Gunn stepped into the ring for the second time in eleven years. "I'll never forget it," recalls Joe Mack, his promoter at the time. "Bobby hit this guy with a left hook to the body that sounded like a drum hit. The whole crowd went '*Oh!*' and the guy went down—that got us started on our ride."

Continuing his streak against low-tier opponents in Mack's backyard—the South—Gunn defeated guys like Jimmy Garrett, a forty-five-year-old journeyman with a 3-28 record, in Memphis, and Jeff Holcomb, an Iraq War vet and policeman with a 10-3 record from Fort Oglethorpe, Georgia, before taking on his first major fight, against Shelby Gross for the International Boxing Association cruiserweight title belt, in Nashville in March 2006.

While not one of the premier titles in boxing, the IBA belt was a respectable stepping-stone victory, an honorific won by champions including Oscar De La Hoya, Roy Jones Jr., and James Toney on their way to the top. For Gunn, it represented everything, and now, with a career record of 15-2, he finally felt ready to take on a real opponent. "I was feeling good," Gunn says. "Knocked Jeff out in the fifth round, broke his spleen—pissed blood on the canvas. What a beating I gave him. And then the corruption started again."

A roughhouse boxer from South Carolina with a 16-3 record, Shelby Gross came to the fight with baggage. In 2000, he wore a wire to a meeting with Las Vegas promoter Robert Mitchell, taping Mitchell's attempt to bribe him with $8,000 to lose a match, and then handing the evidence to the FBI.[1] The taped meeting resulted in a string of fighter arrests, and the first time a boxer was ever convicted of a fight-fixing scheme in Nevada.[2]

That ordeal, however, would soon be overshadowed by Gross's fight against Gunn—"one of the wildest affairs ever seen in a professional ring," according to the IBA.[3] In front of a screaming crowd at Music City's nine-thousand-seat Municipal Auditorium, Gunn and Gross fought with abandon, exchanging haymakers and knockout shots while careening across the ring. In the first round, Gunn knocked Gross down twice. Then, in the second, the South Carolina boxer returned the favor, dropping Gunn, pouncing onto him, and hammering him with shots—a completely illegal move—until the referee picked Gross up and body-slammed him to the canvas. Unable to recover from the illicit pummeling, Gunn was ultimately knocked flat on his back as the bell rang. The referee declared Gross the winner by technical knockout, and his entourage stormed the ring in victory. The win would be short-lived, however. The next month, Gross failed a drug test for an illegal substance, resulting in a no-contest ruling by the Tennessee Athletic Commission—a decision backed by an angry IBA and national Association of Boxing Commissions over the sloppy refereeing of the bout.[4] "The integrity of this event [was] somewhere between 'ear biting' and a 'post fight mugging,'" the IBA stated.[5]

Gunn was upset, embarrassed, and heartbroken over the fight, his one chance at a world title belt transformed into a bizarre spectacle. "I was shell-shocked," he says. Yet six months later, Joe Mack set him up to fight again for the same IBA world title belt, this time against Shannon "the Sandman" Landberg, a respected veteran with a 58-11 record, at the Lac Courte Oreilles Reservation in northern Wisconsin. Landberg, forty-one, was even more washed up than Gunn. But the clean-shorn, muscle-bound former army boxer had also never won a world title and was hungry to defeat Gunn.[6] "Landberg was a very cagey guy, a veteran," Gunn recalls. "And I had just broken my thumb."

In the days before the match, Gunn had been sparring and caught his right thumb in his opponent's headgear, breaking it at the tip. "The skin was just holding it together," Gunn recalls. "It went black." Knowing he could never pass the state medical inspection for the fight with a broken, blackened thumb, Gunn concealed his injury with makeup from his wife's purse. When the half-distracted doctor tugged on it during his inspection, Gunn bit his lip to keep from crying out. "I thought I was going to bite my fucking tongue in two," he recalls. "Oh, the pain." For Gunn, fighting with a broken wing was nothing new. "I went into a lot of fights with broken hands," he says. "To keep the doctor's mind off any thought of injury, I'd grab his hand and shake it right—that was always the most nerve-racking part."

Cleared for the fight, Gunn entered the ring wearing tartan trunks and following a lone bagpiper he'd hired for the occasion. He was determined to win the belt. Cradling his right hand, he mostly fought with his left for the first couple rounds, picking Sandberg apart. Then, his adrenaline surging, Gunn says he stopped feeling any pain. "It sounds weird, but sometimes that happens," he says. "The right hand starts numbing and the swelling acts like a case—I started plugging away with it." Now blending his bare-knuckle street tactics with boxing skills, Gunn landed jab after jab while also throwing in a few shots below the belt and even headbutting Landberg at one point, getting deducted for the penalty. In retaliation, Landberg threw power shots at close range, opening cuts above Gunn's eyes. Both men were sweating and bleeding onto the canvas as the Midwestern crowd cheered. In the end, however, Gunn prevailed. "By the fifth round, I felt the life leaving him, and by the sixth I knew it was a matter of time," Gunn says. "I broke him down." Just thirty-six seconds into round seven, Landberg—stumbling with a chipped tooth and a broken right eye socket—threw in the towel. Gunn was crowned the new IBA cruiserweight champion of the world. "I reached down and put my boy on my shoulders," Gunn says. "Once a champ, always a champ."

That night, Gunn shared a double room with his father-in-law, Hugh Keith, and Bobby Jr. (Gunn's father, Robert, had not shown up.) Sleeping in the same bed as his son, Gunn put the giant belt between them, watching as the boy fell asleep with the trophy in his arms. "I stayed up until two in the morning, just looking at my wee boy and reminiscing on the fight," Gunn recalls. "Becoming a world champion for my son was priceless—there's no money that could beat that night."

The win skyrocketed Gunn into the top fifteen national rankings, capping an incredible run for the aging unknown. Now, just two short years after resurrecting his career, Gunn was given a shot at real stardom in an HBO televised fight against Enzo Maccarinelli, the 6'4", 200-pound Welsh cruiserweight champion, in a World Boxing Organization title bout at the 74,000-seat Principality Stadium in Cardiff, Wales. At the last minute, Maccarinelli's opponent had dropped out, clearing the way for Gunn—who, despite being written off by the

[Figure 17.1] Winning the IBA cruiserweight title in 2006 (Photo courtesy of Bobby Gunn)

UK press, saw this as his long-awaited chance for glory. "This is my shot," he said in an interview. "I've got a couple more years to make the best of it and I feel like a million dollars."[7]

If Gunn's IBA belt was considered a stepping-stone, then the WBO was the ultimate prize—one of just four world championships recognized by the International Boxing Hall of Fame. For the match, Gunn had been flown in by powerful UK promoter Frank Warren to fight Maccarinelli—a twenty-six-year-old hometown favorite and rising European star raised just down the road in Swansea—on the undercard match for Joe Calzaghe, another local champion. Trying to gain traction with US audiences, Maccarinelli, the son of an Italian immigrant boxer, looking to pad his record after having a couple of big fights fall through, was taking on Gunn as the heavy favorite. "I have had a few disappointments in the past year," Maccarinelli said at the time. "But I am focusing my frustration and am in the shape of my life . . . Soon enough I will be the main man and Bobby Gunn will find that out."[8]

In April 2007, Gunn arrived in Cardiff and immediately knew that something was wrong. Historically, Travelers have long been derided in Wales as throughout the UK—and the day of the fight, he arrived at the stadium to find a particularly hostile crowd. "People yelling, calling me *pikey,*" Gunn says, referring to the ethnic slur for Travelers.* "It was horrible." He was then given a note from management. Gunn would have to change his trunks because they were too similar in color to Macarinelli's. Also, one more thing: he would have to prepare for the fight in a public restroom. In boxing, underdog opponents are often treated as second-class citizens by promoters looking to give the edge to their star fighters, trying all sorts of schemes to undermine their opponents. But Gunn and his camp contend that the fight in Wales was over the top.

"These promoters pull all sorts of tricks," says Mike Hopper, Gunn's cut man for the fight. "When we arrived, all jet-lagged, they put us five grown men in a compact car and drove us around the hills for over three hours before taking us to the motel—and, needless to say, the accommodations sucked. Sometimes they put stuff in your food to give you the runs. Hell, I had one fighter get sent three hookers to his door the night before his fight, trying to throw him off—The A guy gets the hotel and the B guy gets the shithouse."

Gritting his teeth, Gunn, then thirty-three, walked into the bowels of the stadium, found a bench in a concrete public restroom, and put on his backup trunks and gloves as a steady stream of drunken fans passed through to use the urinals. "Here comes a drunk to take a piss as I'm getting my hands wrapped," Gunn recalls. "'Hello, mate, good luck!'"

---

* The term "pikey," dating back to the nineteenth century, is a reference to Travelers who once roamed along pikes, or toll roads, in the UK.

[Figure 17.2] Prepping for Maccarinelli (Photo courtesy of Mike Hopper)

From there, things only got worse. Not only was Gunn's opponent, Maccarinelli, a hometown favorite, but he was also a far more accomplished fighter, a defending world champion cruiserweight almost a decade younger than Gunn, with a 25-1 pro record, who was at the prime of his career. By comparison, Gunn, with an 18-2-1 record spanning almost twenty years, was largely seen as a fluke—a bare-knuckle sideshow with no business being there at all. "He's a colorful character," the TV broadcast announcer, John Rawling, said about Gunn as the fight began. "Got some real bloodcurdling stories about what went on during his bare-knuckle days, which I think probably, for the good of all concerned, are not repeated on air."[9]

As the fight began, the crowd roared for Maccarinelli, who immediately began pummeling Gunn with a right to the temple and two hooks to the ribs.[10] Gunn moved quickly on the canvas, retaliating with body shots, but was clearly outmatched. With forty-three seconds left in the first round, Gunn was already leaning back against the ropes, his sweaty black hair in his eyes, his right nostril pouring blood as the referee gave him an eight count. "That nose is a legacy of the unlicensed days," Rawling deadpanned on air. "He's not got too much cartilage in there. It's not a particularly pleasant sort of sight." Gunn bounced off the ropes and walked toward Maccarinelli, his face a bloody grin—and was immediately hit with a hard right followed by a devastating left. The fight was called. Gunn never made it through the first round. "Gunn is outgunned," the other commentator, Duke McKenzie, said. "He just doesn't have it."[11]

When asked about the fight, Gunn will admit he was outboxed. However, he says, that was the strategy. "The whole plan was to let Enzo punch himself out," he says. According to Gunn and his team, he was aiming to lose the first few rounds in the hope of tiring out Maccarinelli, who, he hoped, would then leave himself open to a knockout punch. In Gunn's view, the fight was stopped prematurely.

Yet watch the two minutes, thirty-five seconds of the fight on YouTube, and it is impossible to think Gunn had anything remotely resembling a chance. In the end, a fighter, after losing a match, will, of course, say he was robbed. He *has* to assign blame—humility can literally get a man killed in the ring. But in Gunn's case, the worldwide consensus was plain: the aging journeyman fighter had simply gotten in over his head. "The eccentric American pug Bobby Gunn," summarized UK boxing writer David Payne. "A fighter plucked from obscurity . . . and then plunged back to the tank-town circuit following his one-round massacre at the hands of the towering Welshman."[12]

In the end, Gunn left the match, bloodied, bruised, and embarrassed—he had flopped disastrously in his one big shot on the world stage. "I mean, we were on HBO, man," Mack recalls. "It was humiliating. It was tough on him."

There would be one upshot, though. Morose in the motel room, icing his wounds and biding his time for the cab ride to the airport, Gunn was approached by his father, who had been drinking steadily through the day. "Told ya," Robert said, sitting down beside him, a cigarette hanging from his mouth. "The fix is in. You got fucked, boy."

Gunn sat still, not saying a word, playing the fight over and over in his mind, wondering what he could have done differently. "I was mad at myself," he says. The last thing he wanted to hear was gloating from his father. But to his shock, something unexpected happened—his father opened up. "He told me he was proud of me, gave me a kiss," Gunn recalls. "He was a dad that time, more than ever. 'Hold your head high and walk out of here,' he told me. 'You're a fighting Traveler man.'"

Gunn would never fight an international match again.

CHAPTER 18
A GUN, A PAIR OF PLIERS, AND A LIFETIME OF PAIN

Here, in all likelihood, is where Gunn's story should have ended—the slow shuffle of a journeyman fighter off into the sunset, a life of paving driveways and tarring roofs and hustling the backstreets of New Jersey ahead of him.

But then a funny thing happened.

In March 2008, less than a year after his loss to Maccarinelli, Gunn was in Arizona for the winter, laying asphalt, when he decided to meet with a hard-luck promoter who would ultimately change his life and upend the fight world. Theirs was a friendship that began at a P.F. Chang's in Scottsdale. "It was our first meeting," says David Feldman, a pro boxing and MMA promoter. "And Bobby tried to con me."

At the time, Feldman was a struggling promoter out of Philadelphia, hustling for shows anywhere he could, living fifteen weeks a year on the road, staging boxing, MMA, and tough-man events from the back streets of Atlantic City to the gambling boats of the Carolinas, to the outskirts of Reno. When he first met Gunn, Feldman was looking to put on a pro boxing show at Fort McDowell, a 150,000-square-foot casino on the Yavapai Nation

Indian reservation at the edge of the Sonoran Desert. Once a feared band of tribesmen who ranged as far north as the Grand Canyon, the Yavapai now consisted of roughly nine hundred members who lived on or around the sprawling tribal resort, a forty-square-mile fiefdom of golf clubs, RV parks, and casino slots amid the saguaro cactus and volcanic mountains north of Phoenix.[1] Desperate to fill the room, Feldman was scouring the local scene for fighters when he suddenly heard from an aging cruiserweight, a boxer who had recently returned to the ring, a man he'd heard rumors about for years—Gunn. "I was like, 'Yeah, let's meet,'" Feldman recalls. "I'd heard he was a good draw."

Like many Northeast Travelers fleeing winter, Gunn had arrived in the desert for a few months to work asphalt jobs when he saw the news about the upcoming fight—and immediately began his hustle. Since his disastrous loss to Maccarinelli in Wales, Gunn was perhaps the only person on the planet who hadn't written off his career. Just two months later, he had returned to the ring, having to start all over again at the bottom. In June 2007, he demolished Elija Dickens, a hapless cruiserweight with an 0-5 record, at a pro boxing match held in a recreation center in Springfield, Virginia. Then, in August, he defeated Benito Fernandez, a journeyman southpaw, in a bout held in a *high school gym*. By all accounts, Gunn could not have fallen any lower. Yet, despite the odds, he was determined to vindicate himself, to show the world he was still a contender—and saw the fight in Scottsdale as the beginning of a comeback. But first, he had to negotiate his fee. "Dave was a hard guy," Gunn says. "So I tried to work him a little."

In the fight game, boxers and promoters are in a constant struggle. Boxers want to be paid a flat fee for their appearance, while promoters want to cut them a percentage of ticket sales, risking less money up front. At Fort McDowell, Feldman was bringing in fighters from out of town while also cherry-picking local talent, giving the regional contenders a wad of tickets and a promise to cut them in on the profit. Typically, whoever has the most clout—the fighter or the promoter—gets to dictate the deal. And in this instance, both Gunn and Feldman thought they were that person. "You want me to put my money where my mouth is?" Feldman says. "You put your money where your mouth is."

Over noodles and dim sum, the negotiations began. Gunn asked for $20,000 up front, citing his 9-1 pro record in the four years since his comeback. Feldman scoffed, saying he had nowhere near that budget but would cut him a deal—half of all the tickets Gunn could sell. Gunn declined. "He was like, 'Nah, forget that,'" Feldman recalls. "So I called his bluff and said, 'All right, man, see you later.'"

Then something unexpected happened.

They both cracked grins.

"He started laughing, and I started laughing, and we both kind of knew the score," Gunn recalls. "I said, 'Okay, you want to be a hard-ass? Give me the tickets.'"

Gunn went on to sell $25,000 worth of tickets, filling the room with Travelers and then fighting to a draw against Kentucky boxer Cory Phelps, surviving a vicious head butt over his left eye in the first round. "Blood was pouring down, so I couldn't see," Gunn says. "I was lucky to pull it out."

But the real takeaway was his friendship with Feldman, a mutual respect that would soon lead to their collaborating on more pro boxing matches before taking on the craziest scheme in fight-world history—one that would change both their lives forever. "Bobby introduced me to bare knuckle," Feldman says. "And bells started going off in my head—'Wow, are you kidding me? This is unbelievable.'"

He grins.

"I knew this could be the next great American sport."

* * * * *

Behind every great fighter, there is a great promoter. And then you have David Feldman. "My life is fucked, dude," he says, sitting in his Spartan two-room office in west Philadelphia in May 2016. "You just don't understand."

Feldman, a former pro welterweight boxer with a 4-1 record, has a reputation. Early in his promotion career, when one of his pro boxers didn't show, he would change into old middleweight trunks he lugged around in the trunk of his car, and step into the ring himself. In later years, he would do the same at underground bare-knuckle matches he organized, taking off his shirt and flooring fighters half his age when one of his guys backed out. "No other promoter steps in the ring like I do," Feldman says. "I understand these fighters. I know what it feels like to get punched in the face. And they respect me for it."

Born in 1970 as the youngest son of Marty Feldman, a hard-ass boxing trainer in Philly, Feldman, forty-seven, was raised in a fight factory. At one point, after his mother had left Marty, he and his brother lived with ten boxers—all Black and all from impoverished inner-city neighborhoods—in the family's three-bedroom house in Broomall, a white middle-class suburb on the western edge of Philadelphia. "Just about the only Blacks in Broomall were the ones in our house," Feldman says. By day, his father ran a denim shop, Marty Feldman's Jeans, selling pants and work boots. By night, starting at eight, he ran grueling training sessions. These were the days of Vietnam and Watergate and segregation, a time when changing race relations and social mores were inciting controversy, and a Jewish family living with a houseful of Black men in an all-white subdivision did not sit well.

"We'd be running down West Chester Pike, people yelling 'nigger lover,'" recalls Charles Williams, a former world heavyweight champion who trained under Marty. "That didn't bother Marty. He'd punch you in a heartbeat or pull out his pistol and shoot you." If the neighbors didn't like the fact that Marty oversaw a homegrown gym, didn't like that he occasionally shot bullet holes in the ceiling to get his boxers' attention, didn't like that he housed young Black fighters on their manicured streets, they could go to hell. "The neighbors would call the cops," Feldman says. "And my dad would be like 'Yo, they're fighters—get the fuck out of here.'"

[Figure 18.1] **David Feldman** (Photo by author)

Feldman smiles. He is dark-eyed handsome with a fighter's build, favoring jeans, a T-shirt, and sneakers. He works out every morning. Twice a week, he sees a doctor for a pinched nerve in his left shoulder—an ailment caused by his years as a boxer, his head getting snapped back so often, it condensed the vertebrae in his back. He is divorced, has two grown children, and is currently engaged to a stunning younger hairdresser. Most afternoons, he visits Marty at the Broomall Rehabilitation Center, now helping his eighty-three-year-old father fight the toughest opponent of his life: dementia. "I had a fucked-up thing with Dad," Feldman says. "But he was a badass motherfucker—he never would have wanted to be in a place like this."

Feldman, at heart, is a survivor. He has been a pro boxer, a bartender, a night-school student at Temple. He owned a night-club at twenty-four, went broke at twenty-six, and, after telling his old man he needed money and getting only a five-dollar bill, paid his rent by selling custom suits for six months, making 150 cold calls a day until some doctor mouthed off to him and he quit. He then did what he always does—endure—by buying a mechanical bull, hauling it around to bars, and making $10,000 a week, back on top. "Chicks would get naked on the bull," he says. "It was crazy. Look, I used to sell candy in high school. I'll never not make money."

But if Feldman is going to succeed in life, it is for one reason and one reason alone: he won't let himself dishonor the memory of his mother, Dawn. "She is the strongest person I've ever met," he says. "I always stayed close with her." In his office, he keeps a painting she once made, a small, delicate watercolor of a blue rose. Dawn created it by gritting a brush between her teeth—a testament to her strength after surviving a horrible tragedy: the loss of use of her arms and legs. "With bare knuckle, I'll be like 'Fuck this, it's too hard,'" he says. "Then I'll look at that painting my mother made with a brush between her teeth and say, 'Too hard? You're a pussy.' And I'll go back and try harder."

For Feldman, the seminal event of his life happened not in the boxing world, but near a cemetery on a deserted highway in the dead of night. In 1974, Dawn had left Marty and began dating another local man. One night, according to Feldman and his older brother, Damon, and backed in part by a 1981 newspaper account, Dawn got into an argument with her new boyfriend at a club.[2] On the way home, he stopped alongside a graveyard and began hitting her, eventually beating her head against a tombstone and running her over with the car. He then put her back in the passenger's seat and, while driving down the highway, pushed her out the door. The fall broke her neck, leaving her a quadriplegic. "She had a black-and-blue footprint across her chest," the newspaper story states. "She faded in and out of consciousness for almost a month."[3] Ultimately, Dawn wound up in a coma. The man went into hiding. Marty served his wife divorce papers while she was recuperating in the hospital. "My brother and I went through adversity like most people never see," says Damon Feldman. "When our mom got injured and became a quadriplegic in a wheelchair, we weren't able to bond with her that well. It was devastating."

As a child, of course, Feldman didn't know any of the details of Dawn's attack. At age four, all he knew was that his mother had suddenly disappeared. "It was tough, man," he says. "I don't remember that happening as much as I remember not being with her. A long time would go by and I wouldn't see her."

For a period, Feldman and his brother lived with friends of the family, until returning to live with their father. While Feldman would ultimately reconcile with Marty, he says their relationship during his youth was difficult. Aside from training him to fight, Marty rarely showed Feldman love, instead flinging pots and pans at him while drinking half-gallon bottles of scotch at the kitchen table. "There was this corner of the kitchen that was my corner," Feldman recalls. "I'd stand there and get fucking hit with pots and pans and plates and everything. He beat the fuck out of me with shit every day." Pushed away by his father, Feldman began visiting his mother in her assisted-living homes. He admired her bravery, how she had briefly contemplated suicide after the accident until deciding to live her life anew, returning to school, taking up painting, trying out for the Special Olympics, even getting three poems published in a local book—all without the use of her limbs. "I loved Mom," Feldman says. "I always stayed close with her because I had a really bad relationship with my dad. She just did everything. It was unbelievable."

Feldman drew on his mother's strength, watching her persevere as he helped her through her ailments—the kidney infections, the colostomy bags, her inability to eat sometimes due to the medication. Her disability became a fact of life, a tragic car accident that had left her paralyzed. Then, when Feldman turned fourteen, his mother finally told him the truth about what had happened by the cemetery that night, why she had nearly died—and his life changed forever. "I was like, 'Okay, I gotta do something,'" he says. "I saw all the ailments my mom went through. It was such a fucked-up way to live. I was going to try to find him."

All Feldman had to go on was the man's name. For the next twenty-six years, he searched for clues, asking around town, chasing down leads, trying to find his mother's abuser but never turning up a trace. Then, one night in 2006, after his own boxing career had fizzled and he was running a dive bar, a beautiful woman walked in and asked for a drink. "She was so attractive, I just started talking with her," he says, grinning. "All I knew was her first name, Chrissie." The two flirted for months, Chrissie becoming a regular, until one night he asked her last name—and his heart froze. "It was the attacker's last name," he says. "I asked if she knew him and she said, 'Yeah, he's my uncle. He lives around the corner.'" Feldman pauses. "He was only fifteen minutes from here."

Walking to the man's door, Feldman didn't have a firm plan—just a gun, a pair of pliers, and a lifetime of pain and anger building to this moment. "I didn't know what I was gonna do," he recalls. "But I had a vision." His mother, Dawn, had finally passed away just weeks before, and he thought of her as he knocked on the door. After a minute, it opened. An old man looked at him. "I said, 'I'm David Feldman,'" Feldman recalls. "And he looked like he saw a fucking ghost." Feldman leans forward. "'You know my mom, right? I know what happened. I know that you never got in trouble for what you did.' And he was like 'Uhhh, uhhh.' And right then I knew for sure it was him. I grabbed him, put him on the fucking ground, and just started choking his neck." Feldman lets out a breath. "And then I stopped and said, 'Look. I'm not gonna do this to you.' I had a gun on me but I'm glad I didn't do that, either. Instead, I took out the pliers, took his Achilles heel, and I fucking squeezed it and squeezed it and squeezed it until it popped. And then I just left—'Now you can't walk, motherfucker.'"

* * * * *

Around the time of his mother's death, Feldman began working as a fight promoter. Tired of running a nightclub and sports bar in Philly, he was trying to launch a new career staging pro boxing and MMA events but was having little luck. Then he had an idea. An old family friend, Len Hayko, had moved out to Scottsdale to open a line of tanning salons. On a whim, Feldman asked him to set up an interview with the local casino at the Yavapai Nation. To his shock, they said yes. A few days later, Feldman and Hayko—both wearing black pants and black T-shirts with the name of their would-be company, "Bad Boy Promotions," stenciled across the chest—entered the Fort McDowell casino management office. They were ushered into a private room and seated across a conference table from two young Yavapai women. One of them, Ernestine Boyd, was the assistant marketing director for the casino.* According to Hayko, she glanced up, looked them over, and asked one simple question: "What the fuck do you guys want?"

Feldman, jet-lagged and sweating in the desert heat, decided to try humor. "I said, 'My mother's full-blood Choctaw Indian.† Are our tribes cool?' And it was dead fucking silence. I thought, 'Oh shit.' They were not happy."

Defeated, Feldman and Hayko were getting up to leave when something unexpected happened. "They started laughing," Hayko recalls. "I mean, picture us. Here's two Philly guys walking in wearing matching outfits and saying they want to put on a fight. So Dave and I started laughing too. And then Ernestine said, word for word, 'I hate fucking boxing. All you boxing promoters are scumbags.' And I said, 'Well, here's the good news. I'm not a boxing promoter and neither is Dave. He's a fighter. We're just sorta trying to build a business out here. And she started laughing again. 'Ah,' she said. 'That's good.'"

Feldman and Hayko were in. They launched Bad Boy Promotions, staging a wild medley of boxing, MMA, and amateur "tough man" competitions at the casino. Hayko was the local contact and helped with financing while Feldman oversaw the logistics, flying in for events. From the beginning, trying to differentiate themselves from other promoters, they were willing to try anything—a tactic that quickly brought notoriety. Their "tough man" competitions were open-call brawls. Anyone off the street was allowed to sign on,

---

* A representative at the Fort McDowell Yavapai Nation said Boyd had worked at the casino but was no longer employed there. I asked for her contact information but was never given it.
† Feldman says his mother was, in fact, part Choctaw.

don gloves, and duke it out. "Applicants are poorly screened and the officiating isn't consistent," stated a local boxing newsletter in 2012. "The other concern is safety; Bad Boy boxing fans can get very rowdy after a few big gulps of beers."[4] But Feldman deemed any press good press, doubling down on radio promotions and outlandish stunts. And Hayko says Boyd's mother was vice president of the tribe, ensuring they could stage their shows without a problem. Somewhere along the line, everyone became friends, Hayko even once flying Boyd and some other tribal members out for two weeks to vacation at his beach house in Sea Isle, New Jersey. In fact, according to Hayko, it was Fort McDowell's idea to stage one of his and Feldman's most notorious events, a match billing itself as "Extreme Midget Wrestling," at the casino. On the night of the event, amid local protests, Feldman himself stepped into the ring when the appointed referee never arrived. "Dave was like, 'Fuck it, I'll do it,'" Hayko recalls. "He put on the ref shirt, and goddamn if he didn't pull it off." At one point, as part of the show, Feldman had to pretend to get clotheslined by a wrestler. "Dave fell down, smashed his arms on the mat, and it sounded like the whole ring was going to fall apart," Hayko says. "He pretended like he got knocked out cold. God, it was great. That's one thing about Dave—he's a worker."

For years, Feldman would continue to stage fights at the Fort McDowell Casino, the matches becoming more and more outrageous as his career grew. But even he would not be prepared for the blowback from his most daring stunt yet, which he would attempt soon after meeting Gunn: the revival of a sport not legally staged in the USA in over 120 years—bare-knuckle boxing.

"One day, Dave said, 'What do you think about doing a bare-knuckle fight?'" Hayko recalls. "I was like, 'I don't know . . .'"

But Feldman was adamant. "They were the kind of tribe we needed," he says. "The kind to say, 'Fuck you, we're doing what we want.'"

CHAPTER 19

FROM MEDIEVAL TIMES TO THE RUSSIAN MOB

After his win in Arizona, Gunn's comeback did not go as planned.

In February 2009, after defeating a couple more journey-men as well as Shelby Gross in a rematch for a minor USNBC title belt, Gunn fought Kansas cruiserweight Brad Gregory in the last place imaginable: a "Fight Knight" card at a Medieval Times restaurant in Lyndhurst, New Jersey. "The place smelled like horse shit," Gunn recalls. "My dressing room was in a stall."

Following his victory, standing in the ring, Gunn looked at the faux castle facade and decided his career needed a jolt. Since first meeting Feldman in Arizona, he had been working with the aspiring promoter, sometimes having him book his fights, sometimes booking his own fights and then letting Feldman take care of the details. But so far, Gunn was still a long way from contention, fighting no-name opponents in dingy settings ranging from an amateur baseball park by the airport in Atlantic City to this amusement park restaurant in Jersey. Now thirty-five, Gunn faced a stark truth: the Macca-rinelli defeat may have killed his prospects. If he was going to turn things around, he needed to do it himself, and he needed to do it now. He needed to find another blue-ribbon opponent, a legitimate contender, in order to win a top belt. And that's when he thought of Tomasz Adamek, the top cruiserweight boxer in the world.

In 2009, Adamek, a stone-faced 6'2", 200-pound slugger with a bulbous, oft-broken nose, was at the height of his fame. Born in the tiny mountain village of Gilowice, Poland, on the Slovakian border, he had fought for years in Warsaw before moving to the States in 2005, winning the World Boxing Council world title in his debut bout in Chicago. Now he was based in Newark, New Jersey, was ranked number one by *Ring* magazine and ESPN, and had a starring role in an X-Box video game. All of which prompted the question—Why would he ever deign to fight Gunn, an over-the-hill boxer whose most recent match had been at a Medieval Times?

The answer, of course, was hustle. Gunn, like most journeymen, was long used to booking his own fights, calling promoters and making his case in those few seconds before they could slam down the phone. He had to keep in shape at all times, in case a marquee star dropped out of a title fight and they needed a last-minute replacement, as had happened with Gunn against Maccarinelli in Wales. And sometimes, when he truly needed a miracle, he had to go straight to the champions themselves.

Based just down the road in Newark, Adamek, the reigning cruiserweight, was about to fight in a title bout in front of six thousand people at the gleaming new Prudential Center. Gunn bought a ticket and, taking a chance, walked right up to the sweating champ after his victory, breaking through security and challenging him on the spot. "You've been in three really hard fights," Gunn said. "You need something easier. I'll bring the Irish, you bring the Polish, and we'll sell this place out." There was a tense moment, bodyguards and entourage eyeing Gunn.

Then Adamek grinned. "I've heard of you," he said in broken English. "You have good record. Can you meet tomorrow?"

It would take a month before Gunn would get his wish, but finally, after constantly working the phone, going through layers of handlers, he was called in to meet Adamek and his management team at an office near the Willowbrook Mall in Wayne, New Jersey. According to Mike Normile, who accompanied Gunn, Adamek's team didn't want him to take the fight. But the stone-faced champ liked Gunn's moxie and knew that his courage would resonate with Adamek's Polish fans. "This is my business, my choice," Adamek recalls about deciding to fight Gunn. "If you start listening to people around you, then you can't be great. Polish hate when you have weak heart and show blood." He sighs. "Boxing is a tough business. Most fighters who get to big fights and big money bow in the locker room. But Bobby Gunn has a big heart. He told me he love Jesus Christ and he lose a couple fights but he still was strong. He said, 'Tomasz, mentally I'm not done yet. I can bang.'" Adamek grins. "He showed heart. I respected him—Bobby is a warrior."

After the meeting, Gunn, elated, hustled to prepare, training every spare minute for his last big shot in the ring. He hit the gym at dawn, spent his days laying asphalt and tarring roofs and banging nails, and then wore himself out with pushups at night. As always, he took on a couple of bare-knuckle bouts to cover expenses, bruising his hands and then still lacing up the sparring gloves the next morning. At times, despite his drive, the pressure sometimes got to Gunn. The press, calling him a long shot in a trumped-up fight, sank him into funks, into the bad old days of those lonely campground years. But he never let it break him. "In boxing, things can change on the turn of a dime," he said in an interview. "All it takes is one punch—and I am going to throw that punch."[1]

On July 11, 2009, Gunn drove his work truck straight from a construction site to the Prudential Center. Passing Adamek's stretch limo, Gunn parked, wriggled out of his work clothes and into his trunks, and then entered the arena.[2] He had Feldman as his manager, a cornerman of sorts, but that was it. "Smelling like an old dog, I get on the scale," he says. "Not ripped, but in good shape. Adamek's handler is reading contracts, signing things. They're checking the gloves, and paint is coming off my hands. The guy looks at me like 'Where is this paint coming from?' Where is my team?" Gunn pauses. "No team."

In front of six thousand screaming Adamek fans, the stands a sea of red-and-white Polish national flags, the audience chanting "Polska! Polska!" with every punch, Gunn stood alone against the world's top boxer.[3] Planning to tire out the hulking champ, to go the distance and then try for a knockout punch in a later round, Gunn exploded with energy, moving around the ring, dancing, ducking, swinging. But from the beginning, he was clearly outmatched. Methodical, relentless, a towering machine of pale-skinned precision, Adamek picked Gunn apart with devastating jabs. By the fourth round, in trouble, Gunn went for broke, leaning his head forward in an audacious bloody-grinned display, offering a clean shot. Adamek obliged, his punch missing Gunn, who ducked and then went for the kill, a wild haymaker that glanced off the defending champ. Within seconds, Adamek unleashed a powerful overhand in return, buckling Gunn's knees, and pinned him against a corner post, pummeling him with punches, eventually ending the round with seventeen unanswered shots.[4] The ref called the match. Gunn had lost.

[Figure 19.1] Fighting Adamek in 2009 (Photo reprinted by permission from Ed Mullholland)

Soon thereafter, Gunn sat in a bar, nursing a Coke, alongside some Travelers and his father, discussing the fight. According to Mike Normile, who was there, Gunn turned to his father, who had not been able to make the match, and asked, "So, what did you think, Dad?" Robert hesitated a moment and then said, "I think you could have done better. I think you could have won."

"Then Bob looked at me," Normile recalls. "And I just said, 'I think you done great.'"

Normile pauses. "It hurt him," he says. "I could tell."

In the years during his comeback, Gunn had pulled off an astounding feat, winning a legitimate title belt and squaring off against some of the best boxers in the world—but he still hadn't earned the respect of his father. "He was supporting me, but he was never happy," Gunn says. "And even today, if you ask him, he'll say, 'Yeah, he was cruiserweight champion and fought the best, but that wasn't my boy in there fighting those guys. The [younger] Bobby that would've kept fighting would've been like Joe Calzaghe, a super middleweight undefeated king.'" When it came to his son, Robert could never get over the boxing career that should have been, the one that was cut short by the death of his wife and all those years squandered in the underground—a sense of failure that still haunts Gunn today. "I was like, 'Dad, I was a champion,'" Gunn says. "'And he'll say, 'Yeah, but you could have been super middleweight world champion.'"

Gunn shakes his head. "You understand how his mind-set is? It bothers me. But that's his point of view. And the truth is, he's right. I mean, I could get mad about it. 'Dad, I was champ.' But he's right. I gotta call an ace an ace—I am half the man that I was."

Gunn would go on to lose every single one of his few remaining boxing matches, his heart no longer in the sport. "Nobody even talks about my boxing career no more," he says. "But that's what makes me better in bare knuckle. I'm not a barroom brawler—I'm an athlete."

* * * * *

His pro boxing dream dead, Gunn now turned full-time to the one world he had always been able to dominate: the underground. "New York is the capital of the fight world, my hometown, my heart," he says. "For twelve years, I ruled the underground. Warehouses, under subways, empty parking lots, basements, boxing gyms, docks, mansions—I beat everybody they brung in front of me."

Now thirty-six, Gunn entered the underground arena with a growing list of injuries and a new reason to fight: the birth of his baby daughter, Charlene. For years, he and his wife had been trying for another child, when suddenly, twelve years after Bobby Jr.'s birth, Rose became pregnant again. If Gunn, dwelling on the stillbirth of his infant sister, had been nervous about the birth of his son, he became positively obsessed about Charlene, constantly worrying about the health of his coming child and his pregnant wife, now thirty-four. "I was worried because Rose was older," Gunn says. "So I made sure she ate good and exercised."

In the end, his concerns proved unfounded. On October 10, 2009, Charlene Gunn was born without a hitch, in a New Jersey hospital. Standing by his wife, Gunn watched his daughter come into the world and immediately asked the nurse if he could cradle her in his arms. "I was the first one to hold baby Charlene," he recalls. "The nurse gave her to me and I went back and helped bathe her. She was completely different from her brother. She was screaming and squealing. I just remember holding her in my arms, feeling thankful." Gunn smiles. "Charlene runs my life— my baby is my boss."

In 2010, just months after the birth of his daughter, Gunn—more famous than ever in the wake of his pro boxing resurgence—now began approaching his big-money bare-knuckle fights like a pro. "I took my experience from pro boxing and mixed it with the art of bare knuckle, becoming a master," Gunn says. "I was good with my hands, and it was all about the money." For months, he rolled through his opponents, toppling fighters for $10,000 a match under needle-strewn overpasses in the Bronx, in warehouses in Maryland, and on the docks of Newark. At all these fights, he wore his trademark black muscle shirt, blue jeans, and black boots, the better to fade into the crowd if the cops arrived. He made sure no one in his party brought a gun. "We always had a plan," says fellow Traveler Ed Simpson, who often accompanied Gunn to bouts. "No one wants to go to prison." And he always gave a cut to the house, the better to maintain goodwill and keep his name in the game for the next match. "If I win twenty-five thousand," Gunn says, "I may go home with just fifteen. I pay five grand to the guy putting it together and then five grand to my team for going with me. I gotta take care of my people."

[Figure 19.2] After a bare-knuckle fight
(Photo courtesy of Bobby Gunn)

But despite all Gunn's planning, in the end, sometimes things just went to hell. "These guys are scary," Paul Tyler says about organized-crime members. "I remember looking in one guy's eyes and I could just tell he had killed someone. Like, he had a dark soul. He was a total gentleman, a nice guy, but I don't think he would have had any issue putting a bullet in me for thirty grand."

Once, after defeating his opponent in a match organized by the Latin Kings in the Bronx, Gunn was sitting in his truck alongside Bobby Jr. and a couple of other Travelers when a gang member approached, pulling a gun and trying to rob them. Without blinking, Gunn immediately shifted into drive and slammed the gas. "We left at a hundred miles per hour," Ed Simpson recalls. "Guy might've shot, but I wasn't looking."

Gunn shrugs. "Bobby's had guns pulled on him, but he don't get rattled," he says about his son. "He's not the average man."

Gunn's luck would soon turn south again. In early 2011, he received a challenge to fight a brawler backed by the Irish mob for $50,000 in a warehouse in a major northeast city. This was a faction Gunn did not know, so he vetted them by consulting his contacts in the New York underworld, as well as a Traveler in Ireland. "The guys who were putting on the fight go to Ireland a lot—the IRA, the mob," Gunn explains. "So my man says, 'I know them, Bob.'" Satisfied, Gunn agreed to the match but had difficulty raising the stake money until a lawyer, Jim

Westin, an attorney in Upstate New York, volunteered to back him.* A divorce, construction, and criminal-defense lawyer who loves the fight game, Westin first met Gunn after doing legal work for a mutual friend. Soon, he became friends with Gunn as well, driving to meet him in Chili's parking lots to handle boxing contracts, speeding tickets, or anything else involving the law. Tanned and muscled with a perpetual five o' clock shadow, Westin favors boxy suits, Prada sunglasses, and gold belt buckles. Regarding the Irish mob fight, he told Gunn he didn't expect any profit on his investment; he just wanted to see his friend come back alive. So just this once, he would accompany him to the underground match—but would not leave his car. "Now, that was quite a thing, because a criminal attorney don't want to do that shit," Gunn says. "But this is Jim—fucking game, man."

The fight itself was over in seconds. Walking right up to his opponent, a 6'1", 180-pound brawler, Gunn unleashed a vicious left hook to the chin, immediately knocking him unconscious. "When that kind of money is on the line," Gunn says, "you're getting a whole different Bobby Gunn." Stunned, the man's five Irish-mob backers—"two-bit bums with black leather jackets and Vaseline hair"—tried to rouse him and then, exasperated, pulled guns. Accompanied solely by David Feldman and another Traveler bare-knuckle fighter from Ireland, Gunn was outmatched. "Dave tried to stop them and they grabbed him by the shirt and split his head wide open with the butt of a pistol," Gunn recalls. "I says, 'We're fucked.'" When asked about the incident, Feldman shrugs. "I was scared to death," he recalls.

Gunn and his crew faced five loaded guns. Over $50,000 was in a duffel bag on the floor. Their chances of survival were slim.

Then the cavalry arrived.

---

* This is not his real name.

"Out of nowhere, Jim walks in with his hands in his fucking sports jacket, looking like he's going to shoot," Gunn says. "He's so nervous all he can do is yell, '*You ffffuuuucks!*'"

Westin, sensing something was wrong, had left the car and wandered in through the warehouse door. Coming upon the standoff with no weapon, he did the next best thing: pointing his fingers, sticking them inside the pockets of his jacket and bluffing the gangsters. Shocked by the hyperventilating lawyer in a suit— "They were shook up because he was so shook up," Gunn says, laughing—the mobsters momentarily let their guard down, and Gunn and his team pounced. Feldman bloodied the man who had split his head, the other Traveler grabbed the money, and all four men raced to their car and sped away. "Jim was shaking so bad," Gunn says. "He said, 'Look what you made me do, you fuck! I could have died there!' And then he just looked at me. 'I love you!'"

Afterward, Gunn slept a few hours in a motel. The next morning, he drove to Fords Jewelers in Fords, New Jersey, bought his son a $6,000 silver Breitling diver's watch, and went home. "I gives Bobby the watch and then takes them all to the movies at the mall," Gunn says. "I told you, I just want away from it—I want a normal life."

In the following days, Gunn would call his contacts in the Irish mob in New York, explain the attempted robbery, and leave it to them to sort it out. "They said, 'We'll take care of this,'" Gunn says. "I never heard no more about it."

And he didn't want to hear anything more. He may have fought in the underground, may have won dozens of victories without a single loss, but he always made sure to keep his distance. He never counted the money, never asked names, and never overstayed his welcome. Gunn never wanted to get too close. "I never really seen the guys that put it together too much," he says. "It's a world that's run by the mob. I don't know who's putting it on and I don't want to know, because I don't want to get too involved. Remember, the

Bobby Gunn you see today who goes home to his wee wife, that's the Bobby Gunn I am. I don't want that world infected by this world. So I don't get too deep. My grandfather always said to me, 'When you go home, leave the bums at the gym.'"

Gunn went back to work, storing the duffel-bag money for rent, truck payments, and Charlene's school, praying his worst days were behind him. But just months later, he would endure the most dangerous fight of his career, the one night that still haunts him, the match that ultimately forced him to leave the underground—his fight for the Russian mob.

In spring 2011, Gunn arrived at Ike's to find a phone number waiting for him. Returning the call on the gym's ancient landline phone, he spoke to a man with a mysterious accent. "'We got guy we would like to fight you; we pay you very financial good,'" Gunn recalls the man saying in broken English. "I think it's a joke, a weirdo." Nevertheless, Gunn agreed to a meeting at a nearby Starbucks on Route 17, where he was surprised to find "two well-dressed, lovely gentlemen" who made him an offer he could not refuse: another big-money fight, winner take all. "They said they were bringing this guy over from Russia," Gunn says. "Fair enough, no problem. Let's rock 'n' roll."

Gunn knew that the fight was a risk. Even for the underground, the Russians stand out for their brutality. "Those people are hard-core," Tyler says. "They love combat, they love violence, and they're so tough, man. Their whole face will be filled with blood and they keep getting up."

Gunn was more concerned about their reputation outside the ring. "I hear they put guys in fifty-five-gallon barrel drums of acid," he says. "Turn you to syrup and then throw you in a sewer drain. No DNA, no proof." He pauses. "I mean, a lot of their own soldiers have no fingers because they disobeyed something—and that's their *own* guys."

From the beginning, the fight went nothing like Gunn had expected. He arrived late at night to a McMansion in the outer reaches of Brooklyn, with a couple of Travelers and Danny Provenzano, a sometimes bare-knuckle promoter and felon who had served time on a ten-year sentence, handed down in 2003, for racketeering and failure to pay taxes. Upon arriving, Gunn entered a large foyer to find an elegant party under way—men and women in evening wear, live music, and a giant Russian man standing in the corner, waiting to fight him. "A hundred of these guys in suits, and really weird Russian music playing," Gunn says. "And this big hairy bastard, who's six feet, five inches and just wearing shorts. He looked like a water buffalo."

The crowd formed a circle, and the fight began. Gunn would later learn that his opponent was a master of sambo, a Russian mixed-martial-arts form created in part by a trainer for the Red army in the early 1900s, and was expected to dominate the match. But, constrained by the rules of bare knuckle, the Russian grew increasingly frustrated.

"If he'd been able to slam me, he probably would've destroyed me," Gunn says. "And that's what he was wanting to do. But you take a guy out of his element and he don't know how to handle bare knuckle. He took awful shots, *whack, whack,* blood pouring out of him. As big as he was, he had no power." Over the next ten minutes, Gunn knocked his opponent to the ground five or six times, but the crowd would not let him quit. "They started screaming at him, kicking him to get up," Gunn says. "They couldn't accept it."

As the fight began to drag on, Gunn's crew became increasingly worried. "It was serious," says Provenzano, a lanky man with wavy hair, sleepy eyes, and a thick "*Joy-zee*" accent. "Bobby kept knocking him out and these fucking kids would come and lift him back up. We were like, 'Come on, the fight's over.' But this was their territory—and there was a lot more of them than there were of us."

Finally, Gunn knocked his opponent unconscious—and all hell broke loose. "They'd put a lot of money on this guy," Gunn says. One of the younger Russians pulled a gun on the fallen fighter and then turned it on Gunn. "This kid puts a big chrome thousand-dollar gun to my head," Gunn says. "He was going to shoot me. Speaking his language, shaking that thing. The hatred boiled out of him, and that's what makes you nervous, when someone is like that. 'Oh, my God, this is a fool here. Please, God, get me out of here.'" Not carrying any weapons, Gunn's crew stood still, knowing they had nowhere to go.

"It was scary," recalls Traveler Mike Normile, who was there. "I thought we was going to get shot up—I thought we was dead."

Trying to remain calm, Gunn slowly put up his hands. "All I could think about was the last thing my wife and my little girl said to me that morning," he says. "I never felt anything like that in my life. The blood rushing through my body, a gun to my head. I just said, 'Please don't.'"

In that tense, quiet standoff, Gunn made a decision. If he lay down, the Russians would take it as a sign of weakness, robbing him of his money. If he tried to take the gun, they would shoot him. But if he found a way somehow to go over the head of the wild-eyed young man in front of him, to appeal to the head of the Russian organization in a firm but respectful way, then he and his entourage might all walk out with their money in hand. "You can't show any weakness," Gunn says. "You gotta go out and get it like a lion."

Spotting an old man in the corner, Gunn called out to him. "I began talking real loud, 'Sir, this is not right; this is wrong,'" Gunn says. "And the old man was listening." Luckily, Gunn was backed by Provenzano. Provenzano, forty-eight, had orchestrated bare-knuckle fights for years as a younger man, and his reputation in the underground and his reputed family connections to organized crime helped influence the Russians.

"It was too much money to leave behind," Provenzano says. "So we talked it out. I can only imagine if my pedigree wasn't my pedigree. But we settled it." Finally, after a tense standoff, Gunn and his crew were saved.

"The old man didn't even get up from his seat," Gunn says. "Calm, cool, and collected, he said first in Russian and then English, 'Pay that boy his money. He's a good man.' So the kid put the gun down, they handed me a paper bag of money, and I walked out the door."

His payday: $50,000.

CHAPTER 20

FLYING LITTLE PEOPLE, YAVAPAI WARRIORS, AND THE RETURN OF AMERICA'S FIRST SPORT

In June 2011, David Feldman finally had the idea of a lifetime. Gunn may not have been a world champion in boxing, but he did have something no one else could claim: the best record in the underground. "Love it or hate it, bare knuckle always gets people excited," Feldman says. "I knew this could be my way out."

For his entire life, Feldman had been hustling, promoting every kind of fight sport imaginable, in every kind of low-tier casino across the country, and had almost nothing to show for it. But this was different. This was a chance to create his own sport, to legitimize bare knuckle, to follow in the footsteps of his hero, Dana White, the visionary who had helped transform the UFC from an outlaw competition into a $12 billion global phenomenon. This was a chance to create an empire. And he already had a built-in star.

But first, he had to persuade Gunn to do it.

"I was nervous," Gunn recalls about first hearing the idea of bare-knuckle fighting in a public setting. "I didn't think this was something we needed to bring attention to."

Feldman knew otherwise. "I love Bobby, but he doesn't understand business," he says. "He's always thinking about how to make five grand tonight. But I'm working on how to make five million next year."

He grins.

"I knew this could be my last hustle."

* * * * *

The crazy thing is, Feldman has a shot.

Founded in smoky gambling dens during the nineteenth century and never truly organized at the national level, pro boxing remains the only major sport in the United States without a central governing body. It has no equivalent of a modern-day NFL, NBA, or MLB. Instead, the multibillion-dollar sport, along with all other fight disciplines, is governed by a collection of sanctioning bodies that have arisen over the years—each issuing its own championship belts—which are overseen by independent state athletic commissions. These state commissions can choose to align with the national Association of Boxing Commissions, the closest equivalent to a central governing body, but it is a voluntary decision, meaning that the fight world is ruled almost entirely at the state level.

In fact, only in recent decades has there been any kind of national oversight, after the Professional Boxing Safety Act of 1996 and the Muhammad Ali Boxing Reform Act of 2000 brought some measure of protection to fighters' health—but still no safeguards for their fair pay. All of which, according to Feldman, boils down to one fundamental truth: "This is the biggest scumbag business in the world," he says. "Every day it's a fight."

Even Greg Sirb, the stoic Pennsylvania state athletic commissioner, agrees: "It's a billion-dollar industry run like a five-and-dime store."

Fighting's lack of oversight has had an upside, however. It has created one of the greatest opportunities in pro sports: a lawless landscape with no central governing body, in which new leagues can arise. It made possible the wildest, most improbable success story in athletic history—the UFC. And Feldman is convinced that the fight world's anarchic nature will also propel bare knuckle to legitimacy and glory.

After all, far more improbable fight sports have come before. In the combat world, new competitions crop up every few years, typically in poorer states with less to lose. The UFC, for example, held some of its first events in Oklahoma, Wyoming, and Alabama. And in 2015, South Carolina sanctioned something called arena combat, a sport that debuted as a Russian game show in which two-man MMA teams run, jump, and fight each other on a padded obstacle course, in what looks like a group brawl at a gymnastics center. Imported by former MMA fighter Casey Oxendine, the sport had been shopped around to different state commissions until South Carolina finally bit. (By contrast, Andy Foster of the California State Athletic Commission had said, "We're saying no, and there's a period behind the no.")[1]

For a new fight sport, the trick is not in getting approval from federal lawmakers. The trick is to find a state athletic commission that is willing to take a chance on being the first taxpayer-funded entity to approve your creation and that will stand alongside you through bad press, irate governors, political pressure from the national commission, and the threat of lawsuits if someone gets injured in your premier event. And even then there are no guarantees. After two sanctioned matches in Myrtle Beach, arena combat failed to gain national momentum—and promptly vanished back to Siberia. "It's hard," says Art Davie, the founder of UFC. "Everybody says you're crazy."

But Feldman had a plan. Even though bare knuckle was bloody, it proved to be safer than boxing or MMA. Even though it had a reputation for attracting undisciplined barroom brawlers, it often featured pro fighters, many of whom were aged out of other fight sports but could still handle the quick gloveless rounds. And perhaps most importantly, bare knuckle had an outlaw reputation, an illegal blood-soaked mystique that tied into US history—and also just might cut through to jaded Millennials in search of the next extreme sport. "If Dave Feldman stays in it for the long haul, he could make a billion bucks," says Davie. "Now audiences are used to more violence, so he needs to push the brutality of it. He needs to get the eighteen-year-olds to look up from their phones and say, 'Hey, that's cool.' In the end, the business of promoting is really the business of creating a brand—he needs to find a hero."

In June 2011, Feldman had his hero, but convincing him to fight was another matter. In the two years since his crushing loss to Tomasz Adamek, Gunn had been supporting his family with asphalt work and the underground, and he was worried the Arizona match might bring unwanted attention, disrupting his underground income. But more crucially, Gunn had simply lost his drive. His boxing comeback had been a heroic attempt—the middle-aged journeyman rising from high school gyms to state fairgrounds to world-class arenas—but now it was over. Gunn would never be a world-champion boxer. So he had done the same thing he did nearly twenty years before, hanging up his gloves and returning full-time to the one home he had always known: the underground.

"Because of the way that Adamek fight ended, he just wanted to get back into bare knuckle," says Joe "Mack" McEwen, Gunn's former promoter. "He decided to stop cutting weight and just fight at his natural weight, a heavyweight." Now, muscled and relaxed, out of the harsh spotlight and making top money on the bare-knuckle circuit, Gunn could easily have said no to Arizona. But there was still one reason for saying yes: the lure of becoming a top-tier world champion in at least one fight sport.

"I would be recognized as the bare-knuckle world heavyweight champion," Gunn says. "Bare knuckle was in my family blood, and Dave seen an opportunity."

Since their first meeting, Gunn and Feldman had become close, though combative, friends. Feldman had promoted several of Gunn's pro boxing matches—even working his corner for the Adamek bout—while the Traveler champion had continued to educate his "country-person" friend on the underground, taking Feldman to bare-knuckle fights throughout the Northeast.

[Figure 20.1] Close, though combative, friends (Photo courtesy of Bobby Gunn)

They were a funny pair, the sardonic, cynical promoter and his Christ-loving fighter. For weeks, Feldman would go dark, failing to return calls, only to resurface full of sarcasm and jibes, teasing Gunn, sometimes pushing things too far. Once, while in the midst of a divorce, Feldman began cursing Gunn on the lawn of his house in Philadelphia, eventually throwing a jab at the bare-knuckle champ, who retaliated with a hard body shot, crumpling the promoter to the ground. Another time, while the two men were sharing a hotel room for a meeting with promoters in Scotland, Feldman kept ribbing Gunn at 4:00 a.m. for no apparent reason until the fighter finally lost it, splitting his friend's nose. "That's Dave; that's his personality," Gunn says, shrugging. "I can't figure him out."

But Gunn does know one thing: Feldman is there when it matters. The two men come from similar backgrounds, have similar complicated relationships with their fathers, and often confide in each other, sometimes crying and opening up before going back to their usual sparring. "My old man was crazy and rough and his was hard and cold," Gunn says. "I've always known Dave was a top man." After the Adamek match, Feldman didn't pay Gunn his share, $30,000, for almost a week, brushing him off. But then, just when Gunn was about to hunt him down, Feldman showed up with the entire amount, refusing to take even his own 10 percent cut of the deal. "He just wanted to see if I'd flip out," Gunn says. "Sure, Dave has attitude, and I've had to rough him up a little bit. But I've always been sure he's with me all the way."

For his part, Feldman will tell you Gunn can be an endless nag, pestering him daily about getting pro boxing matches, and then, when he *does* get them, showing up with a horde of Travelers, many of whom try to sneak in for free. "Scumbags," Feldman snorts. Yet, when pushed, he will shrug and admit, "Yeah, Bobby's like a brother to me. He'll tell me to go fuck myself, I'll tell him to go fuck himself, and then we'll be pals. It's one of them things." There's just one catch, one hard line that will always divide them. "Bobby doesn't understand business at all," Feldman says. "He gets impatient. I have to remind him of the UFC, that they took years to get started the right way, that if we just make ten percent of that, we're a home run, so we need to start acting like that. But he just ain't never gonna get it, and that's okay. But he has to let me do my job."

In 2011, even before approaching Gunn, Feldman first had to find a venue, and he knew of only one place bold enough to back him: the Yavapai Nation. In 2008, the tribe had been impressed with Gunn for bringing in hordes of Travelers for his boxing match, and they immediately asked about his return. "After that first fight, the Indians were like, 'When's Bobby Gunn coming back? When's Bobby Gunn coming back?'" Feldman recalls. "It was a good night for them in the casino, and that's how I got them to discuss bare knuckle."

If any casino was game enough for gloveless combat, it was the Yavapai at Fort McDowell—a gutsy, independent tribe with a long history of fighting authority. As a people, the Yavapai Nation has a motto: "Never give up. Always give back." But it may as well be "Don't fuck with us." Although relatively small, not even cracking the fifty largest reservations in the country, the Yavapai have been one of the fiercest tribes in Native Americans' latest battle with the federal government: the struggle over casinos.

Once numbering about six thousand members spread across ten million acres in central Arizona, the Yavapai were rounded up by US troops in the 1870s and relocated to an Apache reservation, many dying along the way, before settling in their present location, a former military installation in the Sonoran desert.[2] For decades, the tribe ran a small bingo parlor and casino amid the saguaro cacti and cottonwoods, never making a stir, until one morning in 1992, when Linda A. Akers, a United States attorney appointed by President George H. W. Bush, launched a state-wide raid against Native American casinos in a dispute over video gambling machines.

At issue was a new federal law stating that Indian reservations could offer video gambling only if the machines were sanctioned or already allowed in the states surrounding their land. In Arizona, then-governor Fife Symington had banned the machines from casinos. But the Yavapai, not caring a whit for Symington's blessing, had installed them anyway, soon making about 70 percent of their casino income from them—prompting Arizona and the feds to retaliate.[3]

At dawn on May 12, 1992, FBI agents stormed the Yavapai casino, seizing 349 video gambling machines and loading them into trucks for removal. In response, tribal members rallied to block the roads with pickup trucks, vans, and front-end loaders. The standoff sparked a headline-grabbing week of powwows and protests that reenergized the national Native American movement for sovereignty. "They will not do this to us," a tribal elder told the *New York Times*. "This time, they will not get away with it."[4] After a tense three weeks, Symington relented, ending the standoff, and ultimately signed a bill changing the laws on gambling in Arizona, allowing the Yavapai to keep their machines. The Yavapai—the only tribe to make a stand like this against the government on this issue—had won. To this day, they still celebrate the protest anniversary as a national holiday.[5]

In 2011, knowing the Yavapai's appetite for risk, Feldman asked his business partner, Len Hayko, to meet with the tribe in person about staging Bad Boy's most audacious event yet: the first legal bare-knuckle fight in the United States in over 120 years. It would be the grand finale to a "Bad Boy Fight Night" of boxing and MMA bouts, the headlining bare-knuckle brawl hopefully launching a new sport and freeing Feldman from his bottom-rung roadhouse matches and Extreme Midget Wrestling events. It was a huge risk, in total contravention of all US boxing laws. Despite the tribe's outlaw bent, Feldman was sure they would refuse. Still, he and Hayko figured it couldn't hurt to ask. Arranging a meeting, Hayko went in expecting a quick dismissal—and instead encountered the shock of his life. He recalls his words to the Yavapai tribal commission. "I was like, 'Yeah, we want to do a bare-knuckle fight.' And they just said, 'Aw, that's awesome.' And that was it. Nothing about regulations. Nothing." He laughs. "So we started promoting it."

Scarcely believing his luck, Feldman scrambled to find fighters. He eventually came across Richard Stewart, a bald, flat-nosed 5'7" cruiserweight with a 14-9-2 record, from Wilmington, Delaware.

Stewart, thirty-five, was a bricklayer by trade, who had lost his last five pro boxing matches—getting knocked out in the final three—and was barred from entering the ring again due to concerns over his health. "When a fighter's knocked out successively like that, there's a good sign there are problems," said Stewart's manager, Keith Stouffer, in 2011. "I wanted nothing to do with this [bare-knuckle fight in Arizona]. It's dangerous, too dangerous."[6]

But Stewart, who has his own reputation in the underground, knew that the fight would actually be safer since he wasn't wearing gloves. More importantly, he wasn't about to turn down a paycheck. "Fighting ain't for the rich," he says. "This is a poor man's thing, bro. A lot of working-class guys just trying to pay their bills." He sighs. "I was actually on Rehoboth Beach on vacation when I got that call. That was a last-minute fight. But in bare knuckle, that's the way it is. Money talks."

Stewart may not have been in top shape, but everyone in the boxing world knew he could still throw—and, in bare knuckle, all it takes is one punch. "He's a tough bastard," Gunn says. "A rough fighter."

Finally, with everything set except for his marquee star, Feldman turned to Gunn. Gunn's one goal had been to become a world champion in boxing, not bare knuckle. In fact, he had spent his entire career trying to escape the underground, even barring his son from entering it. And now he was being asked to glorify it, maybe even risking jail time in the process, when everyone knew he was the champion of the underground anyway. Gunn was unsure what to do, when he says he got a surprise call: Bert Sugar, the seventy-five-year-old, cigar-chomping, fedora-wearing founder of the *Ring* magazine belt—boxing's top prize and the very title Gunn had failed to wrest from Adamek—had heard about the potential fight and wanted to talk.

"He said, 'If this fight is certified, you will be the first recognized bare-knuckle champion in a hundred and twenty-two years,'" Gunn recalls. "I told him, 'I already thought I was the bare-knuckle champ.' And he said, 'No, if you get this, then it's your stamp of legitimacy.'" For Gunn, this was the motivation he needed—a chance to become a true world champion. He agreed to take the fight.

On a sweltering hundred-degree night in August 2011, Gunn took on Stewart at the Yavapai Nation reservation in the first sanctioned bare-knuckle boxing match since 1889—a historic event that remained under siege until the final moment. Having caught wind of the outlaw match, the Association of Boxing Commissions, the Arizona Attorney General's Office, and, according to Gunn's camp, even Arizona Senator John McCain—an avid traditionalist boxing fan who once called MMA "human cockfighting"—all tried to shut it down.

"The casino had flooded the airwaves with TV commercials," recalls Hayko. "'Bare-knuckle boxing coming to Fort McDowell!' Well, as soon as that went out, the boxing commission started calling, saying it was a nonsanctioned event. And the tribe's response was, 'We can do what we want. This is our land. Fort McDowell casino is sanctioning it.'" Hayko pauses. "And, I mean, that's the law—it's a sovereign nation."

Unable to gain traction, state authorities apparently decided to try a final desperate tact. In the hours before the fight, George Kokkalenios, a lawyer who sometimes works for Gunn, says he was lying on his bed in the casino hotel room when the phone rang. It was McCain. "John McCain, God bless him, he's a war hero or whatever, but he called the hotel room, trying to shut it down," Kokkalenios recalls. "He said, 'Give me someone higher up.' I said, 'I don't think there is anyone higher up!'"

Even Gunn says he briefly spoke with him. "I was on the phone with him for two seconds," Gunn recalls. "He said, 'What I think you're doing is horrendous.' So I said, 'Not to be disrespectful, but I don't really have time for this.' And I hung up." (McCain's representatives did not respond to requests for comment.)

With pressure mounting, Gunn began having second thoughts. "People was going nuts," he recalls. "It was in the newspaper and ESPN, and things were getting blown out of proportion. I was getting nervous really bad." At 5:00 p.m., sitting in his hotel room in the final hours before the fight, Gunn says he received one last call, this time from an anonymous person threatening him with jail time if he went through with the fight. "They told me that when I left the casino property, I would get arrested by the local police," Gunn recalls. "I thought about it and then just said, 'Fuck it.'"

Gunn had made up his mind. He had come this far and was not backing down—and neither were the Yavapai. "That reservation would have went to war," Hayko says. "The state was never shutting that down." Having essentially told the government to go to hell, Gunn and the tribal elders finally made their way to the fight venue, a makeshift arena in a baking-hot parking lot—where, incredibly, over five thousand people had gathered to watch the event.

"It was a big deal," Stewart recalls. "The place inside couldn't hold the people, so they did it in the parking lot." Neither the Yavapai nor anyone else had ever witnessed an event like this. Even ESPN was touting the match as "reviving a bygone, bare-knuckle era."[7] Available for $10 as an online pay-per-view, the event had been billed as a blood-soaked illegal brawl, its two referees there to ensure, according to one commentator, "the blood doesn't get too out of control."[8]

Yet despite the hype, the fight was a mild affair. Feldman, shocked to get approval from the tribe and worried they might change their minds, had rushed to put the whole thing together in just weeks. Sponsored by a nearby beer-and-wings hangout called McDuffy's Sports Grill, the show had cheesy lighting, bad music, and a ringside staff made up largely of Feldman's friends and family. Wearing a red polo shirt and black pants, Feldman himself announced the fight from the center of the ring. Shannon Ritch, the local bare-knuckle fighter, donned a headset and did the pay-per-view commentary alongside Feldman's nineteen-year-old son, Dave Jr., a college freshman. "The person we had couldn't make it, so I stepped in," Dave Jr. says. "I was announcing local high school football games at the time."

Even the fight itself, billed as a dangerous outlaw showdown, was a disappointment. Toeing a tricky line, Feldman was trying to provide an extreme event while also making sure no one got seriously hurt, which could have caused a public backlash and killed his sport outright. So, to be safe, he limited the rounds to ninety seconds each, giving the fighters a minute break in between, and hired two referees to oversee the match simultaneously.

From the start, Gunn, an underground fighter long accustomed to no rules or time limits, was off. Wearing black trunks emblazoned with a Star of David and the words "Give God the Glory," he circled the ring, waiting, watching. Stewart, visibly out of shape, feinted and weaved but punched little. "I'd never been on that side of the Mississippi," he recalls. "It was like an oven." The slow action drew boos from the crowd, who quickly diagnosed the whole affair as a sanitized version of what everyone had really come to see—a bare-knuckle street fight.

"It's not the big bloodbath everybody thought it was going to be," Ritch lamented from the commentator's booth.[9]

For the first two rounds, Gunn trudged through, seemingly out of his comfort zone, until the bell for the third round rung— and he suddenly came alive. Having at last taken the measure of his opponent, Gunn, now in rhythm, exploded, flooring Stewart with a combo to the body and a tap on the chin. Fully laid out, Stewart tried to stand, fell, and then rose again, wobbling, a nasty cut beginning to bleed under his left eye. Without hesitation, Gunn strode to his staggering opponent, almost gently pushed his hands from his face as if he were brushing back a lock of hair, and unleashed a devastating haymaker directly to the cut eye, flooring Stewart as Feldman waved his arms, calling the match.

"And this fight is over!" Feldman Jr. screamed as a remix of Black Sabbath's "Ironman" blared from the overhead speakers. "Bobby Gunn, an overhand right! . . . There's history, ladies and gentlemen!"[10]

Gunn and Feldman had expected only fifty thousand to live-stream the online event, bringing in about $500,000. Instead, more than a million tried to watch, crashing the fight's payment system and, with it, any chance for a long-awaited payday. "We made very little," Feldman will simply say now, still upset about the mishap.

Still, it was all the evidence they needed that bare-knuckle fighting was ready for the mainstream. Within hours, Gunn's Facebook page was overwhelmed with views, his Twitter followers soon exploding to over forty thousand people. Finally, he had taken a meaningful step toward the fame that had eluded him his entire life.

"I believe this is the sport of the future," he said, smiling, squinting into the desert during a local interview. "I've never been so popular . . . It's like a dream coming true."

CHAPTER 21
DODGING COPS WITH JAY Z'S BODYGUARD

The trouble began almost immediately. Five days after the Arizona fight, Tim Lueckenhoff, then head of the Association of Boxing Commissions, condemned bare knuckle as "abhorrent, barbaric, egregious, in contravention of a multitude of federal, state, and tribal boxing laws and regulations, and, perhaps, criminal."[1] The Arizona Boxing Commission agreed, stating that it would never have allowed the match with its "serious health and safety implications."[2]

Even the governor's office weighed in. "The governor called the tribe and said, 'What the hell are you guys doing there? Bare knuckle?'" Len Hayko recalls. "The casino took a lot of shit for it."

At least one person, however, was overjoyed. Initially, Gunn had been worried about getting arrested by Arizona police, and he couldn't truly relax until he arrived back in New Jersey. "How bad was it?" he says of the backlash. "I thought I'd be arrested at the gate when I gave them my ID." Even back home, he now had to contend with Greg Sirb, the Pennsylvania athletic commissioner, who opposed bare knuckle. "Greg Sirb started harassing me terrible," he says. "All hell had broke loose."

But despite all the threats, Gunn was pleased—for the first

time in his life, he had made the national news. Wanting to capitalize on his victory, he and Feldman immediately tried to stage another event at Fort McDowell. But this time, the Yavapai tribe was spooked. On August 11, less than a week after the fight, the Fort McDowell casino wrote the ABC a letter stating, "There will not be any more Bare Knuckle Boxing events provided by FelKO Promotions."[3] The tribe then went even further, claiming that the fight was not a professional event but an amateur one—and hence not subject to state law—because no "financial compensation was paid to the boxers." At this, the notion that no fighters had been paid, Lueckenhoff scoffed. "It is hogwash!" he stated.[4] (Both Gunn and Stewart say they were paid.)

In the end, the backlash proved permanent. Whether due to natural timing for a regime change, or controversy over the fight, Ernestine Boyd, Feldman's top contact at the Yavapai Nation, and other casino management officials were soon out of jobs. "The casino got enough heat that they said, 'Uh, I don't know if we want to do this again. This was a little over the edge,'" Hayko recalls. "At that time, everything [in terms of management] turned over. Basically, we were out." (Representatives of the Yavapai Nation confirmed that administration members who put on the fight were no longer in power, but would not elaborate.)

Gunn had done something truly historic. Along with Feldman, he had revived a long-dead American sport, making national headlines without getting arrested—all while gaining the notice of other combat sports. Soon after the fight in Arizona, Feldman claims he was in Las Vegas when he happened to run into Dana White, the president of the UFC. "Nice fight," Feldman recalls the UFC president telling him. "'But you'll never get the sport off the ground.' I just smiled because I knew it had hit a nerve. 'Isn't that the same thing they told you?'" (White's representatives declined to comment.)

With the victory, Gunn had resurrected his name, the notoriety making him attractive to promoters once again. Yet now, just when he was finally poised to strike it rich, he faced another, even greater obstacle. He had nowhere to stage a second fight. So, wanting to build on his momentum, he and Feldman improvised. Instead of trying to bide their time and lobby the ABC for approval—a futile mission, as they saw it—they decided to appeal to the masses, hoping popular approval might then sway the fight world to their cause. Instead of hiding in the shadows, they would try a new approach, Feldman booking the bare-knuckle matches and Gunn then fighting in them, everything taped and posted to YouTube. If they couldn't present the underground to the people, then they would take the audience to the underground. "My name was out there," Gunn says. "So I didn't care if the fights were videotaped anymore."

On a cold, clear Saturday night in December 2011, just four months after his victory in Arizona, Gunn, now thirty-eight, faced off against a 6'1", 160-pound pro boxer in a warehouse in a major northeast city. As usual, in the hours before the match, the sixty or so people in the crowd had been texted a location, arriving to find a run-down bar in an inner-city neighborhood. "The bar was definitely a local town place, heavy in immigrants, Blacks, and Hispanics," recalls Steve Janoski, a local journalist who had been invited to the fight by a friend. "And then outside this bar, you had a fleet of people who looked like they'd just walked out of the IRA—older white guys with scally caps and overcoats. Some of them were definitely from the Irish underworld." Janoski laughs. "You just went, 'What's going on here? This isn't right.'"

Arriving straight from a construction site, Gunn saw the crowd and immediately knew he had to move them. "It was all these Travelers and work trucks in the middle of the ghetto," he recalls. "They were going to attract the cops." Waiting nervously for his opponent, Gunn took a seat at the bar and began eating his prefight meal, the only thing he'd had time to grab: a double-bacon cheeseburger. "I said, 'I wouldn't eat that shit right before a fight,'" recalls Mike Normile, who had been paving roads with Gunn. "But Bob said, 'Hey, man, I haven't eaten all day, and it was a long drive down here. Doesn't bother me at all.'"

Finally, in walked Gunn's opponent, a muscled super middleweight boxer nearly a decade younger and probably twenty pounds leaner, with a shaved head and unflinching brown eyes. Walking straight up to Gunn, the thirty-year-old fighter issued a challenge. "He said, 'I want to bet my share that I'm going to knock you out,'" Normile recalls, meaning the young fighter was staking all his prize money on dropping Gunn unconscious. "And Bob just smiled: 'Of course I'll take that bet.'" Everyone assembled, Gunn and the promoters, including Feldman, led the crowd into a nearby warehouse, walking them up a flight of stairs and into a cavernous space. The tracksuit-and-scally-cap crowd didn't like the young man's lip. But Gunn admired him. He and his three backers had arrived vastly outnumbered and were the only Black people there, to boot. Gunn, having walked alone into hostile territory all his life, knew the feeling. "It took a lot of guts to go in there," he says.

Now, with the warehouse doors locked, Gunn and his opponent, who was brawling under the false name "Ernest Jackson," began their final preparations. Wearing his trademark black muscle shirt, jeans, and sneakers, Gunn paced the floor, wiping down his face, neck, hair, and arms with Vaseline. Jackson, wearing a gray muscle shirt, gym shorts, and knee-high black socks and sneakers, stretched his torso and swung his arms. Unlike most bare-knuckle bouts, this one was being taped—potbellied men in track suits holding up smartphone cameras. Finally, the fighters toed the line. "Fair and square, fair and square, no biting," said the ref, a short man in a backward baseball cap. "You ready? You ready? *Let's fight!*"[5]

By bare-knuckle standards, the match was epic: a nine-minute war amid a screaming crowd in a frigid warehouse. For the first few minutes, Jackson moved quickly, landing fast strikes and opening cuts above Gunn's eyes, keeping him at bay with long jabs. By contrast, Gunn advanced slowly, absorbing the shots, feet firmly planted, taking the measure of his man, noting his weak spots. At the three-minute mark, Gunn unleashed two successive body blows, the wet slap of skin on skin eliciting groans and whoops from the crowd. Shortly thereafter, now revved, both fighters tumbled into the spectators, grappling and hugging each other while nearly colliding with a concrete pillar beneath the harsh industrial lights. "Watch the pole! Watch the pole!" the crowd yelled.

Finally, five minutes into it, the fight turned. Jackson punched Gunn in the nose. The bare-knuckle champ, squinting and shaking his head as if about to sneeze, suddenly charged, retaliating with two body shots and a left jab to the head. The crowd screamed, all restraint lost. "Come on, Bobby! Come on!" *"Bob-by! Bob-by! Bob-by! Bob-by!"* Gunn, now reenergized, focused on his mark, knocking Jackson down with a combination.

From the sidelines, Dom, Gunn's trainer, began screaming, motioning his fighter to take the kill shot. "Double jam right hand!" Dom called, meaning a double right-hand combination. "Double jam!" Finally, after a few more give-and-takes, including a moment where Gunn lifted Jackson entirely off his feet during a clench, the bare-knuckle champ dropped his man with a combination to the liver and heart.

Knowing that the fight was over, Gunn immediately dropped his fists and walked away, breathing hard. Behind him, Jackson got to his knees, tried to stand, and then fell into the arms of the ref. It was done. *"Whhhaaaaooooooo!"* the crowd cheered, embracing Gunn as he fell back into them with his arms up high in a victory pose.

Afterward, spent and sweating, Gunn and Jackson entered the warehouse's makeshift office to sort out the money. Gunn hugged his opponent. "Good fight," he said.

The young man remained sullen. "I guess you won," he muttered. Because Jackson had bet everything on himself, he had forfeited his guaranteed stake in addition to the side bet he had made with Gunn.

But Gunn, not wanting his opponent to walk away empty-handed, threw him some change. "I gave him four thousand," Gunn says. "It took a lot of guts to go in there."

Gunn was almost done stuffing his $25,000 of prize money inside a duffel bag when someone yelled, "Cops! Cops!" The crowd, who had been milling about the warehouse, scattered so quickly that one Traveler who had driven in from South Carolina fell and knocked his head in a stairwell, dropping unconscious, to wake up the next morning unable to remember how he'd gotten there.

"Everybody streamed out those doors as fast as you could imagine," Janoski recalls. "That warehouse was emptied in about four seconds flat." Clutching his cash, Gunn and Bobby Jr. sped out through a back door, blending into the streets and making their way back to his work truck.

In many respects, the warehouse bout resembled every other fight of Gunn's life. A seedy neighborhood. A bloody duel. Scores of Travelers and brawlers and mobsters. Yet this night had been different. Within days, for the first time in Gunn's career in the underground, videos of his fight began appearing online. Along the way, "Jackson" was tagged as one of Jay Z's bodyguards—a falsehood likely intended to gin up interest online. Despite the outrageousness of the claim—Jackson was a lean fighter, nowhere near the gargantuan girth of most bodyguards—the ruse worked as international sites began picking up the story and tacking on further exaggerations, leading to millions of online views and further snowballing the legend of Gunn.

According to the UK newspaper the *Independent*, Gunn had "easily" defeated "Ernest 'Mine's a Nine' Jackson," a fighter with "a fearsome reputation as a former bodyguard of Jay Z," and a towering seven-foot, one-inch build.[6] On YouTube, "The Ballad of Bobby Gunn," an acoustic-guitar-and-tambourine tribute by a Traveler singer named Hughie Rose, debuted, the song further transforming the aging fighter into a full-blown folk hero:

> "*The Ballad of Bobby Gunn,*
> *He is our Celtic Son,*
> *Born his Father's Fighting Boy,*
> *Mother Jackie's Pride and Joy*
> *With Traveler Heart and Fist of Stone,*
> *He will Bring his Title Home.*"[7]

For Gunn, everything was happening quickly, the newfound fame rocketing him from washed-up has-been to international outlaw. But it was also bringing something else, which would threaten everything: a powerful new enemy with the authority to bring it all down.

CHAPTER 22
CAT AND MOUSE WITH THE NAPOLEON OF PENNSYLVANIA

In the wake of Gunn's bare-knuckle bouts going viral, a curious thing happened: pro boxing promoters were suddenly interested in him again, calling to put him back in the ring.

In February 2012, just two months after dropping Jackson in a warehouse, Gunn found himself announcing his first pro boxing match in nearly three years. It would be a heavyweight title fight against former three-division world champion James "Lights Out" Toney at the Landers Center, an 8,400-seat arena twenty miles south of Memphis. "JAMES TONEY TO RUMBLE WITH BARE KNUCKLE CHAMP BOBBY GUNN," the headlines proclaimed.[1]

At the February press conference, Toney, a former world number-one-ranked boxer with a 77-7-3 record, who was now on something of a senior tour, immediately made a point of calling out Gunn's illicit reputation. "I don't get paid to fight in the street," Toney, forty-three, said from the podium. "You gypsy pig."[2]

Gunn, wearing a black tracksuit, rushed the former champ. "Gypsy pig?" Gunn yelled. "I am a gypsy *fighter*! We'll go outside in the street right now!"

Gunn meant it. In preparation for his fight, determined to

finally defeat a world champion legend in pro boxing, Gunn threw himself into round-the-clock training at Ike's gym in Paterson, New Jersey, sparring whenever he wasn't laying asphalt or taking his daughter to school. But no matter how hard Gunn tried, the underground could never escape him. Just three weeks before his pro boxing match against Toney, hard up and needing money to cover the costs of his training, Gunn took on a bare-knuckle fight orchestrated by the Irish mob.

"I went down to Hell's Kitchen late at night, walked through the bar, down through a door in the floor, and fought," Gunn recalls. "Only the elite was allowed in." The Irish were staking Gunn against a fighter brought by the Italian mafia—the main event in an evening of gambling and drinking between the two criminal organizations. Gunn, in top shape due to his training, made short work of his opponent. "They brought in some big Italian guy, a little soft in the midsection," Gunn recalls. "I fought him with a double left hook, split his eye right open, and he went down." Gunn thought the fight was finished. But, after forty seconds, the Italian suddenly roused from the floor, wanting to fight again. "The Irish started freaking out," Gunn recalls. "'*Bobby Gunn! Fucking good! Fuck him uuuup!*'" Gunn shrugs. "So I come on again and we rock and roll." Gunn soon knocked him out, winning the fight and pocketing $10,000. But he didn't walk away clean—he had broken his hand on the man's skull. "I'd hurt my hand," Gunn says. "It was fucked up, swollen."

Despite the injury, two days later, Gunn entered the ring. After weigh-ins and press events in a smoky, mildewed casino along the Mississippi River, Gunn fought Toney in front of four hundred beer-drinking locals in the mostly empty Landers Center. The turnout for the nontelevised event was a resounding thud.[3] Early on, Gunn got in some heavy jabs, but his decision to fight for the money with a fractured right hand—as he had done so many times over the years—proved fatal, shattering his fist. Toney, despite being a lumbering 248 pounds, went on to pick the bare-knuckle champ apart. After struggling through five rounds, Gunn's corner— overseen by Feldman—threw in the towel. The reason? A broken hand. "I'm gonna get it x-rayed," Gunn said afterwards, his eyes bruised, his face bleeding, his dreams dashed yet again. "I lost big."

* * * * *

For the next few years, Gunn abandoned boxing almost entirely. Instead, he began to play a dangerous new game, fighting in underground matches (some taped, most not) while trying to launch it as a new sport—all while dodging Greg Sirb, executive director of the Pennsylvania State Athletic Commission, every step of the way. "That fucking Greg Sirb," Gunn says, shaking his head about it even now. "He tortured me."

Gunn's battle with Sirb began in Arizona, in 2011. During the buildup to the match, headlines had focused on the federal commissioners and Arizona politicians trying to stop the bare-knuckle fight. But in truth, it had been Sirb, a lesser-known but ambitious state commissioner three thousand miles away, who helped instigate the trouble.

According to the notes of a national meeting of the Association of Boxing Commissioners, held just days before the bout, Sirb had given a lecture on "bare-knuckle fighting" in which he "urged all 14 tribal members of the ABC to send the Fort McDowell Tribe a letter noting that such activity contravenes the laws and regulations attendant to professional boxing."* Then, according to Gunn, Feldman, and others involved with the event, Sirb began

* By "tribal members," Sirb is referring to representatives from various Native American reservations across the United States who had joined the ABC.

prodding various politicians to contact the casino, trying to shut it down. And afterward, in the wake of the overwhelming backlash against the fight, the Fort McDowell representatives reportedly wrote their apology not to Tim Lueckenhoff, then president of the ABC, but to his vice president, Sirb.[4] On the face of it, a Pennsylvania state athletic commissioner trying to stop a bare-knuckle fight in Arizona—and then spending the next few years trying to take down Gunn and destroy the sport altogether—would seem unlikely. But, as Gunn and Feldman would soon discover, Sirb lived and breathed the sport of boxing and would stop at nothing to protect it from potential threats.

Sirb, the main commissioner against bare knuckle, is the lone authority in Pennsylvania fight sports, the man who oversees careers and licenses and permits in the nearly $1 million annual state industry, and he runs his jurisdiction with the hard-ass discipline of a drill sergeant.[5] "I'm probably one of the only commissioners who came up boxing and wrestling," he says. "I'm not some punk-ass political appointee."

A former wrestling coach who grew up in the steel town of Sharon, Pennsylvania, Sirb, fifty-seven, is a short man with a high forehead and dark circles under his eyes—the result of endlessly crisscrossing the state since 1990 to oversee its sixty-odd annual boxing, wrestling, MMA, and kickboxing events. At ringside, he is a fixture, his tucked-in polo shirt buttoned to the chin, his back ramrod straight, his face an intense don't-fuck-with-me glare. An old-school boxing guy, Sirb helped build Pennsylvania into a pugilistic powerhouse with over 400 licensed boxers, the third highest number of boxing events in the US, and one of the highest revenues in the country, earning him accolades from US Olympic boxing associations, and a seat on the Governor's Council on Physical Fitness and Sports.[6] In 1997, he even testified before Congress in an effort to create a pension system for pro boxers and to protect them from exploitation and injury.[7]

Safeguarding fighters is a difficult job, and Sirb takes it seriously, his gruff exterior sometimes masking the fact that it keeps him up at night. "My job is a very tricky balance," he says. "If we're talking about risk for the dollar—football, drag-car racing, rodeo—the biggest risk is boxing. You just can't whitewash it." He pauses. "I think it's a legitimate sport, a great sport. If you grew up in the inner city as I did, you gravitate towards these physical confrontations. I love it. But that drive home after a fight is brutal. Hoping that the kid that got beat up isn't hurt. Hoping that you don't get that call at two in the morning from the kid's trainer or mother or father that they took him to the hospital. We had one death. And, you know, that's tough even to talk about. That's still with me. It won't ever leave."

Sirb sees himself as the lone protector of boxing. But in his quest to safeguard it, he has also, among some fighters and promoters, cultivated another reputation—for running his commission like a dictatorship, bullying underlings, waging vendettas, and, most damningly, supporting only boxing while working to keep new fight sports from entering Pennsylvania, one of the last states in the country to sanction MMA. Look up his name, and a host of headlines arise: "Remove Abusive PA Athletic Commission Exec Dir. Greg Sirb From Office."[8] "I Was Assaulted by PA Commissioner Greg Sirb."[9] "Greg Sirb is the devil!"[10]

That last one makes Sirb laugh. "I love MMA," he says. "Guys probably say we're too strict, because they came here and got their ass whipped." But there is one rumor Sirb will confirm: bare-knuckle boxing won't be making its debut in PA—and that's how he says it, "P. A."—anytime soon. "No, I'm not supportive," he says. "Look, because of the success of MMA, which everyone thought was crazy, I have to keep an open mind. But I don't think there's enough data yet on bare-knuckle fighting to make any conclusions about its safety." He pauses. "Dave is always pushing the envelope, and it's my job as commissioner to rein him in—'That's not going to happen.'"

For years, Sirb has been battling the Feldman family, a clan of fight promoters known for pushing the boundaries of the law. "Both brothers are hustlers," he says. "Always looking for something new: the next kid, the next champ, the next sport." The athletic commissioner respects the old man, Marty, who was "tough and mean . . . a stand-up guy." In 2010, however, he filed criminal charges against Damon, Feldman's older brother, a celebrity boxing promoter who pits D-list stars (José Canseco, Danny Bonaduce, Michael Lohan) against each other, for fixing fights.[*11]

[Figure 22.1] Greg Sirb. Photo courtesy Pennsylvania Department of State. Public domain.

Around that same time, Feldman says Sirb came after him, nearly ruining his career by trying to shut down his first pro MMA event, an Xtreme Fight Event at the now defunct Tri-State Sports Complex in Aston, just hours before it was about to start—all due to a personal grudge. "He didn't like my brother, so he tried to take it out on me," Feldman recalls. "I had every dime in that show. So I told Greg, 'Everybody calls you

---

* In 2011, Damon pled no contest to the charges and was prohibited from promoting events in Pennsylvania for two years.

a Napoleon motherfucker and I stand up for you. I work my ass off. Give me respect!' And he apologized, letting me do the show." (Sirb says this did not happen.)

But of all the battles, nothing compared to the war that erupted over bare-knuckle boxing. According to Feldman, the 2011 fight in Arizona infuriated the commissioner, making him look as though he couldn't get a handle on a promoter from his own state. Then, following the Ernest Jackson bare-knuckle fight that went viral, Gunn and Feldman say Sirb threatened to take away their boxing licenses, launching an investigation to pin down whether they were holding underground fights in Pennsylvania. (Sirb acknowledges the investigation but denies making threats.) For years, a cat-and-mouse game ensued, Sirb trying to catch Gunn and Feldman in the underground.

While the duo did not collaborate on every bare-knuckle fight for Gunn—"Remember, I brought him into *my* world," Gunn says—Feldman oversaw enough to get a taste for the sport, bringing in boxers and MMA fighters while trying to devise a plan for launching it as a legal business. "The first one I ever did, I was nervous that we were gonna get jammed up by the cops," Feldman recalls. "And then when we left, I was just like, 'Wow, that was fucking unbelievable. We need to video this and sell it on the Internet.'"

Making it all the more dangerous, Gunn and Feldman continued to collaborate on pro boxing matches, meaning they would sometimes see Sirb on the same day as an underground fight. At one point, Feldman went straight from a bare-knuckle bout to a pro boxing match, where the Pennsylvania commissioner promptly tried to bust him on a tip he'd heard about a warehouse fight. "He knew I was doing it, but could never prove it," Feldman says. "He'd say, 'I'm going to bring you in front of the board for the bare-knuckle thing,' and I'd say, 'I was home sleeping; what are you talking about?'" Feldman laughs.

"I'd fuck with him about bare knuckle: 'You better make sure no one gets killed in that shit.'"*

Finally, after years of evading Sirb, Gunn and Feldman decided to pull off their most audacious underground match yet: a fight to be taped by *60 Minutes Sports.* In a bid to create groundbreaking publicity and, with luck, push bare knuckle to public approval, they teamed up with Danny Provenzano, the felon and bare-knuckle promoter who also had expertise in another world: show business.

In 2003, right before going to jail, Provenzano had released a self-penned, self-directed mob flick, *This Thing of Ours,* featuring James Caan, which included a scene mirroring one of the forty-four indictments that had been leveled against him—that he once ordered a thieving employee's thumb to be smashed with a hammer.[12] And now Provenzano was launching his own media company, Genco.TV, named after the olive oil company that Vito Corleone uses as a business front in *The Godfather*—hoping to help Gunn and Feldman legalize bare knuckle and maybe launch a fight-world reality series in the process. According to Gunn, Provenzano was the one who reached out to *60 Minutes,* inviting them to film his match. So once again, Gunn was going to do what was once unthinkable: shine a light on the underground.

On a Saturday night in March 2014, walking through snow on trash-strewn sidewalks, Gunn entered an auto-body shop in a major northeastern city. Wearing a gray hoodie and baseball cap, he went up a flight of stairs and into a large cavernous room, blending with the crowd of fifty. On the concrete floor, two parallel strips of tape had been laid, the undercard fighters squaring off with their toes to the lines, surrounded by cameras.

---

* For his part, Sirb denies, downplays, or replies "no comment" to the above accusations, simply saying he will crack down on anything illegal. "Yeah, we've made some calls," is about the sum of his description about the investigation.

As the opening bout began, Gunn took off his hoodie and began going through his prefight routine, working his hands, stretching his neck, and trying to keep his mind clear.

Inviting the cameras had been risky. But Gunn felt he needed to make something happen. In the coming weeks, his son, Bobby Jr., would debut as a pro boxer, fighting a thirty-year-old middleweight with an 0-3 record, in a match at a Boys and Girls Club in Annandale, Virginia. Although only seventeen, Bobby Jr. had already amassed a 25-2 record as an amateur and was almost assured of victory, and Gunn had to start thinking about the long term.[13] Pro boxing managers were beginning to swoop in, offering the boy contracts, and Gunn, ever protective, had turned them all down. Some wondered whether Gunn was being too cautious, keeping Bobby Jr. from reaching his potential. But Gunn was adamant. He was trying to build a foundation for his son, the kind he had never enjoyed, and he would personally oversee Bobby Jr.'s pro boxing career until he was good and ready to entrust it to someone else.

The only ingredient Gunn needed was more cash—and maybe taping today's match would help with that, spurring another major bare-knuckle fight and bringing home a payday. "Nobody will have my boy," Gunn says. "I'm bringing him up the way I should have been brought up myself—by giving him everything I've never had."

Now, with the final undercard match over, Gunn squared off against his opponent, a thirty-five-year-old pro heavyweight boxer fighting under the name "George Streeter." Standing a few feet apart, Gunn and Streeter—both about two hundred pounds, both in muscle shirts and jeans, both longtime vets of the underground—sized each other up. "All right, let's do this," Provenzano yelled, clapping his hands. "Let's *fight!*"[14]

Almost immediately, Gunn drew first blood, hitting Streeter

with a left jab to the nose. But Streeter, a seasoned fighter with a rumored 33-6 bare-knuckle record, hardly flinched, countering with jabs to the body. For the next two minutes, the pair moved around and around the concrete floor, exchanging blows and dodging feints. Finally, after punching little for nearly a minute, biding his time, Gunn saw an opening. Like a sniper, he suddenly unleashed a precise left hook to Streeter's right eye, sending the pro heavyweight toppling to the ground, clutching his face, the crowd in an uproar. Before Streeter even hit the ground, Gunn was already walking away, knowing the fight was over. "He's out," Provenzano called. "That's it."

That night, Gunn left with a reputed $40,000, a nest egg allowing him to properly train Bobby Jr. and lead him to a 5-0 pro boxing record—a stunning debut with four knockouts and a world youth title. "By the time this boy is twenty-one, he'll be fighting for a world middleweight title," Gunn told me months later. "From my mouth to God's ears, I hope it happens that way."

The price of Gunn's victory, however, had been steep. When it debuted, the *60 Minutes Sports* piece was a shadowy thirteen-minute segment that emphasized the underground and included interviews with Provenzano, Gunn, and an ex-con known as Johnny "Knuckles."[15] The host claimed that the show had captured "the bloody sport in its rawest form."[16]

After it aired, Sirb redoubled his efforts. Now Gunn could go nowhere near another sanctioned bare-knuckle fight. In fact, he says the TV spot actually *worsened* his chances at another respectable match, the show's depiction of the underground keeping all potential bare-knuckle venues at a wary distance, none wanting to be associated with the sport. To avoid harassment and potential prosecution from Sirb, Gunn's accomplice, Feldman, did not renew his promoter's license in Pennsylvania. Joey Eye, the Philly cut man who had been at the underground match, says he himself was ultimately banned in six states thanks to Sirb, racking up thousands in legal fees and remaining out of work for nearly a year. "He had his people haul me out of a locker room at a pro boxing match and then he called me up screaming," Eye recalls. "He's a total Napoleon!" ("That's his interpretation of it," Sirb says about the incident.)

For the next three years, Gunn would do little fighting. "I was scared," he says. "We were under the gun."

CHAPTER 23
GO OUT AND TAKE IT LIKE A LION

"I'm the boss, I'm the boss, I'm the boss, I'm the boss."

In February 2017, in an empty banquet room backstage at the Chase Center in Wilmington, Delaware, Gunn repeats his mantra while shadowboxing, his face hidden behind a tiger-skin print hood.

Bap! He sinks a hard left jab into the pads of his trainer, Ossie Duran, who whispers in his ear.

Bap! Bap!

"Come on, Dad, dig, dig!" Bobby Jr. yells, his arms crossed, his eyes worried. "Fuck Roy Jones!"

Bap! Bap! Bap!

Gunn breathes, punches, dances as Patsy Cline's "Sweet Dreams" plays on smartphone speakers.* Around him, a steady stream of Travelers, some from as far away as Scotland, stop in to wish him good luck. In an adjoining room, his opponent blares

---

* Gunn's prefight playlist is Patsy Cline, Dolly Parton, Johnny Cash, the Eurythmics, Dean Martin, Bing Crosby, Concrete Blonde's "Joey," Elvis, Kim Carnes's "Bette Davis Eyes," Europe's "The Final Countdown," *The Last of the Mohicans* theme song, and endless traditional Irish Traveler ballads. "Bobby is the only fighter you'll ever see who gets pumped up to music like *that*," says a New Jersey trainer, smacking his gum, raising an eyebrow.

rap music, the wall shaking like an angry heartbeat. And farther in the distance, in the bowels of the arena, the sold-out crowd of 2,400 roars for the undercard matches, awaiting the night's main event. But right now, ensconced in his custom-made tiger-print hood, Gunn is oblivious of it all. He is here to fight Roy Jones Jr. in a sold-out cruiserweight title match on pay-per-view, put together by David Feldman. At age forty-three, Gunn is about to begin the most high-profile boxing bout of his career—a fight that could finally lay the groundwork for the launch of bare knuckle as a legal sport—and he will not be distracted. "To beat Roy puts me on a different level," Gunn says, rolling his neck. "Makes me one of the best gypsy fighters of all time. Everything in my life has brought me up to this moment."

[Figure 23.1] Prepping for Jones (Photo by author)

In the three years since his underground match against Streeter, Gunn has been working steadily, taking fewer bare-knuckle fights while biding his time for a sanctioned match, focusing on his family. He has led Bobby Jr. to an 8-0 pro boxing record and bought his daughter, Charlene, a keyboard piano. He has spoiled Max every day, carting around the highest-quality dog food in the back of his truck and outfitting him in a purple camouflage harness. And he has even surprised his wife, Rose, with a family trip to Cancún, taking everyone to one of those all-inclusive resorts, returning with a sunburn and a straw hat.

But things have not been easy. The Cancún trip was a sponta-neous splurge, a break everyone needed from the heart of a Jersey winter, but it seriously drained Gunn's bank account. Since then, he has been working long weeks, taking jobs as far afield as Texas and North Dakota, roaming with bands of Travelers and sleeping in his truck while saving every dollar. But it never seems enough. And now, on top of everything else, his father, Robert, has been steadily getting worse, his declining health often forcing Gunn to drop everything and drive the six hours up to Niagara Falls to check on him. "The booze is a terrible thing," Gunn says, shaking his head. "Last time I saw him, he was drinking and crying, embarrassed that he was drinking, that he looked like that in front of his grandson." He sighs. "He's a broken man."

For a fight, though, everyone rallies. Today, just hours before the match, Gunn took a rest in his hotel room, snuggled Max, and then left him watching the Animal Channel. Arriving backstage, he lay prostrate on the floor for a full twenty seconds, praying, before calling Rose and Charlene, who are watching at home. And just now, he rang his father, who managed to get in yet another barroom brawl last week and is currently watching the under-card match from a bar stool in Niagara Falls, ready to give his son pointers. "Near the ropes he's not worth a fuck," Robert says about Gunn's opponent, Jones. "And remember to have a good shit if you can." Gunn shakes his head. "Don't get in no fights tonight, Pop."

Now, everything set, Gunn nears the end of his prefight routines. He moves around the room, strategizing with Duran— who has prepped him to wear down Jones before surprising him with a knockout shot—as well as his old trainer, Dominick Scibetta, who offers blunter advice: "Try to nail him right in the balls, then come right back uptown." Gunn smacks his gum, moving, moving, moving, wearing only the tiger-print hoodie, a black T-shirt, black boxer briefs, a black jockstrap the size of a miner's harness, and tall black boxing shoes with a photo of his family tucked between the laces. He is jacked and in tune and totally absorbed, when suddenly he snaps back to the present.

"Where's my boy?"

Gunn walks over to his son, favoring the right hand he recently sprained, the one he has broken countless times over the years, the one now covered in thick white tape, and puts it on Bobby's shoulder.

"Don't worry, Bob," he says, leaning in, looking his son in the eye. "I've fought five world champions. I'll be okay."

Bobby Jr. says nothing. His father turns, grinning to the backstage crowd of

[Figure 23.2] "I feel nervous. Always." (Photo by author)

Travelers and ex-fighters, grinning to himself. "I'm a bare-knuckle guy," he says. "Just when I think I'm done, they pull me back in!"

Bap!

Bobby Jr. wipes his face.

Bap! Bap!

"I feel nervous," Bobby Jr. whispers. "Always."

Bap! Bap! Bap!

"I'm the boss, I'm the boss, I'm the boss, I'm the boss."

Gunn may grin, but he is a long shot, and he knows it. He is forty-three. Jones is forty-eight. Both fighters are past their prime, but Jones is on a different level. He is a former Olympian who has held six world titles in four different weight classes, a man whom

ESPN dubbed the "pound-for-pound king" of the sport during his reign from 1994 to 2004.[1]

A future Boxing Hall of Famer and truly one of the all-time greats, Jones caused an uproar when he announced his intention to fight Gunn. For years, the boxing world has been calling for Jones's retirement, aghast that he is still fighting, taking on opponents who are beneath him, who normally wouldn't have survived a round with him. In their eyes, Gunn is deemed a new low, a journeyman who hasn't laced up in three years, a novelty act best known for the underground. "In a fight that simply has disaster written all over it," sneers sports site East Side Boxing, "Jones, or what's left of him, will face tough bare-knuckle KO King Bobby Gunn."[2]

Sure, Jones never would have fought Gunn ten years ago, never would even have considered it. And yes, he can probably use the money, the rumors still swirling about failed investments in real estate, tax liens rumored to be as much as $3.5 million, and mysterious ventures in Russia, where he retains a dual citizenship.[3] (Jones has denied having any financial problems.)[4]

But what none of the beat reporters realize is that for Jones, the fight also represents something else: a lifelong fascination with the underground. Raised on a pig farm in the coastal pine scrub north of Pensacola, Florida, Jones was brutally trained in a makeshift backyard ring by his father, a Vietnam vet who used PVC pipe to repeatedly knock down his son, to toughen him up against the local rednecks, to prepare him for the world.

Jones was carrying a shotgun at age six, driving a tractor by seven, and fighting in unsanctioned boxing matches on the beaches of Pensacola before he could drive. From his father, he also learned to breed fighting cocks, to respect blood sport, to nurture the terrible affection one can feel for animals raised to fight to the death.[5] For all these reasons, Jones has long admired Gunn and other underground knucklers even though he—with a onetime reported net worth of

$45 million—has never had to remove the gloves. "It's only because of how good Bobby is at bare knuckle that I'm giving him this opportunity," Jones says before the fight. "Come on, man, that's a bad dude."

* * * * *

Standing in the doorway, watching Gunn, Feldman has a different take. Although the promoter has given nothing but support to Gunn, promising him this is *his time* to shine, *his time* to take home the belt, in truth, Feldman has no illusions. Gunn, who truly wants to win, is going to lose. Feldman is just worried Gunn will lose *bad,* ruining the promoter's other, more secret motives for the night: to announce the launch of a legal bare-knuckle fight league. "This could be bad for Bobby," he says, shaking his head. "And bare knuckle."

Feldman wears a gray three-piece suit, open-collar shirt, and giant neon lanyard that says "Promoter." He looks Vegas cool and radiates a hard-ass vibe, but lingering in the gaunt lines of his face, the dark circles beneath his eyes, is a different story. In the past few years, he has battled through both brain and skin cancer, surviving rounds of chemo that left him bald, weak, and emaciated—disorienting, soul-searching territory for the alpha promoter. It made him spend more time with his kids and fiancée, made him resolve to finally step out of the shadows and stage another sanctioned bare-knuckle match. And now, just three days ago, just when everything was starting to fall into place, his father, Marty, died after a years-long struggle with dementia. Feldman was there to hold his hand as he slipped away. "I've been going on eight hours of sleep for the last three days," Feldman says, rubbing his temples. "Actually, the fight is helping. It's taking my mind off him."

Feldman will have to mourn later—tonight is the biggest show of his career. It is the first time he has overseen everything, from the bout to the venue, to the pay-per-view contracts, to the sweaty rubber-banded rolls of ticket money his fighters bring him in shoeboxes. All told, he is in for $400,000—more than any fight he's put on in his entire life. It is a huge risk, a public attempt to step up to the next level, and his right-hand man, his son, the only person in the world he trusts, Dave Feldman Jr., has just told him they've sold out the house.

And yet Feldman looks pissed.

"This don't look good for our boy," he says, watching Gunn. "Jones has been training hard for this one."

What no one outside this backstage room realizes—from the sold-out crowd to the fighters, to the hundreds of thousands of people watching on pay-per-view and online across the world—is that all of it, *all of it,* is being put on to set the groundwork for Feldman's real plan: resurrecting bare knuckle. For the past eight months, he has been secretly working with athletic commissioners, promoters, industry veterans, and an undisclosed backer to launch bare knuckle in a huge and legal way, in a state-sanctioned event in Kansas. The Kansas Athletic Commission, long tired of being overlooked in the heartland, is interested in taking a chance on the sport, betting it may become a surprise hit like MMA, and is talking with Feldman about staging the first legal bout in the United States.

Working to meet their requirements, Feldman has drafted a rulebook for bare knuckle. He has filed patents on a ring, logos, equipment. According to Feldman, he has even made peace with the national Association of Boxing Commissions, the same entity that once called his sport "abhorrent, barbaric, egregious . . . and, perhaps, criminal." He has even gotten the blessing from their new commissioner that bare knuckle won't have political problems. In short, he is doing everything he did not do in 2011. This time, he is going through the front door. This time, he is launching not only a sport, but a specific company like the UFC, one that will hold all the patents and connections and legal rights, ensuring that any event with the words "bare knuckle" will be staged by one entity: David Feldman Promotions.

Tonight's event is a dry run, a chance to prove to Kansas, the ABC, and his moneymen that Feldman can put on a quality show. But there's just one hitch. If Gunn, the public face of his new sport, does not put on a good fight tonight, does not look like the superstar they need him to be, then the whole enterprise may be cast into doubt. It's not that Feldman needs Gunn to win. Hell, Jones has been training for months in a private gym on an eighty-eight-acre compound in Florida, while Gunn has been banging nails in the Jersey winter, grabbing bag time when he can. Winning is not expected for Gunn. But Feldman does need Gunn to go down swinging, not to play it safe. He needs him to *fight*.

Feldman's phone rings. He looks at it, takes one last look at Gunn, and then turns to go out the door.

"I just need him to make it a good fight."

* * * * *

In the end, Gunn goes out and does the opposite. Under the bright lights, in a screaming arena, the aging journeyman throws a three-punch combination—a left to Jones's face, a right to his body, a left to his face again—in the first round and then falls apart. There are a series of halfhearted charges, a strong left hook in the sixth, but Gunn seems to arrive totally exhausted, totally spent. For his part, Jones doesn't look much better, but he at least begins to warm up in the fourth, sniping with single shots, until the last seconds of the seventh, when the former world champion unleashes a devastating right-left combination, staggering Gunn and leaving him bleeding from the eyes, mouth, and nose. A minute later, Gunn's corner throws in the towel.

[Figure 23.3] Watching Dad fight
(Photo courtesy of Bobby Gunn)

[Figure 23.4] In the ring
(Photo by author)

Blood flowing from both nostrils, down his chin, and onto the canvas, Gunn leaves the ring with Bobby Jr. Backstage, his eyes glazed, a vicious gash across his face, he calls his wife and daughter as the room fills with Travelers, the air as still and solemn as at a funeral.

"I'm sorry," Gunn says, slumping in a chair, tears starting to mix with the blood. "I let you down; I let you down."

[Figure 23.5] "I'm sorry. I let you down." (Photo by author)

CHAPTER 24

MIDNIGHT BRAWL AT THE WESTIN

Around midnight, after his lopsided loss, Gunn lies on a bed. He is tired and bloodied and doesn't want to leave his hotel room at the Westin Hotel, located next to the Chase Center boxing arena. But he needs to take Max outside one last time, so he decides to go ahead and also check on his son. Usually a quiet kid, Bobby Jr. had been infuriated by his father's loss, rushing into the center of the ring and screaming at Jones, "You never got him down! You never got him down!" Gunn, totally surprised, had stepped between his son and Jones, not sure of what to expect. But Jones, knowing something about a son's love for a father, had just calmly looked at the boy, the swirl of cameras around them, and agreed. "No, I didn't," Jones told him. "He's a tough motherfucker." The teenager relented.

Now Gunn—his eyes blackened, nose bruised, a long cut running like a knife scar down his right cheek—rises from bed, throws on a black tracksuit, and scoops Max into his arms. He is forty-three and feels sixty-three, and the last thing he wants to do is leave this room. But he needs to check on his son and knows exactly where he will be: the bar. For nights on end, the bar at the Westin has been a Traveler gathering site, the various Scottish,

Irish, and English clans convening to put aside their differences, sing songs, and drink until someone pisses someone else off and the fighting resumes all over again. "You here for the boxing?" a housekeeping woman asks me in the hotel elevator one morning. "I got here at six in the morning and they was still cleaning up the lobby from the fight last night."

Gunn steps off the elevator, Max tucked under his arm, and walks into the packed bar. It's a sweaty sea of techno music, clinking drinks, and loud conversation, everyone riding the high of the fight. After wading through endless Travelers, all wanting to shake his hand or take a photo, Gunn finds Bobby Jr., who does not drink but is hanging out with friends. Blood still stains the boy's sweatshirt—a remnant from the ring incident—but now he seems happy, so Gunn decides to sit a moment and enjoy the conversation. He orders a water. At one point, when he blows into a Kleenex, he leaves a bloody mess. But there is a calm in the fighter. A new resolve, a sad acceptance. "I'm done with boxing," Gunn says, shaking his head. "I think Roy was taking it easy on me."

Gunn had left the ring by the time Feldman took the microphone, announcing to the sold-out crowd, the world, that bare-knuckle boxing would return this year. And, of course, that meant one thing: Gunn, the aging marquee star, would rise to the canvas one last time. He shook his head, looking older. His father would continue brawling until he could no longer stand, and now his own son had tried to rough up a future Hall of Famer on a national pay-per-view broadcast. Bare-knuckle boxing was just in his blood. And if he couldn't go out a champion in the ring, then he at least would go out one while not wearing gloves. There had to be one final fight.

"I still got it," Gunn says. "I'm still the best out there. None of these other guys can get in the ring with Roy. This year, I defend my title—I put bare-knuckle boxing on the map."

Gunn is relaxing, petting Max, thinking on his next move, when someone tells him three Irish Travelers are looking for him. Standing, Gunn approaches the men. They are from Ireland, not well known to the community, and seem drunk, agitated, and looking to start something. "Hey," one of them says to Gunn, leaning in too close, shoving a smartphone in his face. "My sister wants to say hello."

Gunn doesn't see the empty beer bottle in the man's hand, doesn't see him begin to swing it at his face. But his son does. Grabbing the man, Bobby Jr. pushes him back, punching him as the crowd swarms. Gunn's son is fighting with abandon, as if something has been unleashed within him, when one of the other two men steps in to take a cheap shot at the boy.

Wrong move.

Gunn swivels, his bloodshot eyes suddenly in focus, and grabs the man. Smooth as a greased piston, he inserts two fingers into the man's nostrils and then pulls up and up and up, hearing a crunch and then a pop of severed cartilage and then watching as the tip of the nose rips right apart.

The third man runs away.

PART III:
LAST STAND
IN THE WILD WEST

CHAPTER 25

FIGHTING IS THE UNIVERSAL LANGUAGE

Gunn stands alone in a ring, shadowboxing, sweating, breathing hard. "*Huh!*" he grunts, throwing three left jabs, ducking an imaginary foe, advancing. "*Ha!*" he exclaims, pivoting on his good leg, starting the sequence all over again. At ringside, Bobby Jr. remains engrossed in his smartphone. Outside, Gunn's French bulldog, Max, is asleep in the truck. On this Saturday morning in July 2017, in an arena in south Philadelphia, the only person paying attention to the bare-knuckle champ is a heavily tattooed young fighter from Rahway, New Jersey, a part-time pizza delivery guy who, along with dozens of other fighters, has traveled here for one reason: to meet Gunn and, he hopes, follow in his footsteps. "This guy's a legend," the kid says, staring up at Gunn. "You're a warrior!"

Gunn shakes out his hands, rolls his neck, and steps down from the ring. He is not here to compete—he's wearing a black baseball cap, black polo shirt, and jeans—and jumped in the ring only out of habit, an almost physical need to tread the canvas whenever he sees it. No, Gunn is here for a far more important reason, one he never thought would happen: to help launch the

Bare Knuckle Fighting Championship, a new professional combat league debuting in the coming months.

Today, thirty fighters from across the United States, all wearing black jerseys with gold fists on the front and numbers on the back, will compete for a limited number of slots in the league. Under Gunn's and Feldman's watchful eyes, the prospects will undergo a series of tests—sparring with pads, working bags, measuring their strength against a "punch meter"—all in a bid to secure a spot on the league's first bare-knuckle event, a pay-per-view match that Gunn will headline in Kansas in the coming months. Orchestrated by Feldman, today's tryout, from the officials to the uniforms, to the five-man crew taping everything for a possible reality series, feels full of promise—a new endeavor on the cusp of success.

Not that Gunn feels a shred of it.

"I'm dead broke," he says, smiling tightly as yet another young fighter approaches for a picture. "A quick fight for ten grand sure would be good about now."

Gunn, in perhaps the greatest irony of his life, is finally about to transcend the underground, and all he can think about is getting back into it. "I used to just take one on when I needed the money," he says, eyeing the cameras and promoters. "But I can't do stupid stuff no more. There's just too much at stake."

If this is going straight, it is killing Gunn. Last night, after a week of paving roads and painting barns in far upstate New York, he slept in his truck by the side of the highway, awakening to cicadas and sweat to drive the three hundred miles south for the tryout here. As always, he has been working overtime to survive—and he's barely managing that. In two weeks, Gunn must pay $3,000 to renew the professional tags and licenses on his truck. And then there's the upcoming rent payment, the mounting $10,000 in credit-card debt, and, God help him, Charlene's private school tuition for the fall, which is just around the corner. Rubbing his face, Gunn pulls out his smartphone and looks at a family photo from the recent Cancún trip, everyone smiling in matching Hawaiian shirts. "I don't know where I'm going to get the money," he says. "Things are getting desperate."

Unable to fight in the underground, Gunn is doing the next best thing: returning to the boxing ring. In a week, he will fight Gilberto Domingos, a thirty-one-year-old Brazilian heavyweight with a 22-8 record, for $2,500, in a makeshift ring at a Harley Davidson dealership in Huntington, West Virginia. It's a long way from Caesar's Palace—a long way from Gunn's recent fight against Roy Jones, for that matter—and the desperation of the bout is underscored only by Gunn's current haphazard training regimen. Unable to hit the gym at Ike's, he has instead been preparing for the match by standing on the bed of his truck and doing one-arm rows with fifty-five-pound buckets of asphalt sealer. "It weighs a lot," Gunn says. "But it's still not proper training."

[Figure 25.1a, b, c] Training with asphalt sealer (Photos courtesy of Bobby Gunn)

Gunn sighs, surveying the arena—mostly millennial fighters who have all memorized his YouTube fights. In addition to the twenty-eight-year-old pizza-delivery brawler, there is John Hernholm, twenty-nine, a hulking 6'6", 350-pound bouncer from Knoxville, Tennessee, who recently achieved fame for knocking out a drunk hooligan at a bar. The resulting smartphone video racked up 23 million views and led him to drive the ten hours here in search of a new career. Next to him is Sam Shewmaker, thirty-three, a 6'3", 250-pound construction worker from Kansas City, Missouri, who flew here with his trainer, a seventy-two-year-old junkyard owner, in the hope of making a better future for his three children. "I got an offer to fight from a biker gang last month," Shewmaker says, posing for a photo alongside Gunn. "Human nature is brutal."

The contestants even include two fighters who have lost to Gunn in the underground. Mike Liberto, the thirty-three-year-old steelworker and MMA fighter, took on Gunn in a warehouse match. "Bobby's punch angles come from nowhere," he says. "He split my head wide open."

And Jim McClendon, the former marine who fought Gunn in a New Jersey auto-body shop in 2015, says losing to the champ skyrocketed his cred in the underworld, leading to more bare-knuckle fights and money toward his goal of buying a house. "I'm just trying to fight my way into a home," he says. "I see opportunity in this."

Gunn smiles at everyone, posing for the photos. "Keep doing what you're doing," he says. "In order to win in life you have to go through things you wouldn't wish on your worst enemy."

* * * * *

Gunn taps a ringside bell ten times with a hammer and says a prayer, and the contest begins. The thirty aspiring fighters go to work, the arena quickly becoming a maelstrom of punches, swinging bags, and the screaming exertions of combatants striking the "punch meter," a force plate mounted to a wall to quantify strength. "Total waste of time," says Dom, Gunn's longtime trainer, his arms crossed over his belly, frowning at the punch meter. "Like it matters how hard you can hit someone in bare knuckle. It's all about precision."

A man in a fedora disagrees. "This is great," says Art Davie, founder of the UFC. "We had a punch meter at UFC One. It just looks cool. Marketing is everything."

Perhaps the craziest part about Gunn's scheme to transform his life by turning bare knuckle into a worldwide professional sport is that it's not so crazy. Davie, seventy, has done it before. Wearing a houndstooth jacket and holding an unlit Cuban cigar the size of a baton, the Brooklyn-born Davie, at first glance, resembles some sort of carnival huckster. *No way this guy is on the level,* you will think. But Davie is responsible for one of the greatest sports achievements in modern history, a magic trick of epic proportions: helping to transform MMA, a fringe outlaw competition, into a mainstream sport and a $12 billion worldwide phenomenon. "Art Davie is here," Gunn says, still shaking his head in disbelief. "This is about to blow up!"

Gunn should be excited. Davie, who is here as an adviser, knows every trick to pulling this off. In 1993, while working as an adman in Los Angeles, he stumbled into the fight business after trying to convince a client, Tecate beer, to sponsor a kickboxing event. Realizing there was no real promotion for martial arts exhibitions, Davie thought back to a fight he had heard about as a marine in Vietnam, between a wrestler and a boxer in a Bangkok bar.[1] He began dreaming up a new sport that would pit different styles of fighters against each other, and enlisted Rorion Gracie, a Brazilian jiujitsu expert, and John Milius, the cigar-chomping, gun-loving Hollywood screenwriter of *Dirty Harry, Apocalypse Now,* and *Conan the Barbarian,* to help.*[2] Gracie would work with the fighters while Milius would work on the showmanship. Borrowing heavily from the ancient Greek sport *Pankration*—a contest in which everything but biting, eye gouging, and attacking genitals was allowed—the three men hammered out the Ultimate Fighting Championship, a bloody, showy bare-knuckle no-holds-barred tournament that pitted combatants of all disciplines against each other.

Amazingly, they landed a TV deal with Bob Meyrowitz, a Manhattan-based entertainment executive who had made a fortune staging pay-per-view concerts by artists from Ozzy Osbourne to the New Kids on the Block. A former boxer, Meyrowitz was convinced that the fight world was due for a shake-up. "Everyone says that music is the international language, but it's not true," he said at the time. "With the exception of a few giant acts, music is regional at best. But wherever I go, I see fighting. *Fighting* is the international language . . . Everyone understands it."[3]

Some twenty years later, after overcoming politicians and pundits decrying the bloody sport as the end of civilization, the UFC sold for $4.2 billion to an international group including William Morris Endeavor, the Kraft Group, and Dalian Wanda, the largest private-property developer in the world. In 2023, the UFC was valued at $12.1 billion.[4] And although Davie had sold his interest in 1995 for $1 million, he had gone on to invest in other startups and now thought bare knuckle could be the next UFC. "This could make a billion bucks," he says, watching the

---

* Milius was also the inspiration for John Goodman's character Walter Sobchak in *The Big Lebowski,* which tells you everything you need to know.

fighters at the tryout. "Dave's got the chutzpah, and Bobby is the greatest exponent of the sport."

Davie believes that the key to Gunn and Feldman's success is selling the brutality of bare knuckle, breaking through to a jaded millennial audience with a new sport as raw and vicious and compelling as the streets. It's how Davie succeeded with the UFC, plucking his biggest stars from the meanest regions of the underworld. "I had bare-knuckle fighters in all of my first ten UFC matches," he says, watching a contestant wail on his opponent. "My biggest star back then was Tank Abbott, and I found him in a parking lot near Escondido, fighting for a thousand dollars cash. He destroyed this big Samoan kid out of Orange County, dropping him to the cement, kicking him in the head, and then turning to the guy's posse and saying, 'That was extra.'" Davie grins. "I was like, 'I love this guy!'"

Like Gunn and Feldman, Davie searched everywhere for his first fighters in the UFC, even signing a swastika-tattooed enforcer working at an Amsterdam brothel. "Gerard Gordeau was an ice-cold Dutchman," Davie recalls. "John Milius said he had the soul of a CIA assassin." According to Davie, Gordeau, a world champion kickboxer, was moonlighting as an underworld tough when Davie heard of him through a gym manager and invited him to fight in UFC One in 1993. "Gordeau handled all the muscle jobs for the brothel and rave-club owners," Davie recalls. "He had a .32 pistol in his back pocket, and a razor in his sock—I knew he'd be a real tough guy."

A skinny, pale 6'5", 216-pound fighter with a buzz cut and wispy goatee, Gordeau, at first glance, did not look tough. In fact, he looked as if he would surely get smothered by his opponent, Teila Tuli, a 6'2", 420-pound sumo wrestler from Honolulu. But Gordeau's eyes—dark, deep-set, unflinching—told another story. Less than thirty seconds into the first match at UFC One in Denver, Gordeau, wearing loose white karate pants and nothing else, kicked Tuli with a roundhouse to the teeth, following it with a right jab to his eye, exploding the sumo wrestler's socket and sending his teeth flying out over the audience, including the heads of the Gold's Gym sponsors in the front row. (They never sponsored another match.) The fight had lasted twenty-six seconds.

Davie, delighted by the buzz it had generated, went backstage to check on Gordeau, who was smoking a cigarette while a doctor pulled shards of teeth from his foot with tweezers. "I asked if he was okay, and he just said what he always said," Davie recalls. "'No problem, Art Davie.'" Almost everyone else had serious problems with it. *Sports Illustrated* had sent a reporter to cover the event, but the editors, appalled by the violence, decided not to run the story.[5] "Fighting is not what we thought it was," said a shell-shocked broadcaster at the event.[6]

Ultimately, Davie was proved right: the ultraviolence and speed soon made the UFC one of the most popular sports in the world.[7] But the question remained: could bare knuckle catch on the same way?

* * * * *

Gunn watches the fighters. "He's a wrassler," Gunn says, dismissing a young man's MMA stance in the ring. "See how he squares up? He can only hit one punch at a time."

Gunn doesn't much care for MMA. But he respects Davie and what he has done for the UFC, and hopes his predictions for bare knuckle will come true. If the underground sport is ever going to break through, now is the time. In England, where it is legal, bare knuckle has surged in recent years, even getting staged at one of the UK's most prestigious venues, the O2 Arena in London, in

June.[8] And now, as it gains traction in the States, Gunn has seen the underground sport attract increasingly more MMA fighters, young men used to getting kneed in the face and less bothered by the blood and broken bones that come with bare-fisted shots.

Gunn would prefer to see more young boxers entering the sport, but, thanks to Davie, all the kids, attracted by UFC super-stars like Ronda Rousey, Conor McGregor, and Randy Couture, want to fight MMA. If Davie can do that for bare knuckle, then Gunn is willing to let his own prejudices slide. "It really means something that he's here," Gunn says, looking at the fedora-wearing mogul as he stands next to a representative from the Kansas Athletic Commission. "He wouldn't be here otherwise, would he?"

Gunn is hopeful for the Kansas match. But he has seen his dreams come close before. Several years ago, he had been in discussions to fight Davie's former UFC star Tank Abbott in a high-profile bare-knuckle match. But that bout, like every sanc-tioned bare-knuckle fight Gunn has attempted since his 2011 match in Arizona—from a face-off against Kimbo Slice to his most recent bid against Shannon Ritch—fell through.* Now Kansas says it is interested in him fighting in a major pay-per-view event likely to be staged in the fall.

Davie is on board. Sean Wheelock, a member of the Kansas Athletic Commission, is here at the tryouts. And incredibly, even Gunn's old nemesis, Pennsylvania commissioner Greg Sirb, has come around and is now open to discussing a state-sanctioned event.

"I would never have guessed he would call in a million years," Feldman says, speculating that the commissioner doesn't want to

---

* Slice tragically died of a heart attack in 2016. And Gunn's bout against Ritch, originally slated for the Miccosukee tribal casino on the edge of the Everglades, west of Miami, in June 2016, was canceled just a week before the match. Feldman says the tribe had an unexpected change of heart, likely due to political pressure. (Casino representatives confirmed that a fight had been scheduled, but would not elaborate.)

miss out on bare knuckle after being so late to sanction MMA. "If he wants to do it, then there's *nobody* I can't convince."

But Gunn still isn't sure. If Kansas is staging the fight, then why haven't they set a date yet? Hoping to make some news of his own and spur the heartland state to action, Gunn slips out early, driving back home to prepare for his match. A week later, in West Virginia, he pummels Domingos, the Brazilian heavyweight with a 22-8 record, in under four minutes while the crowd screams, "Finish him, finish him, finish him!" It is a decidedly one-way affair, the outcome Gunn always dreamed for himself in his matchups against world champions—victories that never came. But with this seemingly routine win in the heart of coal country, Gunn has achieved something even greater. He has just won the Canadian Professional Boxing Council International title—an obscure belt but a belt nonetheless—meaning that with the win, Gunn has become the first fighter in US history since John L. Sullivan to simultaneously hold heavyweight titles in both pro boxing and bare knuckle.

Gunn has made history. And now Kansas will surely fall into place, meaning he can finally finish his $100,000 fight against Ritch—the last great bare-knuckle match of his career.

"It felt great to get the W," Gunn says, smiling amid the gleaming Harleys. "The Gunnslinger is back."[9]

CHAPTER 26
THE RISE OF THE SON

"That's it!" Gunn yells. "Come on, son. Right jab!"

Standing on the outside edge of the boxing ring, Gunn holds on to the ropes, his massive hands white-knuckled, eyes gleaming with adrenaline as the surrounding crowd screams in this smoke-stained run-down casino in New Cumberland, West Virginia. In the center of the ring, Bobby Jr. circles his opponent, a veteran forty-four-year-old welterweight with a 44-6 record, named Mike Miranda. It is the second round of this September 2017 headlining pro boxing match at the Mountaineer Casino Ballroom, and Bobby Jr.—only twenty years old with an 8-0 record—is vying for an upset.

His opponent, Miranda, is a seasoned pro with forty confirmed knockouts, several world title fights, and, despite his age, a right hook that can drop an ox. In fact, when Bobby Jr. was first presented with the chance to compete for the World Boxing Council FECARBOX super-middleweight title belt, Gunn, his manager and trainer, refused. "I turned it down instantly," Gunn says. "This was a hardened, seasoned bum."

But after studying Miranda's fights on YouTube, Gunn came to a realization—the veteran had a blind spot. "I seen something,"

Gunn recalls. "The guy's a southpaw. When he fought for his last world title, he got dropped with a left hook to the body—and Bobby loves that left hook; he's a winger."

Now, watching his son fight beneath the lights, Gunn wrestles with an unfamiliar feeling: nervousness. The Mountaineer Casino may be a faded resort in a former mining town in the Appalachian foothills, but the belt is real, a chance for Bobby Jr. finally to put his lifetime of lessons to use and continue the legacy of his birthright. Since childhood, Gunn has been training his son for a moment like this, having him run with five-gallon buckets of asphalt sealant during roadside jobs, having him hit Ike's daily to work the bags and spar. Now it is time for Bobby Jr. to begin his own ascendancy. Now it is time for him to achieve what no member of the Gunn clan has ever accomplished: becoming a world champion boxer at twenty years old—and now his father can barely bring himself to watch. "My heart is in my throat," Gunn says, wiping his face. "My nerves are totally shot."

At home, his wife, Rose, is praying at church, refusing even to discuss her son entering the ring. "It makes Mommy upset when my brother gets hit with the black eye," eight-year-old Charlene says at one point. "It makes me upset too."

Now, standing on the edge of the ring, the air reeking of bloodthirst and cheap well drinks, Gunn wills himself to remain confident. If nothing else, he knows he has offered his son this one surefire strategy—he can anticipate how an aging boxer will attack. "An old pro will squat down, hoping to get a young buck to start swinging wildly," Gunn explains. "Then he'll catch him on the chin." He grins. "Basically, I told Bobby to watch out for what I would do to him."

Bap!

Gunn flinches as Bobby Jr. absorbs a blow. "Come on, son!" he yells, banging his palms on the canvas, the gold "Bobby Jr."

lettering on his black T-shirt blazing under the lights. "Give him the punch!"

In the ring, Bobby Jr. steps toward his opponent. Wearing black shoes, black socks, and black trunks with his name written in gold lettering across the front waistband, Bobby Jr. is the chiseled, lean image of his father's former years. Gone is Bobby Jr.'s usual quiet demeanor. Gone the slouched stance. Like his father, he has become a different animal in the ring, a powerhouse of stone-eyed anger and discipline intent on only one aim: destroying Miranda and claiming his prize. "In the ring, the beast comes out," Bobby Jr. later explains. "The adrenaline just takes over. I know what I want and I know what I'm going to get."

Now, with the crowd on its feet in the second round, Miranda throws a jab, leaving his left side open to attack—and in that instant, Bobby Jr. pounces. Dodging the punch, Bobby Jr. leans forward, hammering Miranda's midsection with organ-battering blows—left, right, left, right—until the aging fighter finally sinks against the ropes, the referee stepping in to begin the count.

"Get up!" Bobby Jr. screams, his face a wild-eyed adrenaline snarl. "Get up!"

"Eight . . . nine . . . TEN!" the ref calls, swinging his arms. "It's over!"

In the center of the ring, Bobby Jr. raises his right arm, leans his head back, and lets out a victorious yell. Ducking the ropes, Gunn rushes to his son, grabbing him by the waist and hoisting him upward, parading him around the ring while staring into his face as the crowd of 1,200 cheers, father and son smiling, lost in the moment, the rest of the world a forgotten blur. "My boy made me so proud tonight," Gunn later says. "I love you, Bobby."

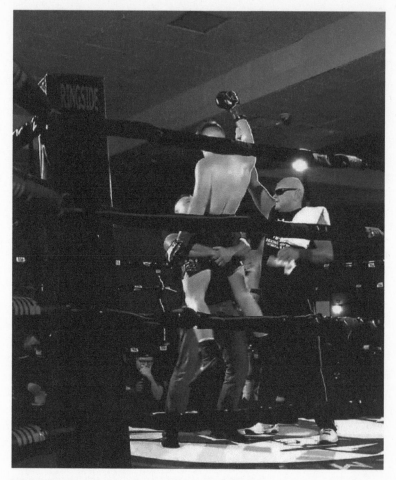

[Figure 26.1] Embracing Gunn Jr. in victory (Photo courtesy of Bobby Gunn)

* * * * *

Eight weeks later, the new World Boxing Association rankings are announced. Bobby Jr. has risen to become the fourteenth-ranked super middleweight fighter in the world. For any boxer, it is a career-making feat. For one trained and managed solely by his father, it is remarkable. "My dad never got the big breaks," Bobby

Jr. says. "Nobody done him no favors." He pauses. "It just makes me thankful. I don't ever take it for granted."

Smiling, Gunn simply shakes his head. "Give God the glory," he says. "My boy is in the world rankings."

It is a chilly morning in November in New Jersey, the temperatures dipping down into the forties, and Gunn and his son are celebrating the news by doing what they always do: heading out to pave another driveway in their dually one-ton truck. "I've been working like a dog," Gunn says, blowing steam from a Dunkin' Donuts cup, his French bulldog, Max, nestled in his lap. "I'm overwhelmed with life, but you know how it is. Just trying to get things going."

For Gunn, Bobby Jr.'s victory is the lone bright spot in an otherwise crushing year. Since losing to Roy Jones Jr. in February, Gunn has returned to his usual hustle, working asphalt while trying to convince someone to take a chance on launching bare knuckle as

[Figure 26.2] "I'm overwhelmed with life."
(Photo courtesy of Bobby Gunn)

a sport. As always, the effort has stalled. Earlier this year, he and Feldman thought they were close to getting approval for a sanctioned bare-knuckle event in a Midwestern state, but the state backed off and the event never happened. Then, this month, Gunn and Shannon Ritch were in talks to fight in a pay-per-view bare-knuckle fight, perhaps on Native American land in the Southwest, but the event broke down over contract disputes, both sides walking away in bitterness.

"I'm done with Gunn," Ritch tweeted. "He backed out and is a pussy."

"Wasters," Gunn replied in his own tweet. "Never had any intentions from the beginning."

Bare knuckle, however, has been the least of Gunn's problems. In recent months, his father, Robert, has steadily declined in health, doing little but trudging to the bar or sitting in his room at the Three Diamond Inn in Niagara Falls, drinking and pining for his wife, Jackie. "A hard life catches up to you," says Jimmy Ruml. "He's got arthritis, diabetes—but won't admit to it—and his vision isn't that great anymore. Now we go for a drink and he gets tears in his eyes, talking about Jackie. When she passed away, it just killed him."

Although Robert spoke recently with Bobby Jr. before his championship fight in West Virginia, offering advice over the phone, he did not make the trip south. So, on a recent morning with an icy wind skimming off Lake Ontario, Gunn drove north to check on his old man. He opened the door to find him drunk and unshaven, his room in shambles. "His eyes were all watered," Gunn says. "He wanted to see his grandson."

Shocked by his father's state, Gunn gave him a shower, shave, and haircut, the old man rebounding, as always—and even, finally, giving Gunn some praise. "Bobby has a natural ability for bare knuckle," Robert says. "He grew up gypsy style, has pro experience, and is a rough-and-tumble man. Now, what his heart wants, my heart wants—we're bringing this back." Soon afterward, Robert even returns to form himself with yet another bar fight. "I might start the Old-Timers Bare-Knuckle Club," he says, laughing. "I'm seventy-three years old and can fuck up most guys. I look at these sixty-year-olds in these coffee shops complaining,

'Jeez, my back, my pain medication.' When I was sixty, I could run five miles and go screw and drink all night. Jesus. What's wrong with these men?"

Grinning, Gunn shakes his head. While he may never figure out his father, he knows that the old man will always battle on, will always survive. Bobby Jr., however, is another matter. While his son has done well in the ring, Gunn has become increasingly worried for his life outside it. In the past year, Bobby Jr. has fallen in love with a teenage Traveler girl, gotten engaged, and, according to custom, prepared to leave the nest and start his own family—only to see the whole thing suddenly called off, seemingly due to differences between the clans.

When asked about it, Bobby Jr. and his father say little, Gunn later simply tweeting, "I pray that my son gets a good decent Christian girl that is humble and puts God first and is not materialistic."

Even more troubling, however, has been the call of the underworld. As Bobby Jr. has gained ground in the ring, he has increasingly drawn threats and challenges to compete in bare-knuckle fights in the Traveler community, a realm Gunn has worked to shield his son from his entire life. While not the mob-run underground that Gunn fought in, the Traveler bare-knuckle world has become more dangerous in its own right, the battles moving beyond fists into more lethal terrain fueled by drugs and alcohol.

According to Gunn, the traditional world of the Travelers is beginning to fall apart. At one point, he receives a shaky smart-phone video of masked Travelers attacking another Traveler over some feud, the marauders ripping open the man's car door and hacking him with a hatchet, screams filling the air as the screen goes black.

"Things are changing," Gunn says, a smartphone earbud

dangling from his face as he drives while trying to call the day's client. "Drugs is taking over a lot of the young gypsy boys. Pills, Oxycontin, heroin. It's really putting the brooms to 'em. Putting them crazy. They'll take a gun and knife and shoot you quicker than they would years ago. That's why I worry about this guy."

In the backseat, Bobby Jr.—head bowed over his smartphone—shrugs. "Ah, they don't do it around me," he says. "I keep good company."

"The younger generation is a lot more violent," Gunn persists. "There's a whole different attitude amongst them."

"That's more in Delaware," Bobby Jr. says. "Nothing to worry about here."

Yet Gunn can't help but worry. As a result, he continues to guard Bobby Jr. from the outside world, saying his son is not quite ready to go out on his own. "He's better with me right now," he says. But others disagree, claiming that Gunn is hampering Bobby Jr. by being overprotective, especially when it comes to his boxing career. Yes, they say, Gunn has raised an undeniable talent in the ring, but it is now time to hand him over to a professional manager and trainer, someone who does this full time, someone who can take him to the next level. In short, it is time for Gunn to let his son go.

"I think Bobby is more protective of his son than he needs to be," says Joe Mack. "Bobby had no one growing up, so he's hypersensitive about him. But he's just got too much going on to also manage his son's career."

Gunn shrugs off such talk. In fact, in the wake of his son's championship title win and the ensuing fight offers from promoters—many of whom, Gunn claims, tried to rip them off with sleazy management deals—he has even conceived a radical idea, one that breaks with centuries of Gunn clan code. He says he loves his son so much, he is willing to give him the

greatest gift of all: his blessing to walk away from the
fight game. "You could slash
me, rip my heart out, and I
come back and win fights,"
Gunn says. "That's my
whole life. If you don't have
that hunger, you'll get hurt."
He pauses. "My boy has the
hunger, but he's disgusted
with the people surround-
ing the game. Yesterday,
he said, 'Dad, you're world
champion and I've gotta
tell you, I don't want to
deal with these guys all my
life. They're scumbags.' And
he's right. So my life now
in legalizing bare knuckle

[Figure 26.3] "I never done as good as I could."
(Photo courtesy of Bobby Gunn)

might mean he doesn't have to do that. If I can make some good
money, do real good, that's my kids' future. I can invest that.
Bobby can do whatever he wants to do in life. I don't tell him
to do the fight game. He's already done great. He's a worldwide
contender. So if he walks away, then I'll back him up because I
love that boy and I understand."

Gunn rubs his face. Sometimes, it all can get to him. Sometimes, he just needs to get away, to turn to the one constant he
has known since childhood, the one refuge in which every outside
worry will fade away and he can stare into the eyes of his opponent
and know the simple electric pleasure of being alive. It's getting
harder to get to that point, even to get in the ring at all. But
when all else fails, he simply puts one mangled foot in front of the

other, heading for that next fight, that next rent check, that next semester of private-school tuition for Charlene. After all, he's only one fight away from that big break.

"I never done as good as I could," Gunn says, disappearing into the wilds of New Jersey, heading to another asphalt job. "But I'm a proper gypsy thoroughbred fighting man."

CHAPTER 27
LAST STAND IN THE WILD WEST

"I'm the boss, I'm the boss, I'm the boss," Gunn says, muttering his mantra to himself, pacing a concrete locker room backstage at the Cheyenne Ice and Events Center on the dusty outskirts of Cheyenne, Wyoming, in June 2018. "Come on, big fucker—let's go."

Gunn, forty-four, is about to take the stage for the fight of his life, the first legal, state-sanctioned bare-knuckle bout in US history. It is being aired live to the world on pay-per-view, introducing him and his underground sport to the mainstream. Yet instead of elation, Gunn—middle-aged, broken down, out of shape—feels something else: doubt. "I didn't have time to properly train," he says, shadowboxing the air, glancing at the other fighters in the room, wondering about his younger and larger opponent, Irineu Beato Costa Jr., a heavyweight boxer from São Paulo, Brazil. "All I do is shovel asphalt. I'm not in shape, and it shows—I'm getting too old for this shit."

Gunn has reason to feel uncertainty. In recent months, his life has changed profoundly, throwing him and his cherished family into chaos. In November, after years living with his wife and children in their apartment in New Jersey, Gunn suddenly uprooted them, packing his family into his extended-cab pickup truck and driving them west to Phoenix. In the past, Gunn would sometimes take his family to Arizona for the winter, leaving the snows of New Jersey to lay asphalt with other Travelers in the desert. But this time was different—Gunn was moving his family west for good. "I just got sick of New Jersey," he says, sitting on a wooden bench in the backstage locker room. "Too many people bringing us down. We needed a fresh scene."

Gunn claims he and his family left their home in New Jersey due to bare knuckle, the local fight world shaking him down to be part of the new sport that was finally becoming mainstream. "Guys kept threatening me for money," Gunn says. "Not that I had it. But they thought I did: 'Come on, Bobby, give me five grand or I'll make sure the sport never happens.'"

In truth, however, Gunn may have left New Jersey for a different reason. In 2017, the breakup of Bobby Jr.'s engagement to a local Irish Traveler girl had rocked his family while also creating rifts within the Traveler community. Bobby Jr., now twenty-one, was heartbroken. Gunn, upset over the ordeal, was at a loss. Perhaps the move was intended as a fresh start—for everyone. "That was very hard on me," Gunn says about the breakup. "My mind was fried. Our house was in chaos."

In November, after arriving in Phoenix, Gunn and Bobby Jr. went to work, scouring the desert to knock on doors and pave driveways with other Travelers, returning every night to Rose and Charlene in their rented apartment. Soon, the family settled into a routine, everything seemingly returning to normal. Then, in March, Gunn awoke to the shock of his life—Bobby Jr. had disappeared in the night, absconding to Las Vegas to elope with a new Traveler girl he had begun dating, getting married at a casino without telling anyone. Gunn, who had spent almost every day of his life with Bobby Jr. for the past ten years, taking him everywhere from gyms to fights, to construction sites, was devastated.

"I was in shock," Gunn recalls. "I was mad. Little Bobby did it without me even knowing—I couldn't believe it."

In April, just weeks after Bobby Jr.'s elopement, Gunn, Rose, and Charlene faced a choice: Should they follow Bobby Jr. to his new home, or go on their own way? After his elopement, Bobby Jr. and his bride had moved to be near her parents' clan in Baltimore. As part of his new life, he was putting his boxing career on hold to work full-time, starting his own paving business to support his family. Now Gunn and his family had to decide their next move. For years, Gunn had dreamed of living and working in Montana, where the clean mountain rivers reminded him of his Canadian youth. "My plan was to go to Montana," he says. "It's a beautiful place right across the border from Alberta and Saskatchewan, where my dad used to take me when I was a kid. I wanted a chance to get away from all the craziness and horseshit."

Yet, in the end, Gunn and Rose decided to keep their family together. "We moved to Baltimore so my wife could be closer to Bobby Jr.," Gunn says. "When you have a chance to be around your kid, then you want to be around them."

In May, as the winter snows melted, Gunn and his family moved into an apartment on the outskirts of Baltimore—a homecoming of sorts for the aging fighter. His mother was originally from the area and had long been buried there, and her clan of people still lived in the region. Now, after settling his family into an apartment, Gunn began visiting his mother's grave, leaving notes tucked inside a crucifix on its headstone, looking for guidance as everything around him seemed to dissolve. "God never promises it'll be a bed of roses," he says of the change.

Gunn, now working alone, found the proximity to his son painful, a reminder of the truth he had been blind to—Bobby Jr. was finally ready to go out on his own. For Gunn, who had always worked to give Bobby Jr. the love and security he himself had never known, the realization was too much to bear. He tried to remain positive—texting Bobby Jr. in the mornings, calling him during breaks on job sites—but there was no getting around it. Gunn was devastated. "I was married young too," he says, rubbing his face. "So it might make him a better person. But it also makes me mad. I have mixed emotions."

Without his son, Gunn poured himself into his work, laying asphalt until well after dark, doing twice the labor as his battered body continued to break down. All around him, bad news seemed to abound. The son of a Traveler friend was killed in a fiery wreck near Brownsville, Texas. All the tools were stolen from Gunn's truck in a Baltimore parking lot. Alone on job sites, Gunn stewed, his tweets taking a darker turn: "Lord, Lord, I need you. I'm all alone."

Finally, in April, good news broke: the return of bare knuckle. Throughout 2017, Feldman had been traveling the country, donning his suit and making his PowerPoint presentation on legalizing the gloveless sport to twenty-eight states in a row, getting rejected by every single one, until a state finally bit—Wyoming. "The commissioner told me, 'I love two things: fighting and capitalism,'" Feldman recalls. "Finally, I found my guy. He's a fighter, a former congressman and a multimillionaire—he's fucking big-time out there."

A rural state with a long streak of western independence, Wyoming, population 570,000, is home to cattlemen, Native Americans, and fracking wildcatters who love to buck tradition—a spirit solidly represented in its state athletic commissioner, Bryan Pedersen. "I take a lot of pride in the three-oh-seven," Pedersen says, referring to the state's area code, as he lifts weights while talking through a headset in March 2018. "We're a rural state and have a sense of independence. I get positive feedback from fighting. It's a sign of being western and tough."

Pedersen, forty-three, is a former state legislator who works as a financial consultant for RBC Wealth Management in the state capital, Cheyenne, population 64,000, in the flat, windswept south-eastern corner of the state. The son of a local RBC consultant whose wife worked on GOP campaigns including former vice president Dick Cheney's, Pedersen has long balanced finance and politics with adventure. After graduating in 1998 from the University of Wyoming with a degree in psychology, he spent his twenties working in Cheyenne while also running with the bulls in Pamplona, studying French cooking at Le Cordon Bleu in London, and climbing Mount Kilimanjaro in Tanzania—a feat he accomplished on the same day he learned he had won the Republican primary for state representa-tive in Wyoming, at age twenty-nine. "There's never a dull moment when you're around Bryan," a friend said in an interview in 2011. "He decides to do things and just does them . . . He takes on things that a lot of people wouldn't even consider."[1]

Of all Pedersen's pursuits, however, none would compare with his true passion: fighting. A bald, beefy 5'11", 185-pound lifelong scrapper, he says, "Fighting was something you did for fun in college bars." Pedersen began formally training in martial arts in his late thirties as a way to keep in shape. Fixated by the sport, he then traveled to Bangkok to learn Muay Thai kickboxing, going on to compete in amateur bouts throughout the West. In 2012, as a state legislator, he wrote a bill to legitimize the sport in Wyoming, creating the nation's first state commission devoted solely to MMA: the Wyoming State Board of Mixed Martial Arts. In 2013, he himself even donned gloves to compete in the state's first sanc-tioned pro MMA event, breaking his nose and bloodying himself before losing in front of a packed arena at the Cheyenne Frontier Days Exhibit Hall. "I whipped wholesale butt for four minutes and twenty seconds," Pedersen recalls. "Then, halfway through the second round, I had a huge adrenaline dump. Afterwards, there was nothing left in my body. So I lost." He shrugs. "I left pro fighting to become the commissioner—I'm excited about combat sports."

For years, Pedersen worked to build MMA into a popular sport in Wyoming, enticing promoters with some of the lowest state fees in the nation. Yet, despite his efforts, he always ran into the same problem: no one wanted to stage events in the least populous state in the country—a landscape so empty, it had even fewer residents than Washington, DC.

Finally, in 2017, Pedersen found his opportunity to put Wyoming on the map, with an upstart sport that combined his love for adrenaline with spectacle and profit: bare knuckle. "In Wyoming, we are driven by an independent western spirit," Pedersen says. "And I'm looking to bring money to my state by taking this mainstream."

In truth, Pedersen wanted to sanction bare knuckle for another reason as well: the sport was already legal and being practiced in his state. In 2012, when he had established an MMA commission instead of a pro boxing commission—which would have outlawed the sport—Pederson had, in effect, made bare knuckle legal in Wyoming. In response, Corey Williams, a general contractor in the six-hundred-person town of Shoshoni, staged bare-knuckle events throughout the state—modest affairs with local fighters, in venues such as town halls.

Although legal, the bare-knuckle bouts were not sanctioned, since Pedersen had never formally recognized the sport. "People found loopholes," he says. "By not making it illegal, we therefore made the sport legal. So people put on small shows throughout the state."

Eventually, bare knuckle began to attract negative headlines in Wyoming, and police chiefs and city councils worked to block events. In 2015, after a bare-knuckle fighter was hospitalized with jaw injuries at one of Williams's bouts in Riverton, the local city administrator, acting on a recommendation by the chief of police, called for the sport to be banned.[2] Soon, the Riverton city council began creating an ordinance to outlaw the sport. Williams filed federal lawsuits in response, the whole ordeal becoming an issue for the state commission.[3] ("I wasn't in violation of any laws," Williams says.) Finally, in 2017, when Feldman arrived with his tightly run format of bare knuckle, Pedersen saw an opportunity—a chance to sanction a sport that was happening in his state anyway, while also making international headlines, jump-starting combat sports in Wyoming.

In December 2017, Pedersen and Feldman began working to make bare knuckle a sanctioned sport—doing everything possible to make it safe, knowing that it would come under scrutiny. Working with Pedersen, state lawmakers, and outside consultants, Feldman drafted a forty-two-page rulebook. He quietly purchased the intellectual property rights to various names for bare knuckle, ensuring that he would own every piece of the sport, anticipating that rival leagues would arise in his wake. He even built and patented a $140,000 ten-ton steel arena, a "squared circle" consisting of a twenty-two-foot-wide ring within a thirty-foot square—an impressive feat of engineering unlike any fight arena in existence.

Technically classifying bare knuckle as a form of MMA—the only type of sport he could legally oversee—Pedersen helped Feldman push it through the tiers of the Wyoming government, at every step giving the lawmakers a simple pitch. "We already regulate MMA and kickboxing," Pedersen says. "In both of those sports you can take a shinbone to the head, which is like getting hit with a baseball bat." He pauses. "A lot of the sanctioning and legality of bare knuckle is due to a misunderstanding. Some places want to say bare knuckle is boxing without gloves, which would make it illegal in most states. But the rules of bare knuckle are different. They allow for striking but also different kinds of things like Muay Thai clinches. So the sport has been misunderstood. It's called bare-knuckle boxing. But in fact, it's bare-knuckle *fighting*."

Finally, in March 2018, Feldman got the call he had long been awaiting. Wyoming had become the first state in the nation to recognize bare-knuckle boxing. Driving in his beat-up SUV in Philadelphia, Feldman tried to remain calm. But after nearly a decade of working to make the sport a reality, he couldn't help himself. "I tried to be polite but then said, 'Fuck that. I'm jumping out of my skin,'" Feldman recalls. "I just yelled, 'Fucking yes, man!'"

Feldman knew he had just been given the opportunity of a lifetime, one that could finally elevate him from the drudgery of low-level promotions to international success. He had a financial backer (an anonymous angel investor in Philadelphia), a state sanction, and a lifetime of fight promotion experience. Now he had just one final hurdle remaining: to pull off a groundbreaking show, one that had never been done before in US history, one that would feature good fights without serious injury, one that would launch a new sport and multimillion-dollar business. If he succeeded, he could be set for life. If he failed, he would be banished back to his anonymous workaday promotions, perhaps even facing criminal charges if a fighter got seriously hurt. On top of everything, however, Feldman had only one nagging concern: would bare knuckle still be compelling once it was taken from the underground?

In the end, Feldman knew that only one man could truly help him pull it off.

* * * * *

"I've got to pee again," Gunn says, waddling toward the urinal, wearing nothing but his padded groin cup, underwear, and boxing shoes. "My God, I sound like a grandfather."

Battle-scarred, out-of-shape, and large of prostate, Gunn finishes up and returns to the backstage dressing room of the Cheyenne Ice and Events Center. It is Saturday, June 2, 2018, and beyond the concrete walls of the dressing room, the evening's ten-card event is already under way, with over two thousand beer-drinking, cowboy-hat-wearing locals screaming for blood, their cries and stomping boot heels shaking the stadium like thunder. Inside the dressing room, however, the mood is subdued as the fighters prep for their bouts by punching air, retreating into their headphones, or saying prayers, the various smartphone boomboxes blaring everything from Elvis to Nas. Overall, the room pulses with nerves, the pro fighters long accustomed to entering the ring but never without gloves—except for one man, whom they all revere: Gunn. "I'm so happy I get to see you fight," says a tattooed young fighter. Gunn smiles. "God bless you," he says. "This is my last one—I'm the oldest fighter here."

Tonight, Gunn is making his last stand. The legend will fight his final bout in an ice-and-roller-skating arena adorned with giant American flags and advertisements for construction companies, taking the stage alongside nineteen other fighters from pro boxing, MMA, and street brawling—all aiming to resurrect one of America's oldest sports. Attended by cheering cowboys, farmers, oil-rig workers, and uniformed soldiers,

[Figure 27.1] Backstage in Cheyenne (Photo by author)

the ten-card event features a mix of up-and-coming contenders like former UFC star Bec Rawlings alongside aging pros like former UFC heavyweight Ricco Rodriguez, everyone fighting in five two-minute rounds while wearing nothing on their hands but wrapping about an inch below the knuckles. The scene is a sort of boulevard of broken-bodied dreams. B-list veterans like forty-one-year-old former army boxer and MMA fighter Eric Prindle, looking for one last shot at glory, fight alongside total unknowns like thirty-three-year-old stonemason Sam Shewmaker from the Missouri Ozarks, wearing US flag trunks and a philosopher's beard.

Only one thing is certain: no one knows what to expect. "You guys are making history," says one of the referees, Dan Miragliotta, to the assembled crowd of fighters before the show, everyone huddled in a quiet corner as the crowd screams for the bouts to begin. "You're pioneers."

Dave Feldman, wearing a blue suit and open white-collared shirt, then gives a blunter ultimatum. "If you don't put up a good fight, you're not getting paid," he says. "If you show some fucking heart, though, that's different—you're getting a bonus."

Now, in the minutes before his fight, Gunn stands ready. Backstage in the locker room, he is approached by a steady stream of fighters, some asking to hold hands in prayer, others seeking advice. While the various fighters all have experience with gloved combat, none have competed much in bare knuckle, so all are trying to gain some last-minute knowledge. Rodriguez, the former UFC heavyweight champ, talks body-shot strategy with Gunn. "I used to spar with Bobby ten years ago in Bayonne, New Jersey," Rodriguez says. "He would clobber me and then take me aside to show me tricks. He's a legend."

Maurice Jackson, a pro MMA fighter from Las Vegas, returns grinning to the locker room after his bout. He knocked out his opponent with a left hook and two right crosses in just over a minute. "Bobby, I did what you said," Jackson says, smiling. "I tapped him with the reach and he was like, 'Oh, shit'—it worked!"

Gunn grins. "I gave advice to both him and his opponent," he says. "Only one listened."

Gunn, the grizzled YouTube legend, smiles, playing the part

of elder statesman. Inside, however, he's a wreck. "I don't like the air up here," he says, breathing heavy in the six-thousand-foot atmosphere while wrapping tape and gauze around his wrists—the only allowed hand protection for the event. "And I don't like wrapping. They don't do no good anyway—I want it old school."

For Gunn, the past few weeks have been a slog. In addition to laying asphalt six days a week, he has been promoting this event constantly, tweeting and doing interviews for outlets including SiriusXM, *Men's Health,* and ESPN. Then, on Wednesday, he flew to Denver, driving the hundred miles north to Cheyenne to continue the press tour, smiling for days alongside Feldman, Pedersen, and the other nineteen fighters for the social-media machine.

In many ways, Gunn finds all this satisfying, the world finally catching up to him and the sport he has practiced for decades. But it is also exhausting. Earlier this week, while driving his truck to Cheyenne, passing the endless wind farms, pumpjacks, and liquor stores of the Great Plains, he felt a loss of confidence—a feeling echoed by Feldman. After Gunn's dismal loss to Roy Jones Jr. last year, the aging journeyman is largely seen as a washed-up fighter. Now, though, he is the defending champion of bare knuckle. He's not even fighting as the headliner, but in a middle-of-the-card bout. Gunn's face is barely on the posters.

"I feel kind of weird headlining," Rodriguez says at one point. "Bobby is the defending champion."

Broke, broken-bodied, and without compass, Gunn is profoundly unsure of himself. For the past few days, when not smiling for the cameras, he has been pacing endlessly, lamenting the absence of his son and his beloved bulldog, Max, who stayed behind with Rose and Charlene. In addition, he is worried about preserving the last concrete thing he has left: his perfect 72-0 bare-knuckle record. "I look better than some of these guys, don't I?" he mumbles to himself at one point, rolling his stump-size neck. "I just can't think about the fight. What's the point? What will happen will happen."

In truth, Gunn can think of nothing else but the fight. He knows he has little chance of winning against his opponent, Costa, a younger, stronger 6'3", 200-pound boxer with seventeen knock-outs in his past twenty-six bouts. Gunn also doesn't like the overall setup of the event. In addition to having to wear wrapping around his wrists—a safety precaution intended to minimize broken hands—he must fight within the event's fast-paced two-minute rounds. It is a change from his usual underground bouts, which have no time limits, allowing him to gauge his opponent before going in for the kill. In response, Gunn has honed a simple strategy, which he formulated on the phone with his father in Niagara Falls. It's the equivalent of a Hail Mary. He will go in fast and close against Costa, aiming for a quick knockout before the giant can decimate him with his longer reach.

"I'm gonna roll the dice," Gunn says, writing the name of his recently deceased Traveler friend on his shirt, dedicating the fight to him. "Go in close and chop him up like a lawnmower—it's my only chance."

"You're up next, Bobby!"

Gunn begins to pace. Wearing a black sleeveless shirt, black shorts, and black shoes, he favors his right foot, the one that was once shattered by a rooftop fall. Moments ago, as a final reminder of his troubles, he had opened his gym bag to realize that his wife, Rose, had accidentally packed him his son's gear instead of his own. After sticking the smaller mouth guard into boiling water and then shoving it in his mouth—grimacing as the hot rubber molded to his teeth—Gunn had shimmied into Bobby Jr.'s cup and shoes, the smaller clothes adding to his discomfort. "Bobby Jr. usually packs my bag," he says. "I miss him."

Now, leaving the backstage locker room, Gunn walks the

concrete tunnel toward the ring. Unlike almost every other fighter, he has no trainer or manager. Instead, he is accosted by a camera crew wanting a quick interview and then by several fighters asking for selfies. But once he gets to his spot in the wings, Gunn stands alone. Letting the outside world slip away, he retreats into himself, going through the same motions that have sustained him since childhood, the mantra he has always repeated like an omen. "I'm the boss, I'm the boss, I'm the boss," he says, punching the air.

Sure, he wants to win in the first state-sanctioned bare-knuckle fight event in US history, solidifying his place in the record books, legitimizing a wayward career. But more than that, as always, Gunn fights for a different reason. Since the departure of Bobby Jr., he now thinks about his children in a different way, dwelling more on their personal goals. So tonight, while shadow-boxing the air, the crowd screaming just beyond the darkness, Gunn focuses his mind on his one true motiva- tion: to take the $10,000 prize money home to his daughter,

[Figure 27.2] Waiting to enter the ring (Photo by author)

Charlene, who, he now says, can buck Traveler tradition to attend private school into her teens. "She's a smart girl, the joy of my heart," he says. "I want her to go to school for as long as she wants."

"One minute, Bobby!"

Gunn bounces from foot to foot, opening and closing his mouth, staring at the ring in the spotlight. Suddenly, he is confronted by a man, the person getting right in his face, whispering in his ear—Feldman. For the duo, the road to this night has been a long one, often marked by conflict. Although Gunn first introduced Feldman to the sport and has helped him grow it over the years, it is unclear whether the aging fighter has any formal stake in Bare Knuckle Fighting Championships, Feldman's company that is producing the event.

Still, Feldman knows he needs Gunn. Twenty-five years ago, just down the road in Denver, the UFC made history by holding its first PPV combat event, a bloody wild affair that was written off by the world until it eventually grew to become a $12 billion cultural juggernaut. Feldman, wearing the necklace of his deceased father beneath his suit, sees that kind of opportunity for bare knuckle—and he needs his star fighter to pull off one last victory.

[Figure 27.3] "The legacy continues." (Photo by author)

"We worked a long time," Feldman says, his mouth in Gunn's ear. "This is your fucking moment. Go out there and do what you got to do. Don't be safe. Don't box. Don't be technical—go knock this fucking guy the fuck out."

Gunn sniffs.

"All right."

The stage goes dark. The aging fighter takes one last deep breath. "I'm the boss, I'm the boss, I'm the boss," Gunn says. "Come on, big fucker, let's go."

Walking out to Whitesnake's "Here I Go Again" in front of a screaming crowd, Gunn takes the stage, squaring off against Costa, a musclebound opponent who towers over him. Standing just feet apart, the men raise their fists. It is a striking image in US sports history—no boxing gloves.

"Knuckle up!" one of the two referees yells.

Charging Costa, Gunn throws a penetrating left hook to the liver, dropping him within seconds. "Down goes Costa!" yells the announcer. The crowd cheers.

Now animated, dancing on his feet, Gunn circles the ring as Costa manages a wobbly rise. Sensing his opportunity, Gunn rushes him again. Costa swings a punch. Gunn ducks and leans forward, this time going for the kill—another deep shot to the liver, topped by a final overhand right hook to the temple as he falls.

The crowd roars.

Costa lies crumpled on the ring.

The fight is over.

"That left hook to the liver—Ooh! That was a nasty shot," an announcer says. "That takes your breath and your legs away, immediately."

In only forty-one seconds, Gunn has proved why he is the champion of this sport, demolishing his opponent with the precision of a surgeon, the victory and the body shots so quick, the Internet will later wonder how he did it. But for Gunn, it's just another victory to add to his lifetime 72-0 record in bare knuckle, only this time with a crucial twist—he won in a legal arena in front of a pay-per-view audience around the world, making history. "Just like that, the legacy continues," says the announcer. "The legend that is bare-knuckle fighter Bobby Gunn."

Smiling, squinting into the lights, Gunn raises his arms in victory.

[Figure 27.4] "The legend that is bare-knuckle fighter Bobby Gunn." (Photo courtesy of Bobby Gunn)

EPILOGUE

Gunn's storybook ending didn't last long.

On September 28, 2019, Gunn was driving his Dodge Ram 3500 truck through Upper Pittsgrove Township, New Jersey, when his truck crossed the median and crashed head-on into a Hyundai Elantra. The collision killed the driver, Polly Tornari, 51, and injured her husband, Robert. At the time, he was interviewed by police and released; a few months later, the New Jersey authorities issued a warrant for his arrest. According to a criminal complaint, Gunn had allegedly been under the influence of a controlled substance,[1] which prosecutors later stated was fentanyl, a synthetic opioid up to a hundred times more powerful than morphine.[2]

"State police are looking for bare-knuckle boxer Robert 'Bobby' Gunn," stated a New Jersey news report. "Police said Gunn was last seen in Maricopa County, Arizona on DEb. [*sic*] 10 and may be working as an independent contractor."[3]

The death of Polly Tornari—a customer service representative with Farmers Mutual Insurance for thirty-one years and a lifelong member of New Jersey's Quinton Baptist Church, according to her obituary[4]—also marks a tragic twist in the story of Gunn.

How did a dedicated father, Christian, and lifelong teetotaler wind up in such a tragic situation?

There are no clear answers. Gunn has refused to comment, citing the ongoing nature of the investigation. According to friends and family, in June 2020 Gunn was traveling in Arizona when a friend showed him a Facebook post that the New Jersey State Police were looking for him. Gunn quickly drove east and turned himself in to authorities in Woodstown, New Jersey. According to reports, he was detained on two charges—second-degree vehicular homicide and third-degree assault by auto. Facing up to fifteen years in prison if convicted on both counts, Gunn hired a lawyer and was granted bail, since he had no prior criminal record. According to his attorney, Gunn subsequently completed a twenty-eight-day program at a rehab facility. In February 2021, a grand jury indicted him on the charges. Gunn's attorney, however, stated he had his own account of the crash. "It's clear in the police report that Mr. Gunn gave a different version of the happening of the accident, which will be dealt with at a later time," his attorney said. "Also, it's set forth that Mr. Gunn attempted to do evasive action prior to the happening of the accident. He was also injured in the accident."[5]

At I write this, Gunn has yet to stand trial, and his future is uncertain to say the least. But bare knuckle, the sport resurrected in part by him, is reaching new levels of success. After the first sanctioned bare-knuckle event in 2018, Feldman used the momentum to attract washed-up MMA fighters looking for redemption and get the sport legalized in twenty-six states, including California, Mississippi, Florida, Kansas, New Hampshire, and Alabama, as well as licensed matches in Thailand and England. In 2022, Triller, a social media app, bought a majority ownership in Bare Knuckle Fighting Championship (BKFC) for an undisclosed sum.[67] Bare knuckle doesn't have a major TV broadcast deal and its sponsors include companies like Nerd Focus Energy Drink. But the sport has over one million followers on Instagram and is being covered by outlets like ESPN—"Blood Sport: Bare Knuckle Fighting Emerges from Shadows,"[8] one headline reads—and is reaching unimagined levels of success compared with only recently being in basements and back alleys. Looking ahead, Feldman says he's still working to make the sport a financial success, but his ambitions are high.

"I can't believe where we're at," Feldman says. "It's been a hard, hard road. But we never quit. And now we're starting a new fight series, we're in talks with networks, and someone even wants to do a movie about me. It's 'pinch-me-I'm-dreaming' stuff." He pauses. "And I won't forget Bobby. We started this idea together, and once he gets this legal situation behind him, we're going to talk."

For Gunn, witnessing the success of the sport he helped create as he faces a potential prison sentence must be devastating. But for now, his focus is likely on just surviving, and on providing for his family should he do time.

There is, however, a ray of hope. In August, Bobby Jr. and his wife welcomed their first child, a daughter named Mary Ann.

"My dad left me a left hook and a lot of memories," Bobby Jr. says. "I watched him win the world title, travel around the world, and do amazing things. It's stuff I'll never forget—and I can't wait to tell my kids." He pauses. "Life isn't easy, but something good will come of this. You know, testimonies don't come without the word *test*."

Gunn's career is probably over, and Bobby Jr. says he is done with the fight world as well.

But in the years ahead, the Gunn lineage could continue on.

In August, Bobby Jr. posted a photo of his weeks-old daughter to Twitter. Lying on a white blanket, swaddled in white and wearing a pink bow, the granddaughter of Bobby Gunn, the undefeated bare-knuckle champion, raises her hands like fists. Tiny pink satin boxing gloves are arranged on either side of her as she stares straight into the camera.

"We're ready for the fights Saturday," the caption reads. "Lets gooooooo."

ACKNOWLEDGMENTS

Thank you to Bobby Gunn and his family for their time and trust. It means a lot.

Thank you to the great editors who helped shape this story, including Mark Healy, Larry Kanter, Ryan Krogh, and Michael Carr.

Thank you to Annie Licata, who did the herculean task of fact-checking this book.

Thank you to Blackstone Publishing for believing in the story and committing to it.

Huge thanks to David Feldman for his time and trust.

Thank you to Shannon Ritch for sharing his time and his invaluable perspective.

Thank you to John Stygles, Max Sparber, Jason Thalken, and everyone else who gave their time for interviews and offered their resources.

Thank you to the bare-knuckle and Irish Traveler communities for letting me in.

Thank you to Don Winslow for his wisdom and support.

Thank you to Shane Salerno, the greatest agent in the world, and his team of superheroes at the Story Factory for their innovative approach with this book.

Thank you to my family and friends for all their love and support.

Huge thanks to my brothers for always having my back, talking writing, and sharing laughs.

Thank you forever to my parents, who always encouraged me to chase my dreams.

Most of all, thank you to Catherine and my children for everything.

AUTHOR'S NOTE

Why did Gunn and others talk to me for this book? A key factor in prosecuting street fighters is establishing the specific date and locale of an underground match. This is the reason I never give exact locations for bouts I witness. Also, when requested, I have omitted fighters' names or used pseudonyms. These instances are noted in the text. When requested by underground fighters and promoters, I have withheld certain details, like match locations and purse amounts.

NOTES

CHAPTER 1

1. Dean Davis, "1st LAR Bn. Marine Shoots to Attain Higher Goal," Defense Visual Information Distribution Service, October 24, 2008, https://www.dvidshub.net/news/25786/1st-lar-bn-marine-shoots-attain-higher-goal.

2. Robert D. McFadden, "Anthony Provanzano, [*sic*] 71, Ex-Teamster Chief, Dies," *New York Times*, December 13, 1988, https://www.nytimes.com/1988/12/13/obituaries/anthony-provanzano-71-ex-teamster-chief-dies.html.

CHAPTER 2

1. Kara Seymour, "America's Most Dangerous Cities: 6 Are in N.J.," Patch, August 29, 2015, https://patch.com/new-jersey/cherryhill/americas-most-dangerous-cities-6-are-nj.

2. Dick Ryder, "Bobby Gunn vs Ernest Jackson for the BKB Title," December 3, 2011, YouTube video, https://www.youtube.com/watch?v=78Bokbfc170.

3. Don Muzzi et al., "Epidemiology of Professional Bare-Knuckle Fighting Injuries," The Physician and Sportsmedicine 50, no. 5

(October 2022): 448–53, https://doi.org/10.1080/00913847.2021
.1955604.

4. Bryan Alary, "Mixed Martial Arts Bloodier but Less Dangerous
than Boxing," Folio, University of Alberta, November 5, 2015,
https://www.ualberta.ca/folio/2015/11/mixed-martial-arts-
bloodier-but-less-dangerous-than-boxing.html.

CHAPTER 5

1. Krishna-Dwaipayana Vyasa, *The Mahabharata*, trans. Protap
Chandra Roy (Calcutta: Bharata Press, 1884), https://books
.google.com/books?id=JxlBAQAAMAAJ&pg=RA1-PA29&
lpg=RA1-PA29&dq=Mahabharata+boxing+clenched+fist&
source=bl&ots=8CUjMpFKVx&sig=9gFolIsDVsX-H80B7Szv
0G0zGB8&hl=en&sa=X&ved=0ahUKEwjwnvvyrbHUAhU
CymMKHaNIC-4Q6AEIQzAE#v=onepage&q=Mahabharata
%20boxing%20clenched%20fist&f=false.

2. Paul MacKendrick and Herbert M. Howe, eds., *Classics in Translation*, vol. 2, Latin Literature (Madison: University of
Wisconsin Press, 1952), https://books.google.com/books?
id=AdzlbYqjp-AC&pg=PA232&lpg=PA232&dq=the+aeneid+
gloves+of+eryx&source=bl&ots=ax1KgowJ5e&sig=01og
IPyZQJe1KAVxDWwSBKQi6f8&hl=en&sa=X&ved=0a
hUKEwj8ja2fv4PRAhUPzGMKHclIBrAQ6AEILjAD#v=
onepage&q=the%20aeneid%20gloves%20of%20eryx&f=false.

3. David Dabydeen, John Gilmore, and Cecily Jones, eds., *The
Oxford Companion to Black British History* (Oxford, UK: Oxford
University Press, 2007).

4. "Tom Molineaux," Virginia Museum of History & Culture,
accessed August 26, 2019, https://www.virginiahistory.org/collec-
tions-and-resources/virginia-history-explorer/tom-molineaux.

5. Elliott J. Gorn, *The Manly Art* (Ithaca, NY: Cornell University
Press, 1986), 35.

6.   Bob Mee, *Bare Fists* (New York: Overlook Press, 1998), 66.

7.   Pierce Egan, *Boxiana; or, Sketches of Modern Pugilism* (London: Sherwood, Jones, and Co., 1824).

8.   Michael T. Isenberg, *John L. Sullivan and His America* (Urbana: University of Illinois Press, 1994), 79.

9.   Robert K. Turnbull, "Boxing," in *Appletons' Annual Cyclopaedia and Register of Important Events* (New York: Appleton, 1889), 100, https://books.google.com/books?id=q95CAQAAMAAJ &pg=PA99&lpg=PA99&dq=gypsy+jem+mace+broken+arm& source=bl&ots=ryu_6JAJ4S&sig=_M7Qa3mmQKwkAdJ6v-GN0A1Hm0g&hl=en&sa=X&ved=0ahUKEwiM1Zi4wu HRAhVT0mMKHa2GBv84ChDoAQguMAc#v=onepage& q=gypsy%20jem%20mace%20broken%20armsulli&f=false.

10. Turnbull, "Boxing," 99.

11. Gorn, *The Manly Art*, 210–16.

12. Randy Roberts, "Sport, Action, and the American Mind," *Reviews in American History* 12, no. 3 (September 1984): 398–402, https://www.jstor.org/stable/2702251.

13. Gorn, *The Manly Art*, 216–28.

14. Mee, *Bare Fists*, 192–93.

15. Elliott J. Gorn, "John L. Sullivan: The Champion of All Champions," *Virginia Quarterly Review* 62, no. 4 (Autumn 1986), https://www.vqronline.org/essay/john-l-sullivan-champion-all-champions.

16. Mike Waters, "End of a Boxing Era: The Tale of Jake Kilrain vs. John L. Sullivan, the Final Bare-Knuckle Heavyweight Title Fight," *Post-Standard*, June 9, 2012, http://blog.syracuse.com/ sports/2012/06/end_of_a_boxing_era_the_tale_o.html.

17. Christopher Klein, *Strong Boy: The Life and Times of John L. Sullivan, America's First Sports Hero* (Lanham, MD: Lyons Press, 2013), 166–7.

18. Richard Hoffer, "Fisticuffs John L. Sullivan & Jake Kilrain

in the Outlaw Brawl That Started It All: How 75 Rounds of Bare-Fisted Boxing in 1889 Crowned America's First Superstar and Transformed the Face of Sport," *Sports Illustrated*, May 6, 2002, https://www.si.com/vault/2002/05/06/81101527/ fisticuffs-john-l-sullivan--jake-kilrain-in-the-outlaw-brawl-that- started-it-all-how-75-rounds-of-barefisted-boxing-in-1889- crowned-americas-first-superstar-and-transformed-the-face-of- sport.

19. Hoffer, "Fisticuffs."

20. Waters, "End of a Boxing Era."

21. "John L. Sullivan and Jake Kilrain in Last Bare Knuckles Boxing Match," *Omaha Daily Bee*, July 10, 1889, http://www.eugene carsey.com/boxingnewspapers/news/sullivan_kilrain1889.html.

22. Waters, "End of a Boxing Era."

CHAPTER 6

1. The Dubliners, "The Ould Orange Flute," *The Dubliners in Concert*, recorded December 4, 1964, https://www.lyrics.com/ lyric/5348117/The+Dubliners/The+Ould+Orange+Flute.

CHAPTER 8

1. T. E. Lawrence, introduction to *Travels in Arabia Deserta*, vol. 1, by Charles M. Doughty (London: Jonathan Cape, 1936).

2. Ian F. Hancock, "Romani Americans (Roma)," Texas State Historical Association, December 1, 1995, https://tshaonline. org/handbook/online/articles/pxrfh.

3. "Census of Population 2022 Profile 5—Diversity, Migration, Ethnicity, Irish Travellers and Religion," Central Statistics Office, Cork, Ireland, October 26, 2023, https://www. cso.ie/en/csolatestnews/pressreleases/2023pressreleases/ pressstatementcensus2022resultsprofile5-diversitymigratio- nethnicityirishtravellersreligion/.

4. "Questionnaire: Tinkers [Travellers]," Irish Virtual Research Library and Archive, 1952–1956, https://digital.ucd.ie/view/ivrla:31691.

5. "Freshwater Pearl Mussel," NatureScot, accessed January 18, 2024, https://www.nature.scot/plants-animals-and-fungi/invertebrates/freshwater-invertebrates/freshwater-pearl-mussel.

6. Timothy Neat, *The Summer Walkers: Travelling People and Pearl Fishers in the Highlands of Scotland* (Edinburgh: Birlinn, 2002), 6; Paul Burgess, "Wiggy (Wisdom) Smith," in CD booklet from *Band of Gold*, by Wiggy Smith and other Smith Family members, 2000, http://www.mustrad.org.uk/articles/smith.htm.

7. Bartley Gorman with Peter Walsh, *Bare Knuckle Fighter: Memoirs of the Undefeated Fighting Champion of Ireland* (Dublin: Maverick House, 2005), v.

8. Sharon Bohn Gmelch and George Gmelch, *Irish Travellers: The Unsettled Life* (Bloomington, IN: Indiana University Press, 2014), 11.

9. Gareth A. Davies, "Tyson Fury's Target after Becoming Heavyweight World Champion? A £4,000 Caravan and Some New Socks," *Telegraph*, November 29, 2015, http://www.telegraph.co.uk/sport/othersports/boxing/12023966/Tyson-Furys-target-after-becoming-heavyweight-world-champion-A-4000-caravan-and-some-new-socks.html.

10. Pierce Egan, *Boxiana; or, Sketches of Modern Pugilism, during the Championship of Cribb, to Spring's Challenge to All England* (London: George Virtue, 1829), 424.

11. Egan, *Boxiana...during the Championship*, 418.

12. Nigel Collins, "Fury's Roots Echo Familiar Story," ESPN, January 9, 2013, http://www.espn.com/boxing/story/_/id/8828342/british-heavyweight-tyson-fury-irish-traveller-roots-echo-familiar-story; Mee, *Bare Fists*, 163–73.

13. AmeriCymru, interview with Lawrence Davies, *The History of Bareknuckle Boxing*, accessed January 19, 2024, http://historyofbkb.weebly.com/mountain-fighting.html.

14. Bartley Gorman, *Bareknuckle: Memoirs of the Undefeated Champion* (New York: Overlook Press, 2011), v.

15. Gorman, *Bareknuckle*, v.

16. Gorman, *Bareknuckle*, v.

17. Gorman, *Bareknuckle*, v.

18. Gorman, *Bareknuckle*, v.

19. Cole Moreton, "Eyewitness: Last Great Bare-Knuckle Champion Is Laid to Rest," *Independent*, January 27, 2002, http://www.independent.co.uk/news/uk/this-britain/eyewitness-last-great-bare-knuckle-champion-is-laid-to-rest-9191383.html.

CHAPTER 9

1. "CBSA Southern Ontario Region: Operational and Enforcement Highlights from 2023," Canada Border Services Agency, modified December 5, 2023, https://www.canada.ca/en/border-services-agency/news/2023/11/cbsa-southern-ontario-region--operational-and-enforcement-highlights-from-2023.html.

CHAPTER 10

1. John M. Stygles, *Scammed by Society: The Contextual Theology and Christian Ethics of the Irish Travelers in the United States of America—A Moral Ethnographic Study* (CreateSpace, 2009), 3.

2. Jared V. Harper, "The Irish Travelers of Georgia" (PhD diss., University of Georgia, 1977, 1984), 35–36.

3. "Traveling Irish Colony: An Interesting Company of Horse Traders Camped Near City," *Morning Herald* (Lexington, KY), June 15, 1901.

4. Harper, "The Irish Travelers of Georgia," 54; "Wanderers Are Wealthy," *Springfield Daily News* (Springfield, MA), May 5, 1911, 7.

5. "Strange Southern Landlords Live as Gypsy Tribe," *Daily Illinois State Register* (Springfield, IL), August 24, 1913, 28.

6. "About Irish Travellers," Irish Traveller Movement, accessed January 19, 2024, https://itmtrav.ie/what-is-itm/irish-travellers/.

7. Penny Owen, "Irish Travelers Linked to Home-Repair Scams," *Oklahoman*, October 21, 2002, https://www.oklahoman.com/ story/news/2002/10/21/irish-travelers-linked-to-home-repair-scams/62074703007/.

8. "Irish Travellers in the United States," Ancient Order of Hibernians, http://www.aohflorida.org/irish-travellers-in-the-united-states/.

9. Michael Wilson, "Rhino Horns: a) Increase Potency; b) Cure Cancer; or c) Bring a Prison Term," *New York Times*, November 8, 2013, https://www.nytimes.com/2013/11/09/nyregion/guilty-plea-in-farflung-wildlife-trafficking-case.html.

10. Christie Ethridge et al., "Second Set of Irish Travelers Plead Guilty to Conspiracy; Bringing Total to Nearly 50 Convicted," WRDW, August 30, 2016, http://www.wrdw.com/content/ news/Nineteen-Irish-travelers-accused-of-racketeering-fraud-enter-not-guilty-pleas-391759251.html.

11. Erin Carlson, "'Dark Knight Rises': Tom Hardy on Playing Villain Bane, Battling Christian Bale (Video)," *Hollywood Reporter*, July 17, 2012, https://www.hollywoodreporter.com/ movies/movie-news/dark-knight-rises-tom-hardy-bane-350187/.

12. William Lindsay Gresham, *Nightmare Alley* (New York: Rinehart, 1946), 65.

13. Genesis 4:12 (King James Version).

14. Gorman, *Bareknuckle*, vii.

CHAPTER 12

1. Maureen Cavanaugh and Pat Finn, "Tijuana Was Once 'Satan's Playground,'" KPBS, July 20, 2010, http://www.kpbs.org/news/2010/jul/20/tijuana-was-once-satans-playground/.

2. Kristen Peterson, "Johnny Tocco's Legendary Boxing Gym Still Thriving, *Las Vegas Weekly*, September 13, 2012, https://lasvegasweekly.com/news/2012/sep/13/johnny-toccos-legendary-boxing-gym-still-thriving/#/0.

3. José Miguel Romero, "Kenny Ellis Calls It Quits after 17-Year Boxing Career," *Seattle Times*, August 2, 2009, http://www.seattletimes.com/sports/other-sports/kenny-ellis-calls-it-quits-after-17-year-boxing-career/.

4. Collins, "Fury's Roots."

5. Bartley Gorman, *King of the Gypsies: Memoirs of the Undefeated Bareknuckle Champion of Great Britain and Ireland* (Reading, UK: Milo Books, 2002); "Boxer Johnny Frankham Jailed for Ripping Off Pensioner," BerkshireLive, February 4, 2010, http://www.getreading.co.uk/news/local-news/boxer-johnny-frankham-jailed-ripping-4230318.

6. Earl Gustkey, "Always a Fight: Canadian Boxer Has His Family in His Corner," *Los Angeles Times*, November 2, 1988, http://articles.latimes.com/1988-11-02/sports/sp-747_1_hilton-family; Sidhartha Banerjee, "Hilton Adds Chapter to Sordid Saga," *Toronto Star*, August 27, 2009, https://www.thestar.com/sports/2009/08/27/hilton_adds_chapter_to_sordid_saga.html.

7. Ian O'Riordan, "How John Joe Nevin Got Back on His Feet to Fight Again," *Irish Times*, March 25, 2015, http://www.irishtimes.com/sport/other-sports/how-john-joe-nevin-got-back-on-his-feet-to-fight-again-1.2152821.

8. "Father of Boxing Champion Tyson Fury Jailed for Gouging a Man's Eye Out after a 12 Year Feud over a Bottle of Beer," *Manchester Evening News*, February 14, 2011, http://www.

manchestereveningnews.co.uk/news/local-news/father-of-boxing-champion-tyson-fury-853780.

9. Matthew Drake, "Tyson Fury Mentor Uncle Was Drug Crime Baron Who Ran Amphetamine Empire from Inside Jail," *Mirror*, January 9, 2016, http://www.mirror.co.uk/sport/boxing/tyson-fury-mentor-uncle-drug-7149892.

10. Terence Dooley, "Peter Fury on His Past Ordeals, Visa Issues and Twitter," BoxingScene, September 3, 2013, http://www.boxingscene.com/peter-fury-on-his-past-ordeals-visa-issues-twitter--69242.

11. Kelefa Sanneh, "Tyson Fury: The Heavyweight Champion We've Been Waiting for," *New Yorker*, November 30, 2015, http://www.newyorker.com/news/sporting-scene/tyson-fury-the-heavyweight-champion-weve-been-waiting-for.

12. Oliver Holt, "Is Tyson Fury Fit to Fight Wladimir Klitschko for the World Heavyweight Title? Read His Vile Homophobic Slurs and Bizarre Rants about Devil Worshippers and Armageddon…" *Daily Mail*, November 7, 2015, http://www.dailymail.co.uk/sport/boxing/article-3308639/Is-Tyson-Fury-fit-fight-Wladimir-Klitschko-world-heavyweight-title-Read-vile-homophobic-slurs-bizarre-rants-devil-worshippers-Armageddon.html.

13. Kent Demeret, "Heiress Josephine Abercrombie Becomes a Contender in the High-Stakes World of Boxing," *People*, May 27, 1985, http://people.com/archive/heiress-josephine-abercrombie-becomes-a-contender-in-the-high-stakes-world-of-boxing-vol-23-no-21/.

14. Christian Giudice, *Beloved Warrior: The Rise and Fall of Alexis Argüello* (Washington, DC: Potomac Books, 2012), 166, https://books.google.com/books?id=YVeOm10uEc8C&dq=gene+hackman+alexis+arguello&source=gbs_navlinks_s; Michael Martinez, "Boxing: Notebook; Barkley and Toney Try the Old

Way," *New York Times*, February 12, 1993, https://timesmachine.
nytimes.com/timesmachine/1993/02/12/602693.html?page
Number=46.

15. Jack Newfield, *The Life and Crimes of Don King: The Shame of
Boxing in America* (New York: Harbor Electronic, 2003), 217,
https://books.google.com/books?id=sWYN6cETROQC
&source=gbs_navlinks_s.

16. Michael Katz, "Don King's Control Grows," *New York Times*,
May 15, 1983, http://www.nytimes.com/1983/05/15/sports/
don-king-s-control-grows.html?pagewanted=all.

17. Katz, "Don King's Control."

18. Christine Pelisek, "The Knockout Shot," *LA Weekly*, February 22,
2006, http://www.laweekly.com/news/the-knockout-shot-2142096;
Romero, "Kenny Ellis Calls It Quits."

CHAPTER 15

1. Luke O'Brien, "The Ultimate Fighter," *Slate*,
June 8, 2016, https://slate.com/culture/2016/06/
kimbo-slice-died-at-age-42-his-street-fights-made-him-a-viral-
video-star-his-mma-bouts-made-him-mortal.html.

2. Earl Gustkey, "Toney's Real Manager Says She Is Gaining Respect
Daily," *Los Angeles Times*, February 13, 1993, https://www.latimes.
com/archives/la-xpm-1993-02-13-sp-1315-story.html.

CHAPTER 17

1. Jack Newfield, "The Great White Dope?: FBI Questions
Promoters in 'Bout-Fixing' Scandal," *New York Post*, August 27,
2000, http://nypost.com/2000/08/27/the-great-white-dope-
fbi-questions-promoters-in-bout-fixing-scandal/.

2. United States Attorney's Office, Nevada, "Boxing Promoter
and Fighter Receive Prison Terms for Fixed Fights," February
22, 2005, https://www.justice.gov/archive/usao/nv/

news/2005/02222005.html; Steve Springer, "Promoter, Boxer Guilty of Bribery," *Los Angeles Times*, November 9, 2004, http://articles.latimes.com/2004/nov/09/sports/sp-boxing9.

3. "Gross Declines Gunn Rematch (for Now)," International Boxing Association, June 21, 2006, https://www.international boxingassociation.com/archive/news0621062.htm.

4. "IBA Rules on Gunn vs Gross: Rematch Ordered," East Side Boxing, April 13, 2006, https://www.boxing247.com/weblog/archives/107777.

5. Norm Longtin, "IBA Rules on Gunn vs Gross," International Boxing Association, accessed January 19, 2024, https://www.internationalboxingassociation.com/archive/news041106gunn.htm.

6. "Shannon Landberg Talks about Bobby Gunn," East Side Boxing, August 23, 2006, https://www.boxing247.com/weblog/archives/109885.

7. "Canadian Gunn Gets Title Shot at WBO Champ Maccarinelli," *Toronto Star*, March 26, 2007, https://www.thestar.com/sports/2007/03/26/canadian_gunn_gets_title_shot_at_wbo_champ_maccarinelli.html.

8. Michael Pearlman, "Bobby Is Gunn-ing for Enzo," *South Wales Argus*, February 23, 2007, http://www.southwalesargus.co.uk/news/1214969.Bobby_is_Gunn_ing_for_Enzo/?ref=arc.

9. John Rawling, "Enzo Maccarinelli vs Bobby Gunn," June 14, 2009, YouTube video, 00:04, https://www.youtube.com/watch?v=dy9VRITQet8.

10. Mike Lewis, "Maccarinelli Wastes Little Time in Spiking Gunn," *Telegraph*, April 8, 2007, http://www.telegraph.co.uk/sport/othersports/boxing/2310613/Maccarinelli-wastes-little-time-in-spiking-Gunn.html.

11. Lewis, "Maccarinelli Wastes Little Time."

12. David Payne, "PR: Bobby Gunn," *BoxingWriter* (blog), May 6,

2007, https://boxingwriter.co.uk/2007/06/06/pr-bobby-gunn-is-a-liar-a-thief-and-a-coward/.

CHAPTER 18

1. Fort McDowell Yavapai Nation, accessed January 24, 2024, https://www.fmyn.org.
2. Jill Porter, "An Abused Child, an Abused Woman," *Philadelphia Daily News*, December 4, 1981.
3. Porter, "An Abused Child."
4. Don Smith, "Boxing News with Don Smith," Knuxx, 2012, https://knuxx.com/boxing-news-with-don-smith-2/.

CHAPTER 19

1. Bobby Gunn, "Quotes from Bobby Gunn Workout—Hackensack P.A.L., Hackensack, NJ," Facebook, July 1, 2009, https://www.facebook.com/notes/main-events/quotes-from-bobby-gunn-workout-hackensack-pal-hackensack-nj/98481852689/.
2. George Kimball, "Easy Night for Adamek; Stops Gunn in Fourth," The Sweet Science, July 12, 2009, https://tss.ib.tv/boxing/articles-of-2009/6995-easy-night-for-adamek-stops-gunn-in-fourth.
3. Associated Press, "Adamek Retains Cruiserweight Crown," ESPN, July 12, 2009, http://www.espn.com/sports/boxing/news/story?id=4321712.
4. Associated Press, "Adamek Retains."

CHAPTER 20

1. Ben Fowlkes, "With Approval from Regulators, 2-on-2 MMA Is Coming—but Where Is It Going?" *MMA Junkie* (blog), *USA Today*, August 16, 2015, https://mmajunkie.usatoday.com/2015/08/with-approval-from-regulators-2-on-2-mma-is-coming-but-where-is-it-going.

2. Dirk Johnson, "Raid on Indian Casino Inflames Issue of Self-Rule," *New York Times*, May 17, 1992, http://www.nytimes.com/1992/05/17/us/raid-on-indian-casino-inflames-issue-of-self-rule.html?pagewanted=all.

3. Associated Press, "F.B.I. Agents Raid Casinos on 5 Indian Reservations," *New York Times*, May 13, 1992, http://www.nytimes.com/1992/05/13/us/fbi-agents-raid-casinos-on-5-indian-reservations.html.

4. Johnson, "Raid on Indian Casino."

5. "Yavapai History & Culture," Fort McDowell Yavapai Nation, accessed January 19, 2024, http://www.fmyn.org/about-fmyn/history/.

6. Tim Mastro, "Fistful of Danger," *News Journal* (Wilmington, DE), August 13, 2011.

7. Michael Woods, "Reviving a Bygone, Bare-Knuckle Era," ESPN, August 5, 2011, http://www.espn.com/boxing/story/_/id/6835788/bringing-back-bygone-bare-knuckle-era-boxing.

8. "Bare Knuckle Boxing Lives," Bobby Gunn vs. Richie Stewart, May 1, 2014, YouTube video, 1:46, https://www.youtube.com/watch?v=bBk6W2hzxbU.

9. "Bare Knuckle Boxing," 8:48.

10. "Bare Knuckle Boxing," 11:29.

CHAPTER 21

1. "ABC Condemns 'Bare-Knuckle Boxing'!" Women Boxing Archive Network, August 10, 2011, http://womenboxing.com/NEWS2011/news081011bareknucklescondemnedbyabc.htm.

2. Norm Frauenheim, "AZ Casino Says No More Bare-Knuckle Boxing, but Commission Association Is Still Angry and Still Has Questions," 15 Rounds, August 11, 2011, http://www.15rounds.com/az-casino-says-no-more-bare-knuckle-boxing-but-commission-association-is-still-angry-and-still-has-questions-081211/.

3. Frauenheim, "AZ Casino."

4. Frauenheim, "AZ Casino."

5. Ryder, "Bobby Gunn vs Ernest Jackson," 1:00.

6. Steve Bunce, "Steve Bunce on Boxing: Explosive Bobby Gunn Ready to Step Out of the Murky Shadows and Fight Roy Jones," *Independent*, November 8, 2013, http://www.independent.co.uk/sport/general/others/ steve-bunce-on-boxing-explosive-bobby-gunn-ready-to-step- out-of-the-murky-shadows-and-fight-roy-8928114.html.

7. Hughie Rose, "The Ballad of Bobby Gunn," October 31, 2013, YouTube video, https://www.youtube.com/watch?v= FxG5ddEYnXg.

CHAPTER 22

1. Leroy Cleveland, "James Toney to Rumble with Bare Knuckle Champ Bobby Gunn," Fight Saga, February 27, 2012, http:// www.fightsaga.com/news/item/1981-James-Toney-to-Rumble- with-Bareknuckle-Champ-Bobby-Gunn.

2. James Toney, press conference in Southaven, Mississippi, February 22, 2012, YouTube video, 3:46, https://www.youtube. com/watch?v=_m9f8nfyysE.

3. "James Toney Wins in the 5th Round by Stoppage because Bobby Gunn Breaks His Hand," Real Combat Media, April 8, 2012, http://realcombatmedia.com/2012/04/james-toney-wins- 5th-stoppage-bro/.

4. Frauenheim, "AZ Casino."

5. Pennsylvania Department of State, "State Athletics," accessed 2019, https://www.dos.pa.gov/OtherServices/State%20Athletics/Pages/ default.aspx.

6. Pennsylvania Department of State, "State Athletics"; Pennsylvania Department of State, "State Athletic Commission to Host Pennsylvania Golden Gloves Tournament Finals on April 8,"

PR Newswire, March 9, 2017, http://www.prnewswire.com/news-releases/state-athletic-commission-to-host-pennsylvania-golden-gloves-tournament-finals-on-april-8-300421261.html.

7. John McCain, "Pension System for Professional Boxers," Hearing of the Senate Commerce, Science and Transportation Committee, C-SPAN video, May 22, 1997, https://www.c-span.org/video/?81494-1/professional-boxing&start=64.

8. Garrett Roche, "Remove Abusive PA Athletic Commission Exec. Dir. Greg Sirb from Office," Change.org, February 22, 2016, https://www.change.org/p/pennsylvania-governor-remove-abusive-pa-athletic-commissioner-greg-sirb-from-office.

9. "I Was Assaulted by PA Commissioner Greg Sirb," *MMA Underground*, November 27, 2013, https://forums.mixedmartialarts.com/t/i-was-assaulted-by-pa-commissioner-greg-sirb/2256343.

10. "Greg Sirb Is the Devil!" Boxing Scene, March 26, 2009, https://www.boxingscene.com/forums/showthread.php?t=256125.

11. Dan Gross, "Damon Feldman Charged with Fixing Celebrity Boxing Fights, Promoting Without License," *Philadelphia Inquirer*, April 9, 2010, http://www.philly.com/philly/blogs/phillygossip/Damon_Feldman_charged_with_fixing_Celebrity_Boxing_fights_promoting_without_license.html.

12. "Crime Imitates Art as Filmmaker Admits to Mobsterlike Behavior," *New York Times*, November 7, 2002, http://www.nytimes.com/2002/11/07/nyregion/crime-imitates-art-as-film-maker-admits-to-mobsterlike-behavior.html.

13. Gerardo Arencibia Jr., "The Family Business: Bobby Gunn Jr. Makes His Pro Debut," *New Jersey Boxing* (blog), updated March 14, 2014, http://blog.nj.com/new-jersey-boxing/2014/03/the_family_business_bobby_gunn.html.

14. Danny Provenzano, "Bare Knuckle Boxing: Danny Provenzano and Bobby Gunn," *60 Minutes Sports*, Showtime, September 2, 2014, YouTube video, 04:24, https://www.youtube.com/watch?v=oTEyW8Z2PpA.

15. Alana Semuels, "A Home for Unlikely Neighbors," *Atlantic*, December 24, 2015, https://www.theatlantic.com/business/archive/2015/12/a-home-for-unlikely-neighbors/421848/.

16. Armen Keteyian, "Bare Knuckle Boxing: Danny Provenzano and Bobby Gunn," *60 Minutes Sports*, Showtime, September 2, 2014, YouTube video, 02:42, https://www.youtube.com/watch?v=oTEyW8Z2PpA.

CHAPTER 23

1. "#P4Prank: No. 4 of Past 25 Years," ESPN, March 14, 2016, http://www.espn.com/boxing/story/_/id/14969875/ranking-top-25-pound-pound-boxers-25-years.

2. James Slater, "Roy Jones Junior–Bobby Gunn on Friday: Another Disaster for the Once Untouchable Great?" East Side Boxing, February 13, 2017, https://www.boxing247.com/boxing-news/roy-jones-junior-bobby/69434.

3. Nick Wong, "Roy Jones Jr. to Fight Bare-Knuckle Boxing Champion in February," *Fightland*, December 13, 2016, https://www.mma-core.com/news/Roy_Jones_Jr._to_Fight_Bare-Knuckle_Boxing_Champion_in_February_FIGHTLAND/1131744 ; "Report: Jones Owes IRS $3.5 Million," Fox Sports, April 7, 2011, https://www.foxsports.com/stories/boxing/report-jones-owes-irs-3-5-million.

4. Wong, "Roy Jones Jr."

5. Gary Smith, "One Tough Bird," *Sports Illustrated*, June 26, 1995, http://www.si.com/vault/1995/06/26/204194/one-tough-bird-roy-jones-jr-the-best-boxer-pound-for-pound-was-raised-under-the-rules-of-cockfighting-win-or-die.

CHAPTER 25

1. Wade Keller and Art Davie, "Interview—Retro: Art Davie— Dana White's Predecessor Discusses Harsh Media Coverage of New Sport (Pt. 2 of 3)," MMA Torch, May 29, 2009, http://www.mmatorch.com/artman2/publish/Interviews_34/article_56.shtml#.V-f9jLWRbBY.

2. Rich Cohen, *The Real Lebowski: The Third Act of Movie Director John Milius* (Amazon Digital Services, 2011), https://www.amazon.com/Real-Lebowski-Director-Milius-Kindle-ebook/dp/B004JN0S74.

3. L. John Wertheim, *Blood in the Cage: Mixed Martial Arts, Pat Miletich, and the Furious Rise of the UFC* (New York: Houghton Mifflin Harcourt, 2009), 57.

4. "Endeavor Announces UFC and WWE to Form a $21+ Billion Global Live Sports and Entertainment Company," World Wrestling Entertainment, April 3, 2023, https://corporate.wwe.com/news/company-news/2023/04-03-2023.

5. Wertheim, *Blood in the Cage*, 60.

6. Art Davie with Sean Wheelock, *Is This Legal? The Inside Story of the First UFC from the Man Who Created It* (Olathe, Kansas: Ascend Books, 2014).

7. Michael J. de la Merced, "U.F.C. Sells Itself for $4 Billion," *New York Times*, July 11, 2016, https://www.nytimes.com/2016/07/11/business/dealbook/ufc-sells-itself-for-4-billion.html.

8. "Bare-Knuckle Boxing Staged at O2 Arena for First Time," BBC News, June 28, 2017, http://www.bbc.com/news/uk-england-40427973.

9. "Bobby Gunn Extends KO Streak and Captures Heavyweight Title," *PhilBoxing.com* (blog), July 27, 2017, http://philboxing.com/news/story-129939.html.

CHAPTER 27

1. Jeremy Pelzer, "Twenty under 40: Bryan Pedersen," *Casper Star Tribune*, April 26, 2012, https://trib.com/business/20underforty/twenty-under-bryan-pedersen/article_388a3e65-7cc0-52e0-b6b2-8f59fc45c626.html.

2. Ben Neary, "Promoter Seeks to Block Regulation of Bare-Knuckle Bouts," Associated Press, *Washington Times*, May 21, 2015, https://www.washingtontimes.com/news/2015/may/21/promoter-seeks-to-block-regulation-of-bare-knuckle/.

3. Neary, "Promoter Seeks to Block."

EPILOGUE

1. Matt Gray, "Boxer Who Was Sought by Cops in Crash That Killed N.J. Woman Arrested," NJ.com, June 23, 2020, https://www.nj.com/salem/2020/06/boxer-who-was-sought-by-cops-in-crash-that-killed-nj-woman-arrested.html.

2. "What Is Fentanyl?" National Institute on Drug Abuse, June 2021, https://www.drugabuse.gov/publications/drugfacts/fentanyl.

3. Dan Alexander, "Update: Pro Boxer Surrenders after Fatal Head-on DWI Crash," New Jersey 101.5, updated June 23, 2020, https://nj1015.com/pro-boxer-wanted-in-deadly-head-on-dwi-crash-cops-say/.

4. "Obituary for Polly Kay Tornari," Sray-Webster Funeral Home, September 28, 2019, https://www.sraywebsterfuneralhome.com/obituaries/Polly-Tornari/#!/Obituary.

5. Matt Gray, "Boxer Charged in Fatal Crash Was under the Influence of Fentanyl, Prosecutors Say," NJ.com, July 12, 2020, https://www.nj.com/salem/2020/07/boxer-charged-in-fatal-crash-was-under-the-influence-of-fentanyl-prosecutors-say.html.

6. "TrillerVerz, Which Is Set to Go Public via Nasdaq Entity

Seachange: SEAC, Acquires Majority Interest in Bare Knuckle Fighting Championship (BKFC)," PR Newswire, February 28, 2022, https://www.prnewswire.com/news-releases/trillerverz-which-is-set-to-go-public-via-nasdaq-entity-seachange-seac-acquires-majority-interest-in-bare-knuckle-fighting-championship-bkfc-301491940.html.

7. "TrillerVerz, which is set to go public via Nasdaq Entity Seachange: SEAC, Acquires Majority Interest in Bare Knuckle Fighting Championship (BKFC)," PR Newswire, February 28, 2022, https://www.prnewswire.com/news-releases/trillerverz-which-is-set-to-go-public-via-nasdaq-entity-seachange-seac-acquires-majority-interest-in-bare-knuckle-fighting-championship-bkfc-301491940.html.

8. John Barr, "Blood Sport: Bare-Knuckle Fighting Emerges from the Shadows," ESPN, February 29, 2020, https://www.espn.com/boxing/story/_/id/28791748/blood-sport-bare-knuckle-fighting-emerges-shadows.

BIBLIOGRAPHY

Alary, Bryan. "Mixed Martial Arts Bloodier but Less Dangerous than Boxing." Folio. University of Alberta. November 5, 2015. https://www.ualberta.ca/folio/2015/11/mixed-martial-arts-bloodier-but-less-dangerous-than-boxing.html.

Alexander, Dan. "Update: Pro Boxer Surrenders after Fatal Head-On DWI Crash." New Jersey 101.5. Updated June 23, 2020. https://nj1015.com/pro-boxer-wanted-in-deadly-head-on-dwi-crash-cops-say/.

AmeriCymru. *The History of Bareknuckle Boxing*. Interview with Lawrence Davies. Accessed January 19, 2024. http://historyofbkb.weebly.com/mountain-fighting.html.

Ancient Order of Hibernians. "Irish Travellers in the United States." http://www.aohflorida.org/irish-travellers-in-the-united-states/.

Arencibia, Gerardo, Jr. "The Family Business: Bobby Gunn Jr. Makes His Pro Debut." *New Jersey Boxing* (blog). Updated March 14, 2014. http://blog.nj.com/new-jersey-boxing/2014/03/the_family_business_bobby_gunn.html.

Associated Press. "Adamek Retains Cruiserweight Crown." ESPN. July 11, 2009. http://www.espn.com/sports/boxing/news/story?id=4321712.

———. "F.B.I. Agents Raid Casinos on 5 Indian Reservations." *New York Times*. May 13, 1992. http://www.nytimes.com/

1992/05/13/us/fbi-agents-raid-casinos-on-5-indian-reservations
.html.

Banerjee, Sidhartha. "Hilton Adds Chapter to Sordid Saga." *Toronto Star*. August 27, 2009. https://www.thestar.com/sports/2009/08/27/hilton_adds_chapter_to_sordid_saga.html.

Barr, John. "Blood Sport: Bare-Knuckle Fighting Emerges from Shadows." ESPN. February 29, 2020. https://www.espn.com/boxing/story/_/id/28791748/blood-sport-bare-knuckle-fighting-emerges-shadows.

BBC News. "Bare-Knuckle Boxing Staged at O2 Arena for First Time." June 28, 2017. http://www.bbc.com/news/uk-england-40427973.

BerkshireLive. "Boxer Johnny Frankham Jailed for Ripping Off Pensioner." February 4, 2010. http://www.getreading.co.uk/news/local-news/boxer-johnny-frankham-jailed-ripping-4230318.

Boxing Scene. "Greg Sirb Is the Devil!" March 26, 2009. https://www.boxingscene.com/forums/showthread.php?t=256125.

Bunce, Steve. "Steve Bunce on Boxing: Explosive Bobby Gunn Ready to Step Out of the Murky Shadows and Fight Roy Jones." *Independent*. November 8, 2013. http://www.independent.co.uk/sport/general/others/steve-bunce-on-boxing-explosive-bobby-gunn-ready-to-step-out-of-the-murky-shadows-and-fight-roy-8928114.html.

Burgess, Paul. "Wiggy (Wisdom) Smith." In CD booklet from *Band of Gold*, by Wiggy Smith and other Smith Family members, 2000. http://www.mustrad.org.uk/articles/smith.htm.

Carlson, Erin. "'Dark Knight Rises': Tom Hardy on Playing Villain Bane, Battling Christian Bale (Video)." *Hollywood Reporter*. July 17, 2012. https://www.hollywoodreporter.com/movies/movie-news/dark-knight-rises-tom-hardy-bane-350187/.

Cavanaugh, Maureen, and Pat Finn. "Tijuana Was Once 'Satan's Playground.'" KPBS. July 20, 2010. http://www.kpbs.org/news/2010/jul/20/tijuana-was-once-satans-playground/.

CBSA Southern Ontario Region: Operational and Enforcement Highlights from 2023," Canada Border Services Agency, modified

December 5, 2023, https://www.canada.ca/en/border-services-agency/
news/2023/11/cbsa-southern-ontario-region--operational-and-
enforcement-highlights-from-2023.html.

Central Statistics Office, Cork, Ireland. "Census of Population 2022
Profile 5—Diversity, Migration, Ethnicity, Irish Travellers and
Religion." October 26, 2023. https://www.cso.ie/en/csolatestnews/
pressreleases/2023pressreleases/pressstatementcensus2022results
profile5-diversitymigrationethnicityirishtravellersreligion/.

Cleveland, Leroy. "James Toney to Rumble with Bare Knuckle Champ
Bobby Gunn." Fight Saga. February 27, 2012. http://www.fightsaga.
com/news/item/1981-James-Toney-to-Rumble-with-Bareknuckle-
Champ-Bobby-Gunn.

Cohen, Rich. *The Real Lebowski: The Third Act of Movie Director John
Milius.* Amazon Digital Services, 2011. https://www.amazon.com/
Real-Lebowski-Director-Milius-Kindle-ebook/dp/B004JN0S74.

Collins, Nigel. "Fury's Roots Echo Familiar Story." ESPN. January 9,
2013. http://www.espn.com/boxing/story/_/id/8828342/british-
heavyweight-tyson-fury-irish-traveller-roots-echo-familiar-story.

Dabydeen, David, John Gilmore, and Cecily Jones, eds. *The Oxford
Companion to Black British History.* Oxford, UK: Oxford University
Press, 2007.

Daily Illinois State Register (Springfield, IL). "Strange Southern Landlords
Live as Gypsy Tribe." August 24, 1913.

Davie, Art, and Sean Wheelock. *Is This Legal? The Inside Story of the First
UFC from the Man Who Created It.* Olathe, Kansas: Ascend Books,
2014.

Davies, Gareth A. "Tyson Fury's Target after Becoming Heavyweight World
Champion? A £4,000 Caravan and Some New Socks." *Telegraph.*
November 29, 2015. http://www.telegraph.co.uk/sport/othersports/
boxing/12023966/Tyson-Furys-target-after-becoming-heavyweight-
world-champion-A-4000-caravan-and-some-new-socks.html.

Davis, Dean. "1st LAR Bn. Marine Shoots to Attain Higher Goal."

Defense Visual Information Distribution Service. October 24, 2008. https://www.dvidshub.net/news/25786/1st-lar-bn-marine-shoots-attain-higher-goal.

Demeret, Kent. "Heiress Josephine Abercrombie Becomes a Contender in the High-Stakes World of Boxing." *People*. May 27, 1985. http://people.com/archive/heiress-josephine-abercrombie-becomes-a-contender-in-the-high-stakes-world-of-boxing-vol-23-no-21/.

Dooley, Terence. "Peter Fury on His Past Ordeals, Visa Issues and Twitter." BoxingScene. September 3, 2013. http://www.boxingscene.com/peter-fury-on-his-past-ordeals-visa-issues-twitter--69242.

Drake, Matthew. "Tyson Fury Mentor Uncle Was Drug Crime Baron Who Ran Amphetamine Empire from Inside Jail." *Mirror*. January 9, 2016. http://www.mirror.co.uk/sport/boxing/tyson-fury-mentor-uncle-drug-7149892.

Dubliners, The. "The Ould Orange Flute." *The Dubliners in Concert*. Recorded December 4, 1964. https://www.lyrics.com/lyric/5348117/The+Dubliners/The+Ould+Orange+Flute.

East Side Boxing. "IBA Rules on Gunn vs Gross: Rematch Ordered." April 13, 2006. https://www.boxing247.com/weblog/archives/107777.

———. "Shannon Landberg Talks about Bobby Gunn." August 23, 2006. https://www.boxing247.com/weblog/archives/109885.

Egan, Pierce. *Boxiana; or, Sketches of Modern Pugilism*. London: Sherwood, Jones, and Co., 1824.

———. *Boxiana; or, Sketches of Modern Pugilism, during the Championship of Cribb, to Spring's Challenge to All England*. London: George Virtue, 1829.

ESPN. "#P4Prank: No. 4 of Past 25 Years." March 14, 2016. http://www.espn.com/boxing/story/_/id/14969875/ranking-top-25-pound-pound-boxers-25-years.

Ethridge, Christie, Lauren Hoar, Robert Magobet, and Joey Gill. "Second Set of Irish Travelers Plead Guilty to Conspiracy; Bringing Total to Nearly 50 Convicted." WRDW. August 30, 2016. http://www.wrdw.com/content/news/Nineteen-Irish-travelers-accused-of-racketeering-fraud-enter-not-guilty-pleas-391759251.html.

Fort McDowell Yavapai Nation. Accessed January 24, 2024. https://www. fmyn.org.

———. "Yavapai History & Culture." Accessed January 19, 2024. http:// www.fmyn.org/about-fmyn/history/.

Fowlkes, Ben. "With Approval from Regulators, 2-on-2 MMA Is Coming—but Where Is It Going?" *MMA Junkie* (blog). *USA Today*, August 16, 2015. https://mmajunkie.usatoday.com/2015/08/with-approval-from-regulators-2-on-2-mma-is-coming-but-where-is-it-going.

Fox Sports. "Report: Jones Owes IRS $3.5 Million." April 7, 2011. https://www.foxsports.com/stories/boxing/report-jones-owes-irs-3-5-million.

Frauenheim, Norm. "AZ Casino Says No More Bare-Knuckle Boxing, but Commission Association Is Still Angry and Still Has Questions." 15 Rounds. August 11, 2011. http://www.15rounds. com/az-casino-says-no-more-bare-knuckle-boxing-but-commission-association-is-still-angry-and-still-has-questions-081211/.

Giudice, Christian. *Beloved Warrior: The Rise and Fall of Alexis Argüello.* Washington, DC: Potomac Books, 2012. https://books.google.com/ books?id=YVeOm10uEc8C&dq=gene+hackman+alexis+arguello &source=gbs_navlinks_s.

Gmelch, Sharon Bohn, and George Gmelch. *Irish Travellers: The Unsettled Life.* Bloomington, IN: Indiana University Press, 2014.

Gorman, Bartley. *Bareknuckle: Memoirs of the Undefeated Champion.* New York: Overlook Press, 2011.

———. *King of the Gypsies: Memoirs of the Undefeated Bareknuckle Champion of Great Britain and Ireland.* Reading, UK: Milo Books, 2002.

Gorman, Bartley, with Peter Walsh. *Bare Knuckle Fighter: Memoirs of the Undefeated Fighting Champion of Ireland.* Dublin: Maverick House, 2005.

Gorn, Elliott J. "John L. Sullivan: The Champion of All Champions."

Virginia Quarterly Review 62, no. 4 (Autumn 1986). https://www. vqronline.org/essay/john-l-sullivan-champion-all-champions.

———. *The Manly Art*. Ithaca, NY: Cornell University Press, 1986.

Gray, Matt. "Boxer Charged in Fatal Crash Was under the Influence of Fentanyl, Prosecutors Say." NJ.com. July 12, 2020. https://www. nj.com/salem/2020/07/boxer-charged-in-fatal-crash-was-under-the-influence-of-fentanyl-prosecutors-say.html.

———. "Boxer Who Was Sought by Cops in Crash That Killed N.J. Woman Arrested." NJ.com. June 23, 2020. https://www.nj.com/ salem/2020/06/boxer-who-was-sought-by-cops-in-crash-that-killed-nj-woman-arrested.html.

Gresham, William Lindsay. *Nightmare Alley*. New York: Rinehart, 1946.

Gross, Dan. "Damon Feldman Charged with Fixing Celebrity Boxing Fights, Promoting Without License." *Philadelphia Inquirer*. April 9, 2010. http://www.philly.com/philly/blogs/phillygossip/ Damon_Feldman_charged_with_fixing_Celebrity_Boxing_fights_ promoting_without_license.html.

Gunn, Bobby. "Quotes from Bobby Gunn Workout—Hackensack P.A.L., Hackensack, NJ." Facebook. July 1, 2009. https://www.facebook. com/notes/main-events/quotes-from-bobby-gunn-workout-hackensack-pal-hackensack-nj/98481852689/.

Gustkey, Earl. "Always a Fight: Canadian Boxer Has His Family in His Corner." *Los Angeles Times*. November 2, 1988. http://articles.latimes. com/1988-11-02/sports/sp-747_1_hilton-family.

———. "Toney's Real Manager Says She Is Gaining Respect Daily." *Los Angeles Times*. February 13, 1993. https://www.latimes.com/archives/ la-xpm-1993-02-13-sp-1315-story.html.

Hancock, Ian F. "Romani Americans (Roma)." Texas State Historical Association. December 1, 1995. https://tshaonline.org/handbook/ online/articles/pxrfh.

Harper, Jared V. "The Irish Travelers of Georgia." PhD diss., University of Georgia, 1977.

Hoffer, Richard. "Fisticuffs John L. Sullivan & Jake Kilrain in the Outlaw Brawl That Started It All: How 75 Rounds of Bare-Fisted Boxing in 1889 Crowned America's First Superstar and Transformed the Face of Sport." *Sports Illustrated.* May 6, 2002. https://www.si.com/vault/2002/05/06/8101527/fisticuffs-john-l-sullivan--jake-kilrain-in-the-outlaw-brawl-that-started-it-all-how-75-rounds-of-barefisted-boxing-in-1889-crowned-americas-first-superstar-and-transformed-the-face-of-sport.

Holt, Oliver. "Is Tyson Fury Fit to Fight Wladimir Klitschko for the World Heavyweight Title? Read His Vile Homophobic Slurs and Bizarre Rants about Devil Worshippers and Armageddon…" *Daily Mail.* November 7, 2015. http://www.dailymail.co.uk/sport/boxing/article-3308639/Is-Tyson-Fury-fit-fight-Wladimir-Klitschko-world-heavyweight-title-Read-vile-homophobic-slurs-bizarre-rants-devil-worshippers-Armageddon.html.

International Boxing Association. "Gross Declines Gunn Rematch (for Now)." June 21, 2006. https://www.internationalboxingassociation.com/archive/news0621062.htm.

Irish Traveller Movement. "About Irish Travellers." Accessed January 19, 2024. https://itmtrav.ie/what-is-itm/irish-travellers/.

Irish Virtual Research Library and Archive. "Questionnaire: Tinkers [Travellers]." 1952–1956. https://digital.ucd.ie/view/ivrla:31691.

Isenberg, Michael T. *John L. Sullivan and His America.* Urbana: University of Illinois Press, 1994.

Johnson, Dirk. "Raid on Indian Casino Inflames Issue of Self-Rule." *New York Times.* May 17, 1992. http://www.nytimes.com/1992/05/17/us/raid-on-indian-casino-inflames-issue-of-self-rule.html?pagewanted=all.

Katz, Michael. "Don King's Control Grows." *New York Times.* May 15, 1983. http://www.nytimes.com/1983/05/15/sports/don-king-s-control-grows.html?pagewanted=all.

Keller, Wade, and Art Davie. "Interview—Retro: Art Davie—Dana White's Predecessor Discusses Harsh Media Coverage of New Sport."

MMA Torch, May 29, 2009. http://www.mmatorch.com/artman2/
publish/Interviews_34/article_56.shtml#.V-f9jLWRbBY.

Kimball, George. "Easy Night for Adamek; Stops Gunn in Fourth." The
Sweet Science. July 12, 2009. https://tss.ib.tv/boxing/articles-of-
2009/6995-easy-night-for-adamek-stops-gunn-in-fourth.

Klein, Christopher. *Strong Boy: The Life and Times of John L. Sullivan,
America's First Sports Hero.* Lanham, MD: Lyons Press, 2013.

Lawrence, T. E. Introduction to *Travels in Arabia Deserta*, vol. 1, by
Charles M. Doughty. London: Jonathan Cape, 1936.

Lewis, Mike. "Maccarinelli Wastes Little Time in Spiking Gunn."
Telegraph. April 8, 2007. http://www.telegraph.co.uk/sport/
othersports/boxing/2310613/Maccarinelli-wastes-little-time-in-
spiking-Gunn.html.

Longtin, Norm. "IBA Rules on Gunn vs Gross." International Boxing
Association. Accessed January 19, 2024. https://www.international-
boxingassociation.com/archive/news041106gunn.htm.

MacKendrick, Paul, and Herbert M. Howe, eds. *Classics in Translation*,
vol. 2. *Latin Literature.* Madison: University of Wisconsin Press,
1952. https://books.google.com/books?id=AdzlbYqjp-AC&
pg=PA232&lpg=PA232&dq=the+aeneid+gloves+of+eryx&
source=bl&ots=ax1KgowJ5e&sig=01ogIPyZQJe1KAVxDWw
SBKQi6f8&hl=en&sa=X&ved=0ahUKEwj8ja2fv4PRAhUPz
GMKHclIBrAQ6AEILjAD#v=onepage&q=the%20aeneid%20
gloves%20of%20eryx&f=false.

Manchester Evening News. "Father of Boxing Champion Tyson Fury Jailed
for Gouging a Man's Eye Out after a 12 Year Feud over a Bottle of
Beer." February 14, 2011. http://www.manchestereveningnews.co.uk/
news/local-news/father-of-boxing-champion-tyson-fury-853780.

Martinez, Michael. "Boxing: Notebook; Barkley and Toney Try the Old
Way." *New York Times.* February 12, 1993. https://timesmachine.
nytimes.com/timesmachine/1993/02/12/602693.html?page
Number=46.

Mastro, Tim. "Fistful of Danger." *News Journal* (Wilmington, DE). August 13, 2011.

McCain, John. "Pension System for Professional Boxers." Hearing of the Senate Commerce, Science and Transportation Committee. C-SPAN video. May 22, 1997. https://www.c-span.org/video/?81494-1/professional-boxing&start=64.

McFadden, Robert D. "Anthony Provanzano, [*sic*] 71, Ex-Teamster Chief, Dies." *New York Times*. December 13, 1988. https://www.nytimes.com/1988/12/13/obituaries/anthony-provanzano-71-ex-teamster-chief-dies.html.

Mee, Bob. *Bare Fists.* New York: Overlook Press, 1998.

Merced, Michael J. de la. "U.F.C. Sells Itself for $4 Billion." *New York Times*. July 11, 2016. https://www.nytimes.com/2016/07/11/business/dealbook/ufc-sells-itself-for-4-billion.html.

MMA Underground. "I Was Assaulted by PA Commissioner Greg Sirb." November 27, 2013. https://forums.mixedmartialarts.com/t/i-was-assaulted-by-pa-commissioner-greg-sirb/2256343.

Moreton, Cole. "Eyewitness: Last Great Bare-Knuckle Champion Is Laid to Rest." *Independent*. January 27, 2002. http://www.independent.co.uk/news/uk/this-britain/eyewitness-last-great-bare-knuckle-champion-is-laid-to-rest-9191383.html.

Morning Herald (Lexington, KY). "Traveling Irish Colony: An Interesting Company of Horse Traders Camped Near City." June 15, 1901.

Muzzi, Don, Anna M. Blaeser, John Neidecker, and Guillem Gonzalez-Lomas. "Epidemiology of Professional Bare-Knuckle Fighting Injuries." *The Physician and Sportsmedicine* 50, no. 5 (October 2022): 448–453. https://doi.org/10.1080/00913847.2021.1955604.

National Institute on Drug Abuse. "What Is Fentanyl?" June 2021. https://www.drugabuse.gov/publications/drugfacts/fentanyl.

NatureScot. "Freshwater Pearl Mussel." Accessed January 18, 2924. https://www.nature.scot/plants-animals-and-fungi/invertebrates/freshwater-invertebrates/freshwater-pearl-mussel.

Neary, Ben. "Promoter Seeks to Block Regulation of Bare-Knuckle Bouts."
Associated Press. *Washington Times*. May 21, 2015. https://www.
washingtontimes.com/news/2015/may/21/promoter-seeks-to-block-
regulation-of-bare-knuckle/.

Neat, Timothy. *The Summer Walkers: Travelling People and Pearl Fishers in
the Highlands of Scotland*. Edinburgh: Birlinn, 2002.

Newfield, Jack. "The Great White Dope?: FBI Questions Promoters in
'Bout-Fixing' Scandal." *New York Post*. August 27, 2000. http://
nypost.com/2000/08/27/the-great-white-dope-fbi-questions-
promoters-in-bout-fixing-scandal/.

———. *The Life and Crimes of Don King: The Shame of Boxing in America*.
New York: Harbor Electronic, 2003. https://books.google.com/
books?id=sWYN6cETROQC&source=gbs_navlinks_s.

New York Times. "Crime Imitates Art as Filmmaker Admits to Mobsterlike
Behavior." November 7, 2002. http://www.nytimes.com/2002/
11/07/nyregion/crime-imitates-art-as-filmmaker-admits-to-
mobsterlike-behavior.html.

O'Brien, Luke. "The Ultimate Fighter." *Slate*. June 8, 2016. https://slate.
com/culture/2016/06/kimbo-slice-died-at-age-42-his-street-fights-
made-him-a-viral-video-star-his-mma-bouts-made-him-mortal.html.

Omaha Daily Bee. "John L. Sullivan and Jake Kilrain in Last Bare
Knuckles Boxing Match." July 10, 1889. http://www.eugenecarsey.
com/boxingnewspapers/news/sullivan_kilrain1889.html.

O'Riordan, Ian. "How Joe Nevin Got Back on His Feet to Fight Again."
Irish Times. March 25, 2015. http://www.irishtimes.com/sport/
other-sports/how-john-joe-nevin-got-back-on-his-feet-to-fight-
again-1.2152821.

Owen, Penny. "Irish Travelers Linked to Home-Repair Scams."
Oklahoman. October 21, 2002. https://www.oklahoman.com/
story/news/2002/10/21/irish-travelers-linked-to-home-repair-
scams/62074703007/.

Payne, David. "PR: Bobby Gunn." *BoxingWriter* (blog). May 6, 2007.

https://boxingwriter.co.uk/2007/06/06/pr-bobby-gunn-is-a-liar-a-thief-and-a-coward/.

Pearlman, Michael. "Bobby Is Gunn-ing for Enzo." *South Wales Argus*. February 23, 2007. http://www.southwalesargus.co.uk/news/1214969.Bobby_is_Gunn_ing_for_Enzo/?ref=arc.

Pelisek, Christine. "The Knockout Shot." *LA Weekly*. February 22, 2006. http://www.laweekly.com/news/the-knockout-shot-2142096.

Pelzer, Jeremy. "Twenty under 40: Bryan Pedersen." *Casper Star Tribune*. April 26, 2012. https://trib.com/business/20underforty/twenty-under-bryan-pedersen/article_388a3e65-7cc0-52e0-b6b2-8f59fc45c626.html.

Pennsylvania Department of State. "State Athletic Commission to Host Pennsylvania Golden Gloves Tournament Finals on April 8." PR Newswire. March 9, 2017. http://www.prnewswire.com/news-releases/state-athletic-commission-to-host-pennsylvania-golden-gloves-tournament-finals-on-april-8-300421261.html.

———. "State Athletics." Accessed 2019. https://www.dos.pa.gov/OtherServices/State%20Athletics/Pages/default.aspx.

Peterson, Kristen. "Johnny Tocco's Legendary Boxing Gym Still Thriving. *Las Vegas Weekly*. September 13, 2012. https://lasvegasweekly.com/news/2012/sep/13/johnny-toccos-legendary-boxing-gym-still-thriving/#/0.

PhilBoxing.com (blog). "Bobby Gunn Extends KO Streak and Captures Heavyweight Title." July 27, 2017. http://philboxing.com/news/story-129939.html.

Porter, Jill. "An Abused Child, an Abused Woman." *Philadelphia Daily News*. December 4, 1981.

PR Newswire. "TrillerVerz, Which Is Set to Go Public via Nasdaq Entity Seachange: SEAC, Acquires Majority Interest in Bare Knuckle Fighting Championship (BKFC)." February 28, 2022. https://www.prnewswire.com/news-releases/trillerverz-which-is-set-to-go-public-via-nasdaq-entity-seachange-seac-acquires-majority-

interest-in-bare-knuckle-fighting-championship-bkfc-301491940
.html.

Rawling, John. "Enzo Maccarinelli vs. Bobby Gunn." June 14, 2009.
YouTube video. https://www.youtube.com/watch?v=dy9VRITQet8.

Real Combat Media. "James Toney Wins in the 5th Round by Stoppage
because Bobby Gunn Breaks His Hand." April 8, 2012. http://
realcombatmedia.com/2012/04/james-toney-wins-5th-stoppage-bro/.

Roberts, Randy. "Sport, Action, and the American Mind." *Reviews in
American History* 12, no. 3 (September 1984): 398–402. https://www.
jstor.org/stable/2702251.

Roche, Garrett. "Remove Abusive PA Athletic Commission Exec. Dir.
Greg Sirb from Office." Change.org. February 22, 2016. https://
www.change.org/p/pennsylvania-governor-remove-abusive-pa-
athletic-commissioner-greg-sirb-from-office.

Romero, José Miguel. "Kenny Ellis Calls It Quits after 17-Year Boxing
Career." *Seattle Times*. August 2, 2009. http://www.seattletimes.com/
sports/other-sports/kenny-ellis-calls-it-quits-after-17-year-boxing-career/.

Rose, Hughie. "The Ballad of Bobby Gunn." October 31, 2013. YouTube
video. https://www.youtube.com/watch?v=FxG5ddE-YnXg.

Ryder, Dick. "Bobby Gunn vs Ernest Jackson for the BKB Title."
December 3, 2011. YouTube video. https://www.youtube.com/
watch?v=78Bokbfc170.

Sanneh, Kelefa. "Tyson Fury: The Heavyweight Champion We've
Been Waiting for." *New Yorker*. November 30, 2015. http://www.
newyorker.com/news/sporting-scene/tyson-fury-the-heavyweight-
champion-weve-been-waiting-for.

Semuels, Alana. "A Home for Unlikely Neighbors." *Atlantic*. December
24, 2015. https://www.theatlantic.com/business/archive/2015/12/
a-home-for-unlikely-neighbors/421848/.

Seymour, Kara. "America's Most Dangerous Cities: 6 Are in N.J." Patch.
August 29, 2015. https://patch.com/new-jersey/cherryhill/
americas-most-dangerous-cities-6-are-nj.

60 Minutes Sports. "Bare Knuckle Boxing: Danny Provenzano and Bobby Gunn." Showtime. September 2, 2014. YouTube video. https://www.youtube.com/watch?v=oTEyW8Z2PpA.

Slater, James. "Roy Jones Junior–Bobby Gunn on Friday: Another Disaster for the Once Untouchable Great?" East Side Boxing. February 13, 2017. https://www.boxing247.com/boxing-news/roy-jones-junior-bobby/69434.

Smith, Don. "Boxing News with Don Smith." Knuxx. 2012. https://knuxx.com/boxing-news-with-don-smith-2/.

Smith, Gary. "One Tough Bird." *Sports Illustrated.* June 26, 1995. http://www.si.com/vault/1995/06/26/204194/one-tough-bird-roy-jones-jr-the-best-boxer-pound-for-pound-was-raised-under-the-rules-of-cockfighting-win-or-die.

Springer, Steve. "Promoter, Boxer Guilty of Bribery." *Los Angeles Times.* November 9, 2004. http://articles.latimes.com/2004/nov/09/sports/sp-boxing9.

Springfield Daily News (Springfield, MA). "Wanderers Are Wealthy." May 5, 1911.

Sray-Webster Funeral Home. "Obituary for Polly Kay Tornari." September 28, 2019. https://www.sraywebsterfuneralhome.com/obituaries/Polly-Tornari/#!/Obituary.

Stygles, John M. *Scammed by Society: The Contextual Theology and Christian Ethics of the Irish Travelers in the United States of America—A Moral Ethnographic Study.* CreateSpace, 2009.

Toney, James. Press conference in Southaven, Mississippi. February 22, 2012. YouTube video, 3:46. https://www.youtube.com/watch?v=_m9f8nfyysE.

Toronto Star. "Canadian Gunn Gets Title Shot at WBO Champ Maccarinelli." March 26, 2007. https://www.thestar.com/sports/2007/03/26/canadian_gunn_gets_title_shot_at_wbo_champ_maccarinelli.html.

Turnbull, Robert K. "Boxing." *Appletons' Annual Cyclopaedia and Register*

of Important Events. New York: Appleton, 1889. https://books.google.
com/books?id=q95CAQAAMAAJ&pg=PA99&lpg=PA99&
dq=gypsy+jem+mace+broken+arm&source=bl&ots=ryu_
6JAJ4S&sig=_M7Qa3mmQKwkAdJ6v-GN0A1Hm0g&hl=
en&sa=X&ved=0ahUKEwiM1Zi4wuHRAhVT0mMKHa2GB
v84ChDoAQguMAc#v=onepage&q=gypsy%20jem%20mace%20
broken%20armsulli&f=false.

United States Attorney's Office, Nevada. "Boxing Promoter and Fighter
Receive Prison Terms for Fixed Fights." February 22, 2005. https://
www.justice.gov/archive/usao/nv/news/2005/02222005.html.

Virginia Museum of History & Culture. "Tom Molineaux." Accessed
26, 2019. https://www.virginiahistory.org/collections-and-resources/
virginia-history-explorer/tom-molineaux.

Vyasa, Krishna-Dwaipayana. *The Mahabharata*. Translated by Protap
Chandra Roy. Calcutta: Bharata Press, 1884. https://books.google.
com/books?id=JxlBAQAAMAAJ&pg=RA1-PA29&lpg=RA1-PA29&
dq=Mahabharata+boxing+clenched+fist&source=bl&ots=
8CUjMpFKVx&sig=9gFolIsDVsX-H80B7Szv0G0zGB8&hl=
en&sa=X&ved=0ahUKEwjwnvvyrbHUAhUCymMKHaNIC-
4Q6AEIQzAE#v=onepage&q=Mahabharata%20boxing%20
clenched%20fist&f=false.

Waters, Mike. "End of a Boxing Era: The Tale of Jake Kilrain vs. John L.
Sullivan, the Final Bare-Knuckle Heavyweight Title Fight." *Post-
Standard*. June 9, 2012. http://blog.syracuse.com/sports/2012/06/
end_of_a_boxing_era_the_tale_o.html.

Wertheim, L. John. *Blood in the Cage: Mixed Martial Arts, Pat Miletich,
and the Furious Rise of the UFC*. New York: Houghton Mifflin
Harcourt, 2009.

Wilson, Michael. "Rhino Horns: a) Increase Potency; b) Cure Cancer; or
c) Bring a Prison Term." *New York Times*. November 8, 2013. https://
www.nytimes.com/2013/11/09/nyregion/guilty-plea-in-farflung-
wildlife-trafficking-case.html.

Women Boxing Archive Network. "ABC Condemns 'Bare-Knuckle Boxing'!" August 10, 2011. http://womenboxing.com/NEWS2011/news081011bareknucklescondemnedbyabc.htm.

Wong, Nick. "Roy Jones Jr. to Fight Bare-Knuckle Boxing Champion in February." *Fightland.* December 13, 2016. https://www.mma-core.com/news/Roy_Jones_Jr._to_Fight_Bare-Knuckle_Boxing_Champion_in_February_FIGHTLAND/1131744.

Woods, Michael. "Reviving a Bygone, Bare-Knuckle Era." ESPN. August 5, 2011. http://www.espn.com/boxing/story/_/id/6835788/bringing-back-bygone-bare-knuckle-era-boxing.

World Wrestling Entertainment. "Endeavor Announces UFC and WWE to Form a $21+ Billion Global Live Sports and Entertainment Company." April 3, 2023. https://corporate.wwe.com/news/company-news/2023/04-03-2023.

YouTube. "Bare Knuckle Boxing Lives." Bobby Gunn vs. Richie Stewart. May 1, 2014. https://www.youtube.com/watch?v=bBk6W2hzxbU.

INDEX